LEADING AND LEADERSHIP

THE ETHICS OF EVERYDAY LIFE

Wing to Wing, Oar to Oar: Readings on Courting and Marrying, ed. Amy A. Kass and Leon R. Kass

The Eternal Pity: Reflections on Dying, ed. Richard John Neuhaus

Everyone a Teacher, ed. Mark Schwehn

Leading and Leadership, ed. Timothy Fuller

Working: Its Meaning and Its Limits, ed. Gilbert C. Meilaender

LEADING
AND
LEADERSHIP

Edited by

TIMOTHY FULLER

UNIVERSITY OF NOTRE DAME PRESS

Notre Dame, Indiana

Library of Congress Cataloging-in-Publication Data

Leading and leadership / edited by Timothy Fuller.
      p. cm. — (The ethics of everyday life)
   Includes bibliographical references.
   ISBN 0-268-01325-X (cl. : alk. paper) ISBN 0-268-01327-6 (pbk. : alk. paper)
      1. Leadership—Moral and ethical aspects. I. Fuller, Timothy, 1940–   II. Series.

   HM1261.L43   2000
   303.3′4—dc21   00-025637

THE ETHICS OF EVERYDAY LIFE
Preface to the Series

This book is one of a series of volumes devoted to the ethics of everyday life. The series has been produced by a group of friends, united by a concern for the basic moral aspects of our common life and by a desire to revive public interest in and attention to these matters, now sadly neglected. We have met together over the past five years, under the auspices of the Institute of Religion and Public Life and supported by a generous grant from the Lilly Endowment. We have been reading and writing, conversing and arguing, always looking for ways to deepen our own understanding of the meaning of human life as ordinarily lived, looking also for ways to enable others to join in the search. These anthologies of selected readings on various aspects of everyday life—courting and marrying, teaching and learning, working, leading, and dying—seem to us very well suited to the task. This preface explains why we think so.

We begin by remembering that every aspect of everyday life is ethically charged. Nearly everything that we do, both as individuals and in relations with others, is colored by sentiments, attitudes, customs, and beliefs concerning "how to live." At work or at play, in word or in deed, with kin or with strangers, we enact, often unthinkingly and albeit imperfectly, our ideas of what it means to live a decent and worthy life. Notions and feelings regarding better and worse, good and bad, right and wrong, noble and base, just and unjust, decent and indecent, honorable and dishonorable, or human and inhuman always influence the way we speak to one another, the way we do our work, the way we control our passions, rear our children, manage our organizations, respond to injustice, treat our neighbors, teach the young, care for the old, court our beloved, and face our deaths.

For many centuries and up through the early part of the twentieth century, there was in the West (as in the East) a large and diverse literature on "living the good life," involving manners, patterns of civility, and the meaning of decency, honor, and virtue as these are manifested in daily life. Moralists, both philosophical and religious, wrote voluminously on the moral dimensions of the life cycle (e.g., growing up and coming of age, courting and marrying, rearing the young, aging and dying); on the virtues of everyday life (e.g., courage, endurance, self-command, generosity, loyalty, forbearance, modesty, industry, neighborliness, patience, hope, forgiveness, repentance); on the moral passions or sentiments (e.g., shame, guilt, sympathy, joy, envy, anger, awe) and their proper expression; on the activities of everyday life (e.g., loving, working, caring, giving, teaching, talking, eating); and on basic moral phenomena (e.g., responsibility, obligation, vocation, conscience, praise and blame). These topics, which once held the attention of great thinkers like Aristotle, Erasmus, and Adam Smith, are now sorely neglected, with sorry social consequences.

The ethics of everyday life have been left behind despite—or perhaps because of—the burgeoning attention given these past few decades to professional ethics and public ethics. Mention ethics today, and the discussion generally turns to medical ethics, legal ethics, journalistic ethics, or some other code of behavior that is supposed to guide the activities of professionals. Or it turns to the need to establish codes of conduct to address and curtail the mischief and malfeasance of members of Congress, generals, bureaucrats, or other public officials. In both cases, the concern for ethics is largely instrumental and protective. The codes are intended to tell people how to stay out of trouble with their professional colleagues and with the law. The latter is especially important in a world in which it is increasingly likely that a challenge or disagreement will be engaged not by civil conversation but by an uncivil lawsuit.

Today's proliferation of codes of ethics, while an expression of moral concern, is at the same time an expression of moral poverty. We write new rules and regulations because we lack shared customs and understandings. Yet the more we resort to such external and contrived codes, the less we can in fact take for granted. "Ethics" and "morality" have their source in "ethos" and "mores," words that refer to the ways and attitudes, manners and habits, sensibilities and customs that shape and define a community. Communities are built on shared understandings, usually tacitly conveyed, not only of what is right and wrong or good and bad, but also of who we are, how we stand, what things mean. These matters are not well taught by ethics codes.

Neither are they communicated, or even much noticed, by the current fashions in the academic study and teaching of ethics or by the proliferating band of professional ethicists. The dominant modes of contemporary ethical discourse and writing, whether conducted in universities or in independent ethics centers, are, by and large, highly abstract, analytically philosophic, interested only in principles or arguments, often remote from life as lived, divorced from the way most people face and make moral decisions, largely deaf to questions of character and moral feeling or how they are acquired, unduly influenced by the sensational or extreme case, hostile to insights from the religious traditions, friendly to fashionable opinion but deaf to deeper sources of wisdom, heavily tilted toward questions of law and public policy, and all too frequently marked by an unwillingness to take a moral stand. Largely absent is the older—and we think richer—practice of moral reflection, which is concrete, rooted in ordinary experience, engaged yet thoughtful, attuned to human needs and sentiments as well as to "rational principles of justification," and concerned for institutions that cultivate and promote moral understanding and moral education. Absent especially is the devoted search for moral wisdom regarding the conduct of life—philosophy's original meaning and goal, and a central focus of all religious thought and practice—a search that takes help from wherever it may be found and that gives direction to a life seriously lived.

Many academic teachers of ethics, formerly professors of moral wisdom, are today purveyors of moral relativism. In the colleges and universities ethics is often taught cafeteria style, with multiple theories and viewpoints, seemingly equal, offered up for the picking. But this apparently neutral approach often coexists with ideologically intolerant teaching. Students are taught that traditional views must give way to the "enlightened" view that all views—except, of course, the "enlightened" one—are culture-bound, parochial, and absolutely dependent on your *point*-of-viewing. The morally charged "givens" of human life—e.g., that we have bodies or parents and neighbors—tend to be regarded not as gifts but as impositions, obstacles to the one true good, unconstrained personal choice. Moral wisdom cannot be taught or even sought, because we already know that we must not constrain freedom, must not "impose" morality. Thus, we insist that our "values" are good because we value them, not that they are valued because they are good. Abstract theories of individual autonomy and self-creation abound, while insights into real life as lived fall into obscurity or disappear altogether. To be sure, not all academic teachers of ethics share these opinions and approaches. But experience and study of the literature convinces us that these generalizations are all too accurate.

The current fashions of ethical discourse are of more than merely academic interest. When teachings of "autonomy" or "self-creation" are disconnected from attention to mores and the cultural ethos and from the search for moral wisdom, we come to know less and less what we are supposed to do and how we are supposed to be. Neither can we take for granted that others know what they are supposed to do and be. Being morally unfettered and unformed may make us feel liberated albeit insecure or lost; but seeing that others are morally unfettered and unformed is downright threatening. Thus, despite our moral codes of ethics with penalties attached, despite the boom in the demand for ethicists and in ethics courses in our colleges, our everyday life declines into relationships of narrow-eyed suspicion. No one can argue that we are as a nation morally better off than we were before professional and academic ethics made such a big splash. Americans of widely differing views recognize the growing incivility and coarseness of public discourse and behavior, the sorry state of sexual mores, the erosion of family life, the disappearance of neighborliness, and the growing friction among, and lack of respect for, peoples of differing ages, races, religions, and social classes. To be sure, contemporary ethicists are not responsible for our cultural and moral difficulties. But they have failed to provide us proper guidance or understanding, largely because they neglect the ethics of everyday life and because they have given up on the pursuit of wisdom.

How to provide a remedy? How to offer assistance to the great majority of decent people who still care about living the good life? How to answer the ardent desires of parents for a better life for their children or the deep longings of undergraduates for a more meaningful life for themselves? How to supply an intellectual defense for the now beleaguered and emaciated teachings of decency and virtue? Any answer to these questions depends on acquiring—or at least seeking—a richer and more profound understanding of the structure of human life and the prospects for its flourishing and enhancement. This series of readings on the ethics of everyday life offers help to anyone seeking such understanding.

The topics considered in the several volumes are central to everyday life. Most of us marry, nearly all of us work (and play and rest), all of us lose both loved ones and our own lives to death. In daily life, many of us teach and all of us learn. In civic life, some of us lead, many of us follow, and, in democratic societies, all of us are called upon to evaluate those who would lead us. Yet rarely do we reflect on the nature and meaning of these activities. The anthologized readings—collected from poets and prophets, philosophers and preachers, novelists and anthropologists, scholars and statesmen; from authors ancient, modern, and contemporary—provide rich materials for such reflection. They are moral, not moralistic; they can yield insights, not maxims. The reader will find here no rules for catching a husband, but rather explorations of the purposes of courting and marrying; no prescriptions for organizing the workplace, but competing accounts of the meaning of work; no discussions of "when to pull the plug," but examinations of living in the face of death; no formulae for "effective leadership," but critical assessments of governance in democratic times; no advice on how to teach, but various meditations on purposes and forms of instruction. The different volumes reflect the differences in their subject matter, as well as the different tastes and outlooks of their editors. But they share a common moral seriousness and a common belief that proper ethical reflection requires a "thick description" of the phenomena of everyday life, with their inherent anthropological, moral, and religious colorations.

The readings in this series impose no morality. Indeed, they impose nothing; they only propose. They propose different ways of thinking about our common lives, sometimes in the form of stories, sometimes in the form of meditations, sometimes in the form of arguments. Some of these proposals will almost certainly "impose" themselves upon the reader's mind and heart as being more worthy than others. But they will do so not because they offer simple abstractable ethical principles or suggest procedures for solving this or that problem of living. They will do so because they will strike the thoughtful reader as wiser, deeper, and more true. We ourselves have had this experience with our readings, and we hope you will also. For the life you examine in these pages is—or could become—your own.

Timothy Fuller
Amy A. Kass
Leon R. Kass
Gilbert C. Meilaender
Richard John Neuhaus
Mark Schwehn

CONTENTS

IV. Recent Reflections

ACKNOWLEDGMENTS

In addition to my colleagues in the Ethics of Everyday Life Project, I want to thank Inger Thomsen Brodey, Michael Gillespie, Robert Ferguson, and David Hendrickson for their helpful suggestions, and Suzanne Tregarthen for both research and editorial work in preparing this book.

INTRODUCTION

Why study leadership, and why are so many today interested in studying it? An ancient, classic answer still pertains to us.

Aristotle taught in his *Politics* that a society of free citizens requires the art of being ruled as well as of ruling. Today especially, we believe citizens must know what those in positions of authority know; the relation between those who lead and those whom they lead must not be obscured in mystery. Those who are led must be able to understand and appraise the work of those who lead; they are, in effect, training themselves for the possible reversal of roles. Those who are led may eventually lead. In a free society, at least, this prospect can never in principle be excluded.

Machiavelli advised Lorenzo de' Medici in the dedication of *The Prince* that "to know well the nature of the people one must be a prince, and to know well the nature of princes one must be a common citizen." Machiavelli thought he had this advantage, and *The Prince* offers us the rudiments of Machiavelli's insight gained by seeing both "from below" and "from above."

The modern answer that complements the ancient one is that we live, work, and define ourselves in a democratic age that emphasizes equal responsibility as well as equal liberty. Leadership is not a substitute for individual, personal responsibility, nor is it a distant activity reserved to a few. It is a widely shared activity, embedded to some degree in the everyday life of most citizens.

It is important for those of us who do not occupy positions of prominence, but who may exercise leadership in our local activities, to take Aristotle and Machiavelli seriously, and to understand from a position of "following" what our responsibilities are. At its best, leadership helps to define what we are to do for ourselves and in association with others; it enhances, but does not supplant, our self-direction.

We are inheritors of the liberal tradition that has emerged in the past five centuries. This means that we are committed to the idea that secure and productive order in social life is possible without the exercise of massive coercion by governments or other agencies. Instead, most of the time we aspire to conduct ourselves under the rule of law rather than under the rule of human beings, no matter how talented they may be.

It also means that we willingly and mutually subscribe to procedural rules that constrain the manner in which we seek to satisfy our personally chosen aims in life, and we try to ensure that the pursuit of aims in common is established by voluntary agreement. We predicate a limited role for government and for the use of coercive power, on the faith we have that most of us, most of the time, are capable of an adequate degree of self-regulation or self-government.

In the context of this book, I associate the terms "self-regulation" and "self-government" with the capacity for "self-leading." George Washington and other American founders emphasized that a republic could not survive unless its citizens had these attributes. A liberal, democratic republic requires those who lead and those who are led to share in the task of directing their energies as they determine jointly to be appropriate. Different individuals will have differing degrees and scope of responsibilities. Nevertheless, there is a strong emphasis on cooperation and mutual regard. Readers will see that many ancient writers were not unaware of, nor did they ignore, these matters. Much of their advice is as suited to "followers" as to "leaders." But in the modern world, we have put a pronounced emphasis on individual responsibility within a framework of procedural rules. In this context, leadership often has little to do with coercion or command. An excellent account of this change in emphasis is to be found in the reading from Benjamin Constant in this anthology.

"Leadership" thus has become a prominent term in American conversation, balanced by other terms such as "participation in decisions" and "accountability of leaders." We speak of leading and leadership in every context from small private groups to the highest levels of government and diplomacy. Our democratic culture avoids words such as "ruling," "governing," and "executing." To many, such terms suggest undesirable hierarchy and elitism. They seem morally ambiguous, and people respond ambivalently or negatively to them.

These terms are replaced in our thinking by the concept of "leadership," a more diffuse concept attached to no particular offices or posts and thus applied to informal as well as formal relationships. The term "leadership" retains elements of the concepts of ruling, governing, or executive action, but also suggests collaboration, team-building, persuasion, dialogue, and management. The preoccupation with leadership identifies something intensely desired today, but it also reveals uncertainty about how we order ourselves, how we define our purposes, and what actions legitimate our ideas of order and purpose.

Leadership is at once both attractive and subject to suspicion. On the one hand, we demand "vision" of those who would lead us, and we demand to know where leaders are "going to take us." Leading thus considered makes it seem as if we are prepared to acknowledge some authority to articulate an end or goal, to organize and express effectively our hopes and desires, perhaps to help define meaning in life. On the other hand, in our century leaders called by such names as *Der Führer* and *Il Duce* have saddled nations with unprecedented demagoguery, imposed despicable goals upon them, and catered to their worst tendencies.

Not surprisingly, then, leading has become a central theme of everyday conversation and debate and a central topic of academic study. Professorships and academic departments devoted to the study of leading and leadership increase in number, parallel to the increasing interest in the subject on the part of large numbers of people removed from the academy. Inspection of any major bookstore reveals that the literature on leadership and management is large and getting larger. Workshops and conferences on leadership abound among professional associations of all sorts. The study of leadership is divided between more professionalized and more popularized presentations, between manuals advising on how to lead and sociological and historical studies of the characteristics of leaders. Yet in speaking positively, often enthusiastically, of leadership, we sometimes conceal from ourselves the ambivalence of attitudes towards actual attempts to exercise leadership.

Leadership is often spoken of as something simply good and desirable. Yet just as often we find public disillusionment at the "lack of leadership," rejection of the leading that is actually attempted, and cynicism about the prospects of leadership and the compromises and necessities of political life which attend even the most creative leadership.

What we too often fail to find is philosophical discussion of what has been thought and said on leadership from ancient times to ours. Nor do we always find thoughtful reflection on why the term "leadership" and the topic of leading enjoy such prominence in a democratic, egalitarian age, which places a premium on individuality, privacy, freedom from direction, majority opinion, and so on. Nor do we find convenient collections of readings from classic writers to balance the current tendency to produce managerial tracts, potted biographies that purport to teach useful lessons, and how-to-do-it manuals.

Writings on leading and leadership frequently offer generic advice, suggestions that are not attached to any particular circumstances. All conduct, however, is particular. We do not "act" in general, but rather we take specific actions in specific circumstances as we understand them, with specific possibilities and limitations so far as we can discern them. General advice is useful insofar as it provides assistance to our reflections on how we shall respond to the conditions in which we operate. It can make us more thoughtful, but we can never simply deduce from general advice what is the right thing to do. What we can do is to take maxims and precepts into account in judging how to deal with the specific situations and concerns we face. It is in our appraisal and judgment that we connect the maxims of conduct to our circumstances.

One needs to be on guard against "rationalism," the belief that thinking is a purely technical skill and that leading is simply a question of finding the right technique and manipulative skill. The peril of rationalism is that it obscures the elements of thoughtfulness and philosophic meditation on concrete experience, and the need for sound judgment, that the classic writers and the best recent writers insist are essential.

The aim of this anthology of readings is to foster discussion of what we can learn about leadership from the reflections of major thinkers of past and present. My own experience and reflection influences what I have to say, as will be seen in the introductions to each section. My field of study is political philosophy, and issues of leadership have been with me in some form for many years. For the last few years I have co-taught a course on leadership with a colleague who holds a chair in Leadership and American Institutions.

As I write this, I am entering my sixth year as the dean of my college. When I began, a distinguished former president of the college assured me that he had only one piece of advice. He made it clear he would not try to tell me what to do about college policy. Instead, his advice was to acquire the works of Epictetus and keep them close by at all times.

Epictetus (50–130) was a freed Greek slave who lived much of his life in exile from Rome. His life was simple and unadorned, and he displayed a "sweetness" of character coupled with religious / moral intensity. He became one of the most famous exponents of Stoicism, combining a powerful aspiration to live a virtuous life with the attainment of serenity before the ceaseless flow of fortune and misfortune encompassing human existence. He believed in rigorous self-examination and in accepting full responsibility for one's actions, cultivating total internal independence while bowing to the external, unavoidable trials of life. He was not a political activist, but he became a great moral and spiritual leader, and his thought, as recorded by his students (like Socrates, he did not himself write anything), has remained a perennial guide. Epictetus emphasized the acceptance of convention and law; at the same time he sought the independence of mind and habit characteristic of one who is a citizen of the universe, of the invisible community of reflective people.

If one's providential dispensation is to find oneself in a position of leadership, according to Epictetus, one should not shrink from its attendant duties (one should be dutiful, even patriotic). However, one should cultivate detachment, not define one's self-understanding by the temporal flow of social life, its fashions and trends, its perils and temptations. The cultivation of strong character, not a checklist of tasks completed or not completed, was central for Epictetus.

The advice of the former president was sound, quite apart from the question whether one is by disposition a Stoic. The experience of leadership responsibilities makes clear the wisdom to be found in the Stoic outlook. If one is called to a position of responsibility by one's community, one can feel honored, but one also discovers what Vergil described in the *Aeneid* as the *lachrymae rerum,* the "tears of things."

It is one thing to accept responsibility both of office and for your every action, and another to learn (often the hard way) how much is not under your control or perhaps under anyone's control. It is one thing to have grand aspirations, another to make them workable in particular circumstances of time, place, and personalities, and to realize how many competing and distracting purposes obscure the central and defining meaning of an institution. It is one thing to know that you never start with a blank slate, and another to learn in daily practice the truth of that truism.

As the Stoic suggests, the rewards often come from the cultivation of one's duty in trying to live up to a conception of virtue and responsibility for a human being. As the ancient thinkers and the best of the modern know, external rewards are given today and taken away tomorrow. One cannot understand or discharge the duties of one's post on the basis of the ups and downs of the quotidian round. One must have an idea of what is needed and seek self-consciously to grasp what one has the capacity to do and what one does not have the capacity to do.

Often, one must act not to fulfill some strategic goal, but simply to maintain the character of the place or the organization amid the multiple conflicting purposes and goals of its inhabitants. This need not lead to discouragement, nor should it prevent anyone from undertaking leadership responsibilities; obviously, leadership is essential and there can be much satisfaction in it.

Moreover, greater thoughtfulness about the elements of leadership is needed in an age of frequently mindless activism. Leadership is not solely about endless activity. Thinking is, in many cases, more appropriate than doing. I hope to convey the excitement and value of thinking to balance the more obvious, sometimes superficial, excitement of acting.

The great writers do not insulate the study of leadership from a larger consideration of the human condition, of the contingencies of historical existence, and of the existence of ineradicable predicaments. They do not think we are free to deal merely with "problems" that can be solved once and for all. They insist on the indispensability of insight based on experience and enlarged by historical and philosophical study. They pay close attention to the appropriate motivations for seeking to lead, and they present a more austere view of leadership than is characteristic of much contemporary discussion. They see the need of profundity in the characters of individual leaders that cannot be acquired by mere reliance on any techniques and that is hard to convey in simple lessons (although simple lessons are a necessary part of achieving thoughtfulness about leading or any subject). One cannot but be struck in reading the reflections of the ancient Greeks and Romans, for example, that even when they glorify leadership, they remain sober about how far human beings can overcome the vicissitudes of time, place, and history. In returning such voices to the conversation on leadership, we hope to deepen our thinking, and to put in perspective current thinking about leading and leadership. To study leadership as proposed, then, is also to seek greater self-understanding.

This anthology urges a sober assessment of the difficulties, possibilities, and limitations of leadership while embracing its centrality in a democratic society. It asks that we thoughtfully understand leadership without discouraging aspirations to leadership. It is for those of us who are led as well as for those who lead.

Part I

CLASSICAL HORIZONS

Part I of this book is called *Classical Horizons*. Each reading in Part I presents a version of what I shall call a classical view of leadership, by which I mean "leadership" as it was understood before the rise of three assumptions integral to modern political thinking: the universal acceptance of the democratic spirit, the belief that the human task is to seek infinite improvement of the human condition, and the belief that human beings can take their destinies into their own hands.

The selections in Part I neither depend on nor presuppose any of these three assumptions, yet what they tell us is clearly pertinent to our reflections on leadership. The classical writers are thus both familiar and unfamiliar. They are helpful, often a source of consolation, but they also challenge some of our assumptions. The dialogue we have among ourselves can be deepened by engaging our predecessors in dialogue.

Confucius

In the selections included from Confucius, the reader will find an emphasis on self-discipline and constant thoughtfulness, a disdain for glory-seeking and popularity, and a focus on effectiveness. The heart of the matter is to cure oneself of anxiety for recognition, cultivating instead that worthiness of recognition which qualifies one to speak with authority. Actual recognition is far less important than having the qualities of character and judgment that make one eligible for recognition. One's worthiness is to be balanced by a sense of one's own unimportance. It is better to be worthy and unrecognized than to be recognized on false premises.

Confucius also emphasizes cultivating a precise kind of civility in one's relations with others that requires the formation of a public persona which is not identical with one's private self. Both here and in the other selections in Part I, this is a project of self-overcoming which is necessary if one is to become fully attentive to one's surrounding conditions and the strengths and weaknesses of those with whom one must deal.

Lao-tzu

Lao-tzu also stresses the importance of the work to be done, not personal glory. One who would lead must be able to discern the characteristics of the group, what it can and cannot do. Strikingly, Lao-tzu urges attention to the group when it is not in action. Hyperactivity obscures the character of the group and makes it difficult to judge when it is or is not operating within its capacities. In hyperactivity one becomes forgetful of oneself in the sense of forgetting to be careful about what sort of self one is, and thus loses the capacity to overcome oneself for the sake of the proper work to be done. Being forgetful in this sense increases the tendency to promote oneself—to glorify what is one's own—and thus to go astray from the true task of leadership. One must be always attentive to the self in order to overcome it, remembering it in the right way and forgetting it in another.

Lao-tzu warns that intervening too much is counterproductive. The lust to have many accomplishments—a checklist to prove oneself a vigorous and successful leader—is dangerous because it too tends to (perhaps inadvertent) self-promotion rather than to the improvement of the group in terms of its actual capacities. People often mistake this taking on of burdens for self-transcendence, when it may be only a manifestation of the anxiety to justify oneself.

The best situation is when what is achieved seems to flow naturally from what has already been going on: the accomplishment is naturally a part of the undertakings of all involved, not of the leader alone. This submersion of the leader's self is both necessary and antithetical to the mentality which reduces the measure of success to the tasks checked off.

In order to get people to do what they "ought to do," one should not constantly preach to them about what they "ought to do," but instead encourage them to catch sight of what is possible because of what they already know how to do. It is when the "ought" is integral to what already "is" that ideas become more than merely ideas and are put into action. It is crucial to see how much can be done with a little.

All of this is a challenge to a certain type of "modern" thinking which, driven by an inability to accept the state of affairs, hankers for an alternative (perfected) world we do not and very likely will not have. The idea is to exemplify rather than preach, and to manifest integrity not by uttering abstract ideals, but by displaying stability of understanding amidst the contingencies of life. There is much about how things happen that we shall never understand, but the more we know of what can be known (through attentiveness, and detachment from preoccupation with "oughts"), the more we can speak and act effectively, and do what we "ought" to do.

Coupled with this is Lao-tzu's insistence on honoring God and tradition. Honoring God and tradition is the way to the self-discipline and self-overcoming that is required for a good leader. In addition, it helps us to remain less vulnerable to bewitchment by abstract theories whose plausibility depends on avoiding the test of actual experience.

Plato

Plato, in his *Seventh Letter,* expresses both the need to unite power with wisdom in a philosophic ruler, and the remote possibility of achieving this lofty goal. He argues that unless and until philosophic insight and ruling power are united, the typical difficulties and disillusionments of political life must persist. He does not mean to say that we should disdain politics or the civic life. We cannot abandon these most characteristically human activities. But he does mean to say that we should approach political involvement with the understanding that the world continually resists our imaginative efforts to see beyond it. Under these circumstances, the virtues of moderation and careful judgment are of high value, but they inevitably produce limited achievements. There are, to be sure, better and worse achievements of this kind, and even if philosophy cannot rule, it can deepen our capacity to assess our circumstances and become more thoughtful in our political and civic conduct.

Cicero

With Cicero we encounter the grand expression of the Stoic understanding, which has a striking resemblance to teachings of Confucius and Lao-tzu: We must detach ourselves from the outwardness of things in order to see beyond current talk and trends and to maintain sight of serious, high purposes.

Cicero reviews the pros and cons of acting in, or retiring from, the world. The decision should not be made on grounds of fear, desire, or love of wealth, but on grounds of careful analysis of what is right for oneself. Those of true philosophic genius have a powerful reason, perhaps a unique duty, to retire from the world. But there is a special virtue in entering the world of public affairs if one has administrative ability and strong moral courage. There may be glory in it, but there is especially a kind of satisfaction that inheres in the noble discharge of a duty to human well-being, a duty which one has because one has the capacity to act in this way.

Cicero also makes clear that one must prepare for public life. One must not dwell on honor, but rather assess one's ability to succeed (how does one do this?), make moral strength an inherent feature of one's existence, and seek a brave and resolute spirit. One must prepare to rule for the good of the whole and develop courtesy, forbearance, and mental poise. Personal courage must be coupled with intellectual ability, a certain philosophic reflectiveness.

Plutarch, Shelley, and Keats

Plutarch, the great essayist and biographer, provides both anecdotal and reflective advice on how to benefit from one's enemies. He notes that enemies often clearly perceive features of our character and conduct which are brushed over or taken for granted by our friends, and he provides sound advice on the conduct of statemanship. He emphasizes nobility of purpose, modesty of expectation for honor and glory, and self-respect through self-control.

The poets Shelley and Keats recall us to the temporality that sweeps all human things away, offering a poetic coda to the reflections both of Plutarch and others of our writers. These poems evoke a disposition which goes against the grain of a certain modern sensibility, though they are composed by modern poets: they represent the appearance, in the midst of the modern aspiration to progress, of the anxiety that accompanies all claims to progress. The paradox of enduring mutability and the experience of rise and decline, of continual change within the apparently stable order of things, give us reasons, with Plutarch, to be modest not so much in our aspirations as in our expectations and wary of evanescent glories. The image of Ozymandias, the "king of kings" who yet is a decayed "colossal wreck," is a physical embodiment of a false stability, a remainder, but lifeless. Fame is both attractive and arbitrary. We may not ever fully know why it is given or refused to those who seek it and who long for it. Stability comes with the acceptance that it is not the victories or the defeats but the manner of conducting a life through both victory and defeat that suffices. The rest must take care of itself.

Montaigne

In his essay "Of Glory," Montaigne is concerned to teach us to shun glory as an object to be pursued, and particularly to shun flattery. We are, he says, "double within ourselves." Glory could either help or hinder us in the pursuit of virtue, which is foremost. If we were to pursue virtue only in public, we would be glory-seeking; virtue would only be a means to recognition. But there is inner glory which may be unrecognized. The cultivation of the inner glory is the protective resource without which the outer glory will lead us astray. Glory is like a shadow—it is an empty presence. Deeds, not fame, are most important, and the contentment of a well-regulated conscience.

Besides, fame, like all earthly delights, is fleeting. Almost everything that ever happened will be forgotten—if it is even lucky enough to be recorded at all by poets or historians. Reflection on the fleetingness of our deeds opens us to a transcending motive for virtue which carries us beyond ourselves by overcoming our misplaced hopes of perpetuating ourselves. Duty comes before honor. The true man of honor is one who would do his duty even at the risk of dishonor. This is a hard demand, and it is difficult to see how one would willingly respond to it if one were moved solely by lust for recognition amidst the changing opinions of mankind.

Bacon

Francis Bacon in his essay "Of Great Place" observes that to occupy great place is to endure a kind of servitude. The true reason to aspire is to do good. Since thoughts are only dreams, the best thoughts are those which become manifest in the reality of life. Man is somewhat like God in that action requires position and power, and rest comes only after accomplishment. Yet those who seek power and get it, because they are not, after all, really God, lose their liberty in so doing. One's standing is slippery, prompting an inward unhappiness which in turn makes external rewards excessively tempting. Also, unlike God, we are mortal, and since natural philosophy or science cannot solve the problem of death, we are drawn to merit and renown in the hope our deeds will perpetuate our memory. However, perpetual remembrance—a meager substitute for immortality—is contingent and unlikely.

For these reasons, according to Bacon, aspirations to power need regulation by thoughtfulness. Yet, while it is the greatest safeguard amidst these perils, thoughtfulness also curtails facile ideas of success and makes one aware of the uncertainty and precariousness of success. As one becomes more known to others, one risks becoming unknown to oneself.

Thoughtfulness requires the study of the wisdom of the ancients in order to know what is best, and the study of modern times to learn what is presently needed. Technically, one must be rule-bound or conventional, departing from rules only for good reasons. Subscription to rules guards against the mistake of trying to direct everything.

Above all, one must seek clarity in policy but maintain reserve about one-self. For Bacon, leadership is not about oneself, and yet the self is always present and so, in a way, cannot help but be about oneself. There is an inner dialectic which is unavoidable and indispensable. Unfortunately, the idea of this dialectic can be expressed, but the capacity to maintain the inner dialectic cannot be taught. In the final analysis, the requirement of success in leadership is not reducible to technique or training. Thus it cannot be known in advance how even the most talented will fare.

Gracián

Balthasar Gracián conveys the sense of the world's treacherousness and the competition of the vulgar with the noble. Above all, one needs the art of prudence or worldly wisdom to pass through the world safely. One needs wisdom, but part of wisdom is cunning. Nor is cunning antithetical either to virtue or to doing good works—rather, it is necessary. This view caused some to accuse Gracián of Machiavellism. What is needed, according to Gracián, is a reflective life that is on guard and always vigilant for the conditions in which one must operate, since the conditions are seldom a matter of choice.

It is part of wisdom to be mindful of the temporality of all things. If one is exposed to the public world, then one must operate with constant awareness and calculation. To philosophize is to temper boldness with self-control. Gracián's advice is as much for the isolated as for the exalted individual; like Machiavelli, he thinks both of the high from the view of the low, and of the low from the view of the high.

Morgenthau

This section closes with Hans J. Morgenthau's essay "Love and Power," from a volume of his essays called *The Restoration of American Politics*. Readers may wonder why "classical horizons" concludes with a twentieth-century essay. We should remember that "classical" here refers only in part to historical periods. It also refers to a way of thinking that might appear in many different times and places. Morgenthau, one of the greatest students of political philosophy and international politics among political scientists of our time, calls us back to the classical writers to gain a critical perspective on our assumptions about the political and social life. When he speaks of the "restoration" of American politics, he means that there are perspectives on the nature of our lives together that have been lost from sight and that we need to recover. He shows us that the "classical horizon" persists as a possibility in our time and that thoughtful contemporaries can still take their bearings from the wisdom of ancient writers.

The premise of this book is that we must become more thoughtful and more philosophical about the meaning of leadership. Morgenthau, in making use of the old authors, brings home their perennial value. They exemplify a way of being thoughtful about what we are trying to do and what we can expect from our public life.

The reader will gain the impression that, for all their sound advice, the classical writers believed that the most important features of leadership cannot be taught or imparted. One cannot know what will happen until one must act and lead. This may seem unsettling. Nonetheless, we moderns, influenced by claims to study social life scientifically, need to consider carefully what we find in these reflections. Thus begins our dialogue with the classical authors.

"The Essential Confucius"

Confucius (551–479 B.C.) was born in China in the state of Lu. Though he held a number of government jobs intermittently throughout his life, he is regarded primarily as a teacher and the founder of Confucianism. Three doctrines form the core of Confucius' teaching: benevolence (treating others as one would like to be treated by others and avoiding doing to others what one would not want done to oneself); the notion of the superior man (one who practices benevolence); and right behavior with others, practiced ritualistically. A collection of Confucius' sayings were first presented in a book called the Analects *in approximately 400 B.C.*

Confucius said, "Don't worry about having no position; worry about that whereby you may effectively become established. Don't worry that no one recognizes you; seek to be worthy of recognition." (4:14)

*

Confucius said, "The way ideal people relate to the world is to avoid both rejection and attachment. To treat others justly is their way of association." (4:6)

*

Confucius said to Zichan, a famous prime minister of the state of Zheng, "The way of exemplary people is fourfold. They are deferential in their own conduct, respectful in their service of employers, generous in taking care of people, and just in employing people." (5:16)

*

Confucius said, "Exemplary people understand matters of justice; small people understand matters of profit." (1:16)

*

A certain pupil asked Confucius about government: "What qualifies one to participate in government?" Confucius said, "Honor five refinements, and get rid of four evils. Then you can participate in government." The pupil asked, "What are the five refinements?" Confucius said, "Good people are generous without being wasteful; they are hardworking without being resentful; they desire without being greedy; they are at ease without being haughty; they are dignified without being fierce." The pupil asked, "What does it mean to be generous without being wasteful?" Confucius replied, "To benefit the people based on what they find beneficial. Is this not generosity without waste?" Confucius continued, "If they work hard after having chosen what they can work hard at, who would be resentful? If you want humaneness and get humaneness, then why would you be greedy? Cultivated people do not dare to be inconsiderate, whether of many or few, of the small or the great, of the young or the old; is this not ease without haughtiness? Cultivated people are proper in dress and solemn in mien, so that others are awed when they look at them; is this not dignity without ferocity?" The pupil asked, "What are the four evils?" Confucius replied, "To execute without having admonished; this is called cruelty. To examine accomplishments without having instructed; this is called brutality. To be lax in direction yet make deadlines; this is called viciousness. To be stingy in giving what is due to others; this is called being bureaucratic." (20:4)

*

Confucius said, "See what they do, observe the how and why, and examine their basic premises. How can people hide? How can people hide?" (2:10)

*

Confucius said, "I do not teach the uninspired or enlighten the complacent. When I bring out one corner to show people, if they do not come back with the other three, I do not repeat." (7:8)

*

Confucius said, "It is all right to talk of higher things to those who are at least middling, but not to those who are less than middling." (6:21)

*

Confucius said, "Enliven the ancient and also know what is new; then you can be a teacher." (2:11)

*

Confucius said, "If you are personally upright, things get done without any orders being given. If you are not personally upright, no one will obey even if you do give orders." (13:6)

*

One of the elder statesmen of Lu asked Confucius, "How would it be to make the people serious and loyal, and thus enthusiastic?" Confucius said, "Preside over them with dignity, and they will be serious. Be filial and kind, and they will be loyal. Promote the good, instruct the unskilled, and they will be enthusiastic." (2:20)

*

A disciple asked Confucius about government. Confucius said, "Dwell on it tirelessly; carry it out faithfully." (12:14)

*

The administrator of a certain clan asked Confucius about government. Confucius said, "Put the officers ahead of yourself, and forgive small errors. Appoint the wise and talented to office." The administrator said, "How can I know the wise and talented to appoint them to office?" Confucius said, "Appoint those you know of. As for those you don't know, will others ignore them?" (13:2)

*

Confucius said, "Cultivated people seek from themselves; small people seek from others." (15:17)

*

Confucius said, "Clever talk disrupts virtue; a little lack of forbearance disrupts great plans." (15:27)

*

Confucius said, "If you are exacting with yourself but forgiving to others, then you will put enmity at a distance." (15:15)

*

A disciple asked Confucius, "How is it when everyone in your hometown likes you?" Confucius said, "Not good enough." The disciple asked, "How about if everyone in your hometown dislikes you?" Confucius said, "Not good enough. It is better when the good among the people like you and the bad dislike you." (13:24)

*

Confucius said, "When I am with a group of people all day and the conversation never touches on matters of justice but inclines to the exercise of petty wit, I have a hard time." (15:17)

*

Confucius said, "Cultivated people have nine thoughts. When they look, they think of how to see clearly. When they listen, they think of how to hear keenly. In regard to their appearance, they think of how to be warm. In their demeanor, they think of how to be respectful. In their speech, they think of how to be truthful. In their work, they think of how to be serious. When in doubt, they think of how to pose questions. When angry, they think of trouble. When they see gain to be had, they think of justice." (16:10)

*

Confucius said, "If you can correct yourself, what trouble would you have in government? If you cannot correct yourself, what can you do about correcting others?" (13:13)

*

Confucius said, "Exemplary people are even-tempered and clear-minded. Petty people are always fretting." (7:36)

*

Confucius said, "When everyone dislikes something, it should be examined. When everyone likes something, it should be examined." (15:28)

*

Confucius said, "If they are directed by government policy and made orderly by punishment, the people will try to get off scot-free and feel no shame about it. If they are guided by charisma and unified by courtesy, they will be conscientious and upright of character." (2:3)

*

Confucius said of two famous purists, "They didn't think about past evils, so they were seldom resented." (5:23)

Lao-tzu, *Tao-te Ching*

According to legend, Lao-tzu (Laozi), who was an older contemporary of Confucius and founder of Taoism, authored the classic Taoist text Tao-te Ching *(Daode Jing) as a condition of leaving his homeland in China for a new life in Tibet. The central teaching of Lao-tzu is the Tao, or Way, to ultimate reality. Lao-tzu teaches that we can achieve a harmony of opposites through a blend of the feminine (yin) and the masculine (yang) forces, and we sustain this harmony through the power (te) of contemplation, or "creative quietude."*

Chapter 9: A Good Group[1]

A good group is better than a spectacular group.

When leaders become Superstars, the teacher outshines the teaching.

Also, very few superstars are down-to-earth. Fame breeds fame. Before long they get carried away with themselves. They then fly off center and crash.

The wise leader settles for good work and then lets others have the floor. The leader does not take all the credit for what happens and has no need for fame.

A moderate ego demonstrates wisdom.

Chapter 11: The Group Field

Pay attention to silence. What is happening when nothing is happening in group? That is the group field.

Thirteen people sit in a circle, but it is the climate or the spirit in the center of the circle, where nothing is happening, that determines the nature of the group field.

Learn to see emptiness. When you enter an empty house, can you feel the mood of the place? It is the same with a vase or pot; learn to see the emptiness inside, which is the usefulness of it.

People's speech and actions are figural events. They give the group form and content.

The silences and empty spaces, on the other hand, reveal the group's essential mood, the context for everything that happens. That is the group field.

1. The chapter numbers used here are the same as those used in other versions of *Tao-te Ching;* the chapter titles are John Heider's [editor's note].

Chapter 17: Like a Midwife

The wise leader does not intervene unnecessarily. The leader's presence is felt, but often the group runs itself.

Lesser leaders do a lot, say a lot, have followers, and form cults.

Even worse ones use fear to energize the group and force to overcome resistance.

Only the most dreadful leaders have bad reputations.

Remember that you are facilitating another person's process. It is not your process. Do not intrude. Do not control. Do not force your own needs and insights into the foreground.

If you do not trust a person's process, that person will not trust you.

Imagine that you are a midwife. You are assisting at someone else's birth. Do good without show or fuss. Facilitate what is happening rather than what you think ought to be happening. If you must take the lead, lead so that the mother is helped, yet still free and in charge.

When the baby is born, the mother will say: we did it ourselves.

Chapter 26: Center and Ground

The leader who is centered and grounded can work with erratic people and critical group situations without harm.

Being centered means having the ability to recover one's balance, even in the midst of action. A centered person is not subject to passing whims or sudden excitements.

Being grounded means being down-to-earth, having gravity or weight. I know where I stand, and I know what I stand for: that is ground.

The centered and grounded leader has stability and a sense of self.

One who is not stable can easily get carried away by the intensity of leadership and make mistakes of judgment or even become ill.

Chapter 31: Harsh Interventions

There are times when it seems as if one must intervene powerfully, suddenly, and even harshly. The wise leader does this only when all else fails.

As a rule, the leader feels more wholesome when the group process is flowing freely and unfolding naturally, when delicate facilitations far outnumber harsh interventions.

Harsh interventions are a warning that the leader may be uncentered or have an emotional attachment to whatever is happening. A special awareness is called for.

Even if harsh interventions succeed brilliantly, there is no cause for celebration. There has been injury. Someone's process has been violated.

Later on, the person whose process has been violated may well become less
open and more defended. There will be a deeper resistance and possibly even
resentment.

Making people do what you think they ought to do does not lead toward
clarity and consciousness. While they may do what you tell them to do at the
time, they will cringe inwardly, grow confused, and plot revenge.

That is why your victory is actually a failure.

Chapter 43: Gentle Interventions

Gentle interventions, if they are clear, overcome rigid resistances.

If gentleness fails, try yielding or stepping back altogether. When the
leader yields, resistances relax.

Generally speaking, the leader's consciousness sheds more light on what is
happening than any number of interventions or explanations.

But a few leaders realize how much how little will do.

Chapter 46: Nothing to Win

The well-run group is not a battlefield of egos. Of course there will be
conflict, but these energies become creative forces.

If the leader loses sight of how things happen, quarrels and fear devastate
the group field.

This is a matter of attitude. There is nothing to win or lose in group work.
Making a point does not shed light on what is happening. The need to be right
blinds people.

The wise leader knows that it is far more important to be content with
what is actually happening than to get upset over what might be happening
but isn't.

Chapter 56: The Leader's Integrity

The wise leader knows that the true nature of events cannot be captured
in words. So why pretend?

Confusing jargon is one sign of a leader who does not know how things
happen.

But what cannot be said can be demonstrated: be silent, be conscious. Consciousness works. It sheds light on what is happening. It clarifies conflicts and harmonizes the agitated individual or group field.

The leader also knows that all existence is a single whole. Therefore the leader is a neutral observer who takes no sides.

The leader cannot be seduced by offers or threats. Money, love, or fame—whether gained or lost—do not sway the leader from center.

The leader's integrity is not idealistic. It rests on a pragmatic knowledge of how things work.

Chapter 60: Don't Stir Things Up

Run the group delicately, as if you were cooking small fish.

As much as possible, allow the group process to emerge naturally. Resist any temptation to instigate issues or elicit emotions which have not appeared on their own.

If you stir things up, you will release forces before their time and under unwarranted pressure. These forces may be emotions which belong to other people or places. They may be unspecific or chaotic energies which, in response to your pressure, strike out and hit any available target.

These forces are real. They do exist in the group. But do not push. Allow them to come out when they are ready.

When hidden issues and emotions emerge naturally, they resolve themselves naturally. They are not harmful. In fact, they are no different from any other thoughts or feelings.

All energies naturally arise, take form, grow strong, come to a new resolution, and finally pass away.

Chapter 62: Whether You Know It or Not

A person does not have to join a group or be a wise leader to work things out. Life's process unfolds naturally. Conflicts resolve themselves sooner or later, whether or not a person knows how things happen.

It is true that being aware of how things happen makes one's words more potent and one's behavior more effective.

But even without the light of consciousness, people grow and improve. Being unconscious is not a crime, it is merely the lack of a very helpful ability.

Knowing how things work gives the leader more real power and ability than all the degrees or job titles the world can offer.

That is why people in every era and in every culture have honored those who know how things happen.

Chapter 72: Spiritual Awareness

Group work must include spiritual awareness, if it is to touch the existential anxiety of our times. Without awe, the awful remains unspoken; a diffuse malaise remains.

Be willing to speak of traditional religion, no matter how offended some group members may be. Overcome the bias against the word "God." The great force of our spiritual roots lies in tradition, like it or not.

The wise leader models spiritual behavior and lives in harmony with spiritual values. There is a way of knowing, higher than reason; there is a self, greater than egocentricity.

The leader demonstrates the power of selflessness and the unity of all creation.

Chapter 81: The Reward

It is more important to tell the simple, blunt truth than it is to say things that sound good. The group is not a contest of eloquence.

It is more important to act in behalf of everyone than it is to win arguments. The group is not a debating society.

It is more important to react wisely to what is happening than it is to be able to explain everything in terms of certain theories. The group is not a final examination for a college course.

The wise leader is not collecting a string of successes. The leader is helping others to find their own success. There is plenty to go around. Sharing success with others is very successful.

The single principle behind all creation teaches us that true benefit blesses everyone and diminishes no one.

The wise leader knows that the reward for doing the work arises naturally out of the work.

Plato, "Epistles"

Plato (428–347 B.C.) is generally regarded as one of the greatest thinkers of all time. Born into a family with associations among Greece's most influential political and scholarly leaders, Plato might have assumed a position of political leadership in Athens, but after the execution of his mentor Socrates in 399 B.C., Plato chose instead to leave Athens and travel. Plato then began writing what have become known as his dialogues, in which he celebrated the life and teaching of Socrates. Plato's Socrates questions opinions held about important matters such as justice, honor, courage, moderation, love, and friendship. Often Socrates deflates the confidence of his interlocutors. Wisdom is hard to gain, and means knowing that you do not know. But this admission opens the soul to a longer, more arduous search for wisdom, restraining the rash leader from ill-considered action.

In 387 B.C. Plato returned to Athens, where he founded the Academy. There Plato taught until 367 B.C., when he moved to Syracuse to become a teacher to Dionysius the Younger. During his years at the Academy and while in Syracuse, Plato composed the writings in which he explores the nature of justice, the nature of being and understanding, and the nature of the soul. The Republic, *Plato's most famous work, was written during this period. In the* Republic, *Socrates inquires into the nature of justice. Justice exists when every being performs the activities most suited to its individual nature. The ideal political community emerges when each citizen performs the functions to which each is suited and individuals recognize and perform their proper function. Reason presides over and ensures harmonious community through the rule of philosopher-kings. The soul is informed by reason through education, particularly through the dialectic that refines and shapes human understanding.*

In the seventh epistle, Plato returns to this theme and his own experience. Note the connection he makes between success in leading and the acquisition of trustworthy friends.

The more I reflected upon what was happening, upon what kind of men were active in politics, and upon the state of our laws and customs, and the older I grew, the more I realized how difficult it is to manage a city's affairs rightly. For I saw it was impossible to do anything without friends and loyal followers: and to find such men ready to hand would be a piece of sheer good luck, since our city was no longer guided by the customs and practices of our fathers, while to train up new ones was anything, but easy. And the corruption of our written laws and our customs was proceeding at such amazing speed that whereas at first I had been full of zeal for public life, when I noted these changes and saw how unstable everything was, I became in the end quite dizzy: and though I did not cease to reflect how an improvement could be brought about in our laws and in the whole constitution, yet I refrained from action, waiting for the proper time. At last I came to the conclusion that all existing states are badly governed and the condition of their laws practically incurable, without some miraculous remedy and the assistance of fortune: and I was forced to say, in praise of true philosophy, that from her height alone was it possible to discern what the nature of justice is, either in the state or in the individual, and that the ills of the human race would never end until either those who are sincerely and truly lovers of wisdom come into political power, or the rulers of our cities, by the grace of God, learn true philosophy.[2]

Such was the conviction I had when I arrived in Italy and Sicily for the first time . . .

. . . These then, were the circumstances that account for my first[3] visit to Sicily and occupied the time of my sojourn there. Afterwards, I came home, only to return again at the urgent summons of Dionysius. Why I returned and what I did, with the explanation and justification of my actions, I will go into later for the benefit of those who wonder what my purpose was in going a second time. But in order that these incidental matters may not usurp the chief place in my letter,[4] I will first advise what is to be done in the present circumstances. This, then, is what I have to say.

When one is advising a sick man who is living in a way injurious to his health, must one not first of all tell him to change his way of life and give him further counsel only if he is willing to obey?[5] If he is not, I think any manly and self-respecting physician would break off counseling such a man, whereas anyone who would put up with him is without spirit or skill. So too with respect to a city: whether it be governed by one man or many, if its constitution is properly ordered and rightly directed, it would be sensible to give advice to its citizens concerning what would be to the city's advantage. But if it is a people who have wandered completely away from right government and resolutely

2. For the expression of this doctrine in the *Republic* see V, 473d, VI, 487e, 499b, 501e.

3. I.e., the first to Dionysius II.

4. These incidental matters (Greek characters) are not really irrelevant, despite this rather formal transition. What has gone before serves as a necessary propaedeutic to the understanding of the advice which Plato now proceeds to give. This second part of the letter extends to 337. The narrative of Plato's third journey to Sicily which begins at that point and occupies the remainder of the letter, except for a defense of Dion's motives at the end, becomes not only an apologia for Plato's actions, but also a dramatic demonstration of the difficulties facing Dion's party in putting Plato's principles into effect.

5. Plato is evidently not very sure of the sincerity of the professed followers of Dion, nor of their willingness to carry out his suggestions. See the opening sentence of this letter.

refuse to come back upon its track and instruct their counselor to leave the
constitution strictly alone, threatening him with death if he changes it,[6] and
order him instead to serve their interests and desires and show them how they
can henceforth satisfy them in the quickest and easiest way—any man, I think,
who would accept such a role as adviser is without spirit, and he who refuses
is the true man. These are my principles: and whenever anyone consults me on
a question of importance in his life, such as the making of money, or the care
of his body or soul, if it appears to me that he follows some plan in his daily
life or is willing to listen to reason on the matters he lays before me, I advise
him gladly and don't stop with merely discharging my duty. But a man who
does not consult me at all, or makes it clear that he will not follow advice that
is given him—to such a man I do not take it upon myself to offer counsel; nor
would I use constraint upon him, not even if he were my own son. Upon a
slave I might force my advice, compelling him to follow it against his will; but
to use compulsion upon a father or mother is to me an impious act,[7] unless
their judgment has been impaired by disease. If they are fixed in a way of life
that pleases them, though it may not please me I should not antagonize them
by useless admonitions, nor yet by flattery and complaisance encourage them
in satisfaction of desires that I would die rather than embrace. This is the principle which a wise man must follow in his relations towards his own city. Let
him warn her, if he thinks her constitution is corrupt and there is a prospect
that his words will be listened to and not put him in danger of his life; but let
him not use violence upon his fatherland to bring about a change of constitution. If what he thinks is best can only be accomplished by the exile and
slaughter of men, let him keep his peace and pray for the welfare of himself
and his city.

6. Cf. Rep. IV, 426c.
7. "Father or mother"; cf. Crito 51c. Plato is doubtless thinking of Athens here. Compare this explanation of his political inactivity at Athens with that implied in Rep. VI, 496b–e. Cicero no doubt
refers to the present passage in Fam. I, 9, 18.

Cicero, *De Officiis*

Marcus Tullius Cicero (106–43 B.C.) is remembered for his masterful essays and speeches on ethics and politics and his active role in ancient Roman political life. Born into an elite family, Cicero made a name for himself in politics at an early age, advancing fairly quickly through the courts, by defending the interests of, among others, Pompey the Great. In 63 B.C. Cicero advanced to the consulship. In this position, he successfully suppressed a conspiracy. Later he secured the execution of some of the conspirators, an act for which he was exiled. He was recalled to Rome a year after being exiled, but after further political humiliations, he turned to more literary pursuits, writing De oratore *in 55 B.C. and* De republica *between 54 and 51 B.C. He returned to public life in 51 B.C. as governor of Cilicia and later returned to Rome just as a civil war was beginning. Cicero took Pompey's side against Caesar, and though Pompey was defeated, Caesar pardoned Cicero. A decision to align himself politically with Octavian (later Emperor Augustus) eventually led to Cicero's being put to death at the insistence of Mark Antony in 43 B.C.*

BOOK I. xx.

XX. The soul that is altogether courageous and great is marked above all by two characteristics: one of these is indifference to outward circumstances; for such a person cherishes the conviction that nothing but moral goodness and propriety deserves to be either admired or wished for or striven after, and that he ought not to be subject to any man or any passion or any accident of fortune. The second characteristic is that, when the soul is disciplined in the way above mentioned, one should do deeds not only great and in the highest degree useful, but extremely arduous and laborious and fraught with danger both to life and to many things that make life worth living.

All the glory and greatness and, I may add, all the usefulness of these two characteristics of courage are centred in the latter; the rational cause that makes men great, in the former. For it is the former that contains the element that makes souls pre-eminent and indifferent to worldly fortune. And this quality is distinguished by two criteria: (1) if one account moral rectitude as the only good; and (2) if one be free from all passion. For we must agree that it takes a brave and heroic soul to hold as slight what most people think grand and glorious, and to disregard it from fixed and settled principles. And it requires strength of character and great singleness of purpose to bear what seems painful, as it comes to pass in many and various forms in human life, and to bear it so unflinchingly as not to be shaken in the least from one's natural state of the dignity of a philosopher. Moreover, it would be inconsistent for the man who is not overcome by fear to be overcome by desire, or for the man who has shown himself invincible to toil to be conquered by pleasure. We must, therefore, not only avoid the latter, but also beware of ambition for wealth; for there is nothing so characteristic of narrowness and littleness of soul as the love of riches; and there is nothing more honourable and noble than to be indifferent to money, if one does not possess it, and to devote it to beneficence and liberality, if one does possess it.

As I said before, we must also beware of ambition for glory; for it robs us of liberty, and in defence of liberty a high-souled man should stake everything. And one ought not to seek military authority; nay, rather it ought sometimes to be declined, sometimes to be resigned.

Again, we must keep ourselves free from every disturbing emotion, not only from desire and fear, but also from excessive pain and pleasure, and from anger so that we may enjoy that calm of soul and freedom from care which bring both moral stability and dignity of character. But there have been many and still are many who, while pursuing that calm of soul of which I speak, have withdrawn from civic duty and taken refuge in retirement. Among such have been found the most famous and by far the foremost philosophers and certain other earnest, thoughtful men who could not endure the conduct of either the people or their leaders; some of them, too, lived in the country and found their pleasure in the management of their private estates. Such men have had the same aims as kings—to suffer no want, to be subject to no authority, to enjoy their liberty, that is, in its essence, to live just as they please.

XXI. So, while this desire is common to men of political ambitions and men of retirement, of whom I have just spoken, the one class thinks they can attain their end if they secure large means; the other, if they are content with the little they have. And, in this matter, neither way of thinking is altogether to be condemned; but the life of retirement is easier and safer and at the same time less burdensome or troublesome to others, while the career of those who apply themselves to statecraft and to conducting great enterprises is more profitable to mankind and contributes more to their own greatness and renown

So perhaps those men of extraordinary genius who have devoted themselves to learning must be excused for not taking part in public affairs; likewise, those who from ill-health or for some still more valid reason have retired from the service of the state and left to others the opportunity and the glory of its administration. But if those who have no such excuse profess a scorn for civil and military offices, which most people admire, I think that this should be set down not to their credit but to their discredit; for in so far as they care little, as they say, for glory and count it as naught, it is difficult not to sympathize with their attitude; in reality, however, they seem to dread the toil and trouble and also, perhaps, the discredit and humiliation of political failure and defeat. For there are people who in opposite circumstances do not act consistently: they have the utmost contempt for pleasure, but in pain they are too sensitive; they are indifferent to glory, but they are crushed by disgrace; and even in their inconsistency they show no great consistency.

But those whom Nature has endowed with the capacity for administering public affairs should put aside all hesitation, enter the race for public office, and take a hand in directing the government; for in no other way can a government be administered or greatness of spirit be made manifest. Statesmen, too, no less than philosophers—perhaps even more so—should carry themselves with that greatness of spirit and indifference to outward circumstances to which I so often refer, together with calm of soul and freedom from care, if they are to be free from worries and lead a dignified and self-consistent life. This is easier for the philosophers; as their life is less exposed to the assaults of fortune, their wants are fewer; and, if any misfortune overtakes them, their fall is not so disastrous. Not without reason, therefore, are stronger emotions aroused in those who engage in public life than in those who live in retirement, and greater is their ambition for success; the more, therefore, do they need to enjoy greatness of spirit and freedom from annoying cares.

If anyone is entering public life, let him beware of thinking only of the honour that it brings; but let him be sure also that he has the ability to succeed. At the same time, let him take care not to lose heart too readily through discouragement nor yet to be over-confident through ambition. In a word, before undertaking any enterprise, careful preparation must be made.

XXIII. That moral goodness which we look for in a lofty, high-minded spirit is secured, of course, by moral, not by physical strength. And yet the body must be trained and so disciplined that it can obey the dictates of judgment and reason in attending to business and in enduring toil. But that moral goodness which is our theme depends wholly upon the thought and attention given to it by the mind. And, in this way, the men who in a civil capacity direct the affairs of the nation render no less important service than they who conduct its wars: by their statesmanship oftentimes wars are either averted or terminated; sometimes also they are declared. Upon Marcus Cato's counsel, for example, the Third Punic War was undertaken, and in its conduct his influence was dominant, even after he was dead. And so diplomacy in the friendly settlement of controversies is more desirable than courage in settling them on the battlefield; but we must be careful not to take that course merely for the sake of avoiding war rather than for the sake of public expediency. War, however, should be undertaken in such a way as to make it evident that it has no other object than to secure peace.

But it takes a brave and resolute spirit not to be disconcerted in times of difficulty or ruffled and thrown off one's feet, as the saying is, but to keep one's presence of mind and one's self-possession and not to swerve from the path of reason.

Now all this requires great personal courage; but it also calls for great intellectual ability by reflection to anticipate the future, to discover some time in advance what may happen whether for good or for ill, and what must be done in any possible event, and never to be reduced to having to say "I had not thought of that."

These are the activities that mark a spirit strong, high, and self-reliant in its prudence and wisdom. But to mix rashly in the fray and to fight hand to hand with the enemy is but a barbarous and brutish kind of business. Yet when the stress of circumstances demands it, we must gird on the sword and prefer death to slavery and disgrace.

XXV. Those who propose to take charge of the affairs of government should not fail to remember two of Plato's rules: first, to keep the good of the people so clearly in view that regardless of their own interests they will make their every action conform to that; second, to care for the welfare of the whole body politic and not in serving the interests of some one party to betray the rest. For the administration of the government, like the office of a trustee, must be conducted for the benefit of those entrusted to one's care, not of those to whom it is entrusted. Now, those who care for the interests of a part of the citizens and neglect another part, introduce into the civil service a dangerous element—dissension and party strife. The result is that some are found to be loyal supporters of the democratic, others of the aristocratic party, and few of the nation as a whole.

As a result of this party spirit bitter strife arose at Athens, and in our own country not only dissensions but also disastrous civil wars broke out. All this the citizen who is patriotic, brave, and worthy of a leading place in the state will shun with abhorrence; he will dedicate himself unreservedly to his country, without aiming at influence or power for himself; and he will devote himself to the state in its entirety in such a way as to further the interests of all. Besides, he will not expose anyone to hatred or disrepute by groundless charges, but he will surely cleave to justice and honour so closely that he will submit to any loss, however heavy, rather than be untrue to them, and will face death itself rather than renounce them.

A most wretched custom, assuredly, is our electioneering and scrambling for office. Concerning this also we find a fine thought in Plato: "Those who compete against one another," he says, "to see which of the two candidates shall administer the government, are like sailors quarrelling as to which one of them shall do the steering." And he likewise lays down the rule that we should regard only those as adversaries who take up arms against the state, not those who strive to have the government administered according to their convictions. This was the spirit of the disagreement between Publius Africanus and Quintus Metellus: there was in it no trace of rancour.

Neither must we listen to those who think that one should indulge in violent anger against one's political enemies and imagine that such is the attitude of a great-spirited, brave man. For nothing is more commendable, nothing more becoming in a pre-eminently great man than courtesy and forbearance. Indeed, in a free people, where all enjoy equal rights before the law, we must school ourselves to affability and what is called "mental poise"; for if we are irritated when people intrude upon us at unseasonable hours or make unreasonable requests, we shall develop a sour, churlish temper, prejudicial to ourselves and offensive to others. And yet gentleness of spirit and forbearance are to be commended only with the understanding that strictness may be exercised for the good of the state; for without that, the government cannot be well administered. On the other hand, if punishment or correction must be administered, it need not be insulting; it ought to have regard to the welfare of the state, not to the personal satisfaction of the man who administers the punishment or reproof.

We should take care also that the punishment shall not be out of proportion to the offence, and that some shall not be chastised for the same fault for which others are not even called to account. In administering punishment it is above all necessary to allow no trace of anger. For if anyone proceeds in a passion to inflict punishment, he will never observe that happy mean which lies between excess and defect. This doctrine of the mean is approved by the Peripatetics—and wisely approved, if only they did not speak in praise of anger and tell us that it is a gift bestowed on us by Nature for a good purpose. But, in reality, anger is in every circumstance to be eradicated; and it is to be desired that they who administer the government should be like the laws, which are led to inflict punishment not by wrath but by justice.

Plutarch, *Moralia*

Plutarch (46–120) was a Greek biographer and essayist. In his Parallel Lives, *forty-six biographies pairing Greek and Roman counterparts, and in his* Moralia, *essays of advice and practical wisdom, Plutarch, in searching character to learn the lessons of human conduct, provided many salutary anecdotes which made his writings a perennial source of practical wisdom and literary inspiration.*

From "How to Profit by One's Enemies"

1. I observe, my dear Cornelius Pulcher, that you have chosen the mildest form of official administration, in which you are as helpful as possible to the public interests while at the same time you show yourself to be very amiable in private to those who have audience with you. Now it may be possible to find a country, in which, as it is recorded of Crete, there are no wild animals, but a government which has not had to bear with envy or jealous rivalry or contention—emotions most productive of enmity—has not hitherto existed. For our very friendships, if nothing else, involve us in enmities. This is what the wise Chilon had in mind, when he asked the man who boasted that he had no enemy whether he had no friend either. Therefore it seems to me to be the duty of a statesman not only to have thoroughly investigated the subject of enemies in general, but also in his reading of Xenophon to have given more than passing attention to the remark that it is a trait of the man of sense "to derive profit even from his enemies." Some thoughts, therefore, on this subject, which I recently had occasion to express, I have put together in practically the same words, and now send them to you, with the omission, so far as possible, of matter contained in my *Advice to Statesmen,* since I observe that you often have that book close at hand. . . .

So look at your enemy, and see whether, in spite of his being in most respects harmful and difficult to manage, he does not in some way or other afford you means of getting hold of him and of using him as you can use no one else, and so can be of profit to you. Many of the circumstances of life are unkindly and hateful and repellent to those who have to meet them; yet you observe that some have employed their attacks of bodily illness for quiet resting, and trials which have fallen to the lot of many have but strengthened and trained them. Some, too, have made banishment and loss of property a means of leisure and philosophic study, as did Diogenes and Crates. And Zeno, on learning that the ship which bore his venture had been wrecked, exclaimed, "A

real kindness, O Fortune, that thou, too, dost join in driving us to the philosopher's cloak!" For just as those animals which have the strongest and soundest
stomachs can eat and digest snakes and scorpions, and there are some even that
derive nourishment from stones and shells (for they transmute such things by
reason of the vigour and heat of their spirit), while fastidious and sickly persons are nauseated if they partake of bread and wine, so fools spoil even their
friendships, while wise men are able to make a fitting use even of their enmities . . .

So the man who knows that his enemy is his competitor in life and repute is more heedful of himself, and more circumspect about his actions, and
brings his life into a more thorough harmony. For it is a peculiar mark of vice,
that we feel more ashamed of our faults before our enemies than before our
friends . . .

If you wish to distress the man who hates you, do not revile him as lewd,
effeminate, licentious, vulgar, or illiberal, but be a man yourself, show self-
control, be truthful, and treat with kindness and justice those who have to deal
with you. And if you are led into reviling, remove yourself as far as possible
from the things for which you revile him. Enter within the portals of your own
soul, look about to see if there be any rottenness there, lest some vice lurking
somewhere within whisper to you the words of the tragedian[8]:

> Wouldn't thou heal others, full of sores thyself?

If you call your enemy uneducated, strive to intensify in yourself the love
of learning and industry; if you call him a coward, rouse even more your self-
reliance and manliness; if you call him unchaste and licentious, obliterate from
your soul whatever trace of devotion to pleasure may be lurking there unper-
ceived. For there is nothing more disgraceful or painful than evil-speaking that
recoils upon its author. So reflected light appears to be the more troublesome
in cases of weak eyesight, and the same is true of censures that by the truth
are brought back upon the very persons who are responsible for them. For as
surely the north-east wind brings the clouds, so surely does a bad life bring
revilings upon itself.

5. As often as Plato found himself in the company of persons whose conduct was unseemly, he was wont to say to himself, "Is it possible that I am
like them?" But if the man who reviles another's life will at once carefully
inspect his own, and readjust it by directing and turning it aside into the opposite course, he will have gained something useful from this reviling, which,

8. Plato.

otherwise, not only gives the impression of being useless and inane, but is so in fact . . .

7. Whenever, then, anything untrue has been said, you must not despise and disregard it just because it is false, but rather consider what word or act of yours, which of your pursuits or associations, has given colour to the calumny, and then be studiously careful to avoid it . . . For there are many things which an enemy is quicker to perceive than a friend (for Love is blind regarding the loved one, as Plato says), and inherent in hatred, along with curiosity, is the inability to hold one's tongue. . . .

11. But even if our enemies by flattery, knavery, bribery, or hireling service appear to reap their reward in the form of dishonourable and sordid influence at court or in the government, they will not be a source of annoyance but rather of joy to us when we compare our own freedom, the simplicity of our life, and its immunity from scurrilous attack. For "all the gold on earth and beneath the earth is not worth so much as virtue," as Plato says, and we must always keep ready in mind the sentiment of Solon:

> But we will not take in exchange
> All of their wealth for our virtue,

nor yet the acclamations of spectators who have dined at our expense, nor honours such as front seats among eunuchs and concubines, and royal governorships; for nothing enviable or noble ever springs from dishonour. But since "love is blind regarding the loved one," as Plato says, and it is rather our enemies who by their unseemly conduct afford us an opportunity to view our own, neither our joy at their failures nor our sorrow at their successes ought to go without being employed to some purpose, but we should take into account both their failures and successes in studying how by guarding against the former we may be better than they, and by imitating the latter no worse.

From "Precepts of Statecraft"

. . . 4. So, then, the statesman who already has attained to power and has won the people's confidence should try to train the character of the citizens, leading them gently towards that which is better and treating them with mildness; for it is a difficult task to change the multitude. But do you yourself, since you are henceforth to live as on an open stage, educate your character and put it in order; and if it is not easy wholly to banish evil from the soul, at any rate remove and repress those faults which are most flourishing and conspicuous . . .

5. However, we should not on this account neglect the charm and power of eloquence and ascribe everything to virtue, but, considering oratory to be, not the creator of persuasion but certainly its coworker, we should correct Menander's line,

> The speaker's nature, not his speech, persuades,

for both his nature and his speech do so; unless indeed, one is to affirm that just as the helmsman, not the tiller, steers the ship, and the rider, not the rein, turns the horse, so political virtue, employing, not speech, but the speaker's character as tiller or rein, sways a State, laying hold of it and directing it, as it were, from the stern, which is, in fact, as Plato says, the easiest way of turning an animal about. For those great and, as Homer calls them, "Zeus-descended" kings pad themselves out with purple robes and sceptres and guards and divine oracles, and although they enslaved the multitude by their grandeur, as if they were superior beings, they wished nevertheless to be "speakers of words" and they did not neglect the charm of speech,

> Nor the assemblies in which men make themselves greatly distinguished,[9]

softening by persuasion and overcoming by charms the fierce and violent spirit of the people. How, then, is it possible that a private person of ordinary costume and mien who wishes to lead a State may gain power and rule the multitude unless he possesses persuasion and attractive speech? . . .

8. Most of all, then, try to employ in addressing the people well-considered, not empty, speech, and to use precaution, knowing that even the great Pericles used to pray before making a public speech that no single utterance foreign to the matter in hand might occur to him. But nevertheless the orator must always keep his speech nimble and in good practice for making apt rejoinders; for occasions arise quickly and often bring with them in public affairs sudden developments . . .

27. But ambition, although it is a more pretentious word than "covetousness," is no less pernicious in the State; for there is more daring in it; since it is innate, not in slothful and abject spirits, but in the most vigorous and impetuous, and the surge which comes from the masses, raising it on the crest of the wave and sweeping it along by shouts of praise, often makes it unrestrained and unmanageable. Therefore, just as Plato said that young people should be told from childhood that it is not proper for them to wear gold on their persons

---

9. Hesiod.

or to possess it, since they have a gold of their own mingled in their souls,—a figurative reference, I believe, to the virtue derived by descent, which permeates their natures,—so let us moderate our ambition, saying that we have in ourselves honour, a gold uncorrupted, undefiled, and unpolluted by envy and fault-finding, which increases along with reasoning and the contemplation of our acts and public measures. Therefore we have no need of honours painted, modelled, or cast in bronze, in which even that which is admired is really the work of another; for the person who receives praise is not the man for whom the "trumpeter" or the "doryphorus," for example, was made, but the man by whom it was made. Cato, Rome then beginning to be full of portrait statues, refused to let one be made of himself, saying, "I prefer to have people ask why there is not a statue of me rather than why there is one." . . .

But if it is not easy to reject some favour or some kindly sentiment of the people, when it is so inclined, for men engaged in a political struggle for which the prize is not money or gifts, but which is a truly sacred contest worthy of a crown, a mere inscription suffices, a tablet, a decree, or a green branch such as Epimenides received from the Acropolis after purifying the city. And Anaxagoras, giving up the honours which had been granted him, requested that on the day of his death the children be allowed to play and be free from their lessons.

. . . For the honour should not be payment for the action, but a symbol, that it may last for a long time, as those just mentioned have lasted. But of all the three hundred statues of Demetrius of Phalerum not one acquired rust or dirt; they were all destroyed while he was still living; and those of Demades were melted down into chamber-pots. Things like that have happened to many honours, they having become offensive, not only because the recipient was worthless, but also because the gift bestowed was too great. And therefore the best and surest way to ensure the duration of honours is to reduce their cost but those which are great and top-heavy and weighty are, like ill-proportioned statues, quickly overturned.

Percy Bysshe Shelley, Selected Poems

Percy Bysshe Shelley (1792–1822) is remembered for his romantic and philo-sophical poetry, and for his lifelong rebellion against English religion and politics. The son of a prosperous country gentleman, Shelley attended Ox-ford University but was expelled in 1811. He spent the next two years in Ire-land with a child bride, Harriet Westbrook, whom he later left for Mary Wollstonecraft, the daughter of the political philosopher William Godwin. During his twenties Shelley was enormously productive, publishing many long and deeply thoughtful political poems, such as "Queen Mab," as well as many shorter poems, such as "To a Skylark." Shelley died in 1822 at the age of twenty-nine as the result of a sailing accident.

Mutability

We are as clouds that veil the midnight moon;
   How restlessly they speed, and gleam, and quiver,
Streaking the darkness radiantly!—yet soon
   Night closes round, and they are lost for ever:

Or like forgotten lyres, whose dissonant strings
   Give various response to each varying blast,
To whose frail frame no second motion brings
   One mood or modulation like the last.

We rest.—A dream has power to poison sleep;
   We rise.—One wandering thought pollutes the day;
We feel, conceive or reason, laugh or weep;
   Embrace fond woe, or cast our cares away:

It is the same!—For, be it joy or sorrow,
   The path of its departure still is free:
Man's yesterday may ne'er be like his morrow;
   Nought may endure but Mutability.

Ozymandias

I met a traveller from an antique land
Who said: Two vast and trunkless legs of stone
Stand in the desert . . . Near them, on the sand,
Half sunk, a shattered visage lies, whose frown,
And wrinkled lip, and sneer of cold command,
Tell that its sculptor well those passions read
Which yet survive, stamped on these lifeless things,
The hand that mocked them, and the heart that fed:
And on the pedestal these words appear:
'My name is Ozymandias, king of kings:
Look on my works, ye Mighty, and despair!'
Nothing beside remains. Round the decay
Of that colossal wreck, boundless and bare
The lone and level sands stretch far away.

John Keats, "On Fame"

John Keats, English romantic poet, was born in 1795 in London and apprenticed at the age of sixteen to a surgeon. He abandoned medicine for poetry, partly as a result of the encouragement of a friend, the poet Leigh Hunt. After a fairly lackluster start in his new avocation, Keats's poetic capabilities emerged with considerable force. No doubt because he was aware of his own imminent death from tuberculosis, Keats possessed an extraordinary ability to express, in his poems and correspondence, the whole of the human experience. Keats died in 1821, just one year before the death of his good friend Percy Bysshe Shelley.

> Fame, like a wayward girl, will still be coy
>   To those who woo her with too slavish knees,
> But makes surrender to some thoughtless boy,
>   And dotes the more upon a heart at ease;
> She is a gipsey, will not speak to those
>   Who have not learnt to be content without her;
> A jilt, whose ear was never whisper'd close,
>   Who thinks they scandal her who talk about her;
> A very gipsey is she, Nilus born,
>   Sister-in-law to jealous Potiphar;
> Ye love-sick bards, repay her scorn for scorn;
>   Ye artists lovelorn, madmen that ye are!
> Make your best bow to her and bid adieu;
>   Then, if she likes it, she will follow you.

Montaigne, "Of Glory"

Michel de Montaigne (1533–1592) is generally regarded the originator of the personal essay as a literary form. Though he served in the parlement of Bordeaux (France) for many years, he is remembered primarily for his Essays, *which were published in three volumes, and which cover a remarkably broad range of subjects. Montaigne's* Essays *were first translated into English in 1603.*

There is the name and the thing. The name is a sound which designates and signifies the thing; the name is not a part of the thing or of the substance, it is an extraneous piece attached to the thing, and outside of it.

God, who is himself all fullness and the acme of all perfection, cannot grow and increase within; but his name may grow and increase by the blessing and praise we give to his external works. Which praise, since we cannot incorporate it in him, inasmuch as he can have no accession of good, we attribute to his name, which is the part outside him that is nearest him. That is why it is to God alone that glory and honor belong. And there is nothing so remote from reason as for us to go in quest of it for ourselves; for since we are indigent and necessitous within, since our essence is imperfect and continually in need of betterment, it is this betterment that we should work for.

We are all hollow and empty. It is not with wind and sound that we have to fill ourselves; we need more solid substance to repair us. A starving man would be very foolish to try to provide himself with a fine garment rather than with a good meal: we must run to what is most urgent. As our ordinary prayers say, *Glory to God in the highest, and on earth peace toward men* [Saint Luke]. We are in want of beauty, health, wisdom, virtue, and suchlike essential qualities; external ornaments will be sought after we have provided for the necessary things. Theology treats this subject amply and more pertinently, but I am hardly versed in it.

Chrysippus and Diogenes were the first and the firmest exponents of the disdain for glory; and they said that of all pleasures there was none more dangerous or more to be avoided than what comes to us from the approbation of others. In truth, experience makes us aware of many harmful betrayals at its hands. There is nothing that poisons princes so much as flattery, and nothing by which the wicked more easily gain credit with them; nor is there any pandering so fitted and so common for corrupting the chastity of women as to feed and entertain them with their praises.

The first enchantment that the Sirens employ to beguile Ulysses is of this nature:

> "Most praiseworthy Ulysses, turn to us here, here,
> Greatest of heroes, whom the men of Greece hold dear."
> *From a French translation of Homer*

Those philosophers said that all the glory in the world did not deserve that a man of understanding should so much as stretch out his finger to acquire it:

> "What's in the greatest glory, if it be but glory?"
> *Juvenal*

I mean for itself alone; for it often brings in its train many advantages for which it may become desirable. It gains us good will; it makes us less exposed to insults and injuries from others, and the like.

It was also one of the principal doctrines of Epicurus; for that precept of his school, CONCEAL YOUR LIFE, which forbids men to encumber themselves with public charges and negotiations, also necessarily presupposes our contempt for glory, which is an approbation that the world offers of the actions that we place in evidence. He who orders us to conceal ourselves and to be concerned only with ourselves, and who does not want us to be known to others, is even farther from wanting us to be honored and glorified. So he advises Idomeneus not to regulate his actions at all by common opinion or reputation, except to avoid the other accidental disadvantages that men's contempt might bring him.

Those arguments are infinitely true, in my opinion, and reasonable. But we are, I know not how, double within ourselves, with the result that we do not believe what we believe, and we cannot rid ourselves of what we condemn. Let us see the last words of Epicurus, which he spoke as he was dying. They are great and worthy of such a philosopher, and yet they bear a certain mark of commending his name and of that humor that in his precepts he had decried. Here is a letter that he dictated a little before his last gasp:

"EPICURUS TO HERMACHUS, GREETING.
While I was passing the happy and the very last day of my life, I was writing this, afflicted all the while with such pain in the bladder and intestines that nothing could be added to its greatness. But it was compensated by the pleasure which the remembrance of my discoveries and my teachings brought to my soul. Now do you, as the affection that you have had since childhood for me and for philosophy requires, embrace the protection of the children of Metrodorus."

There is his letter. And what makes me infer that this pleasure, which he says he feels in his soul over his discoveries, somewhat concerns the reputation that he hoped to acquire from them after his death, is the provision in his will by which he wants his heirs Amynomachus and Timocrates to defray such costs as Hermachus should decree for the celebration of his birthday every January, and also the expenditures that should be made on the twentieth day of each month for the entertainment of his intimate philosopher friends who should assemble in honor of the memory of himself and Metrodorus.

Carneades was the protagonist of the opposite opinion, and maintained that glory was desirable for itself; just as we embrace our posterity for itself, though we have no knowledge or enjoyment of it. This opinion has not failed to be more commonly followed, as those are apt to be which most suit our inclinations. Aristotle gives glory the first rank among external goods: "Avoid, as two vicious extremes, immoderation both in seeking it and in fleeing it." I believe that if we had the books that Cicero had written on this subject, he would tell us some good ones; for that man was so frenzied with this passion that if he had dared, he would, I believe, have readily fallen into the excessive view into which others fell, that virtue itself was desirable only for the honor that always attended it:

> "There is little difference 'twixt buried idleness
> And hidden virtue."
>
> *Horace*

Which is an opinion so false that I am vexed that it could ever have entered the head of a man who had the honor of bearing the name of philosopher.

If that were true, we should be virtuous only in public; and there would be no point in keeping under rule and order the operations of the soul, where lies the true seat of virtue, except in so far as they should come to the knowledge of others.

Is it only a question then of doing wrong—slyly and subtly? "If you know," says Carneades, "that a snake is hiding in the place where, unsuspecting, a person by whose death you hope to profit is about to sit down, you act wickedly if you do not warn him; and the more so in case your action is to be known only to yourself." If we do not derive from ourselves the law of well-doing, if impunity to us is justice, to how many sorts of wickedness shall we not abandon ourselves every day!

What S. Peduceus did in faithfully returning the money that C. Plotius had entrusted to his sole knowledge, and what I have often done in the same way, I do not consider so laudable as I should consider it execrable for him to have failed to do it.

And I find it good and useful to recall in our days the example of P. Sextilius Rufus, whom Cicero accuses of having collected an inheritance against his conscience, not only not contrary to the laws, but by the laws themselves. And M. Crassus and Q. Hortensius, who because of their authority and power had been called in by a foreigner to share in the succession of a forged will, so that by that means he might establish his own share, contented themselves with not being participants in the forgery, and did not refuse to make some profit out of it; feeling sufficiently covered if they kept themselves sheltered from accusers, witnesses, and laws. *Let them remember that they have God as witness, that is to say (as I believe), their own conscience* [Cicero]. Virtue is a very vain and frivolous thing if it derives its recommendation from glory. To no purpose should we undertake to have it keep its rank apart, and disjoin it from fortune: for what is there more fortuitous than reputation? *Truly Fortune rules in all things; she illumines or obscures all things according to her pleasure rather than the truth* [Sallust]. To make actions be known and seen is purely the work of fortune.

It is chance that attaches glory to us according to its caprice. I have very often seen it go ahead of merit, and often surpass merit by a long distance. He who first thought of the resemblance between a shadow and glory did better than he intended. They are always preeminently empty things. The shadow also sometimes goes ahead of its body, and sometimes much exceeds it in length.

Those who teach the nobility to seek only honor in valor—*as if what is not noted were not honorable* [Cicero]—what do they gain thereby but to instruct them never to hazard themselves unless they are seen, and to take good care that there are witnesses who can bring back news of their valor? Whereas a thousand occasions of well-doing present themselves without our being able to be noticed for it. How many fine individual actions are buried in the press of a battle! Whoever wastes his time checking others during such a melee is not very busy in it himself, and produces against himself the testimony he gives of his companions' behavior. *True and wise greatness of soul judges goodness, which our nature mainly seeks, to lie in deeds, not in fame* [Cicero].

All the glory that I aspire to in my life is to have lived it tranquilly—tranquilly not according to Metrodorus or Arcesilaus or Aristippus, but according to me. Since philosophy has not been able to find a way to tranquillity that is suitable to all, let everyone seek it individually.

To what but to fortune do Caesar and Alexander owe the infinite greatness of their renown? How many men has it extinguished at the beginning of their career, of whom we have no knowledge, who brought to their work the same courage as theirs, if the misfortune of their fate had not stopped them short at the birth of their enterprises! Through so many and such extreme dangers, I do not remember having read that Caesar was ever wounded. A thousand have died from lesser perils than the least of those he passed through.

An infinity of fine actions must be lost without a witness before one appears to advantage. A man is not always at the top of a breach or at the head of an army, in sight of his general, as on a stage. He is taken by surprise between the hedge and the ditch; he must tempt fortune against a hen roost; he must root out four paltry musketeers from a barn; he must go out alone from his company and do a job alone, as the need presents itself. And if you watch carefully, you will find by experience that the least brilliant occasions happen to be the most dangerous; and that in the wars that have taken place in our times, more good men have been lost on trivial and unimportant occasions and in fighting over some shack than in worthy and honorable places.

Whoever thinks his death ill employed unless it is on some signal occasion, instead of casting luster on his death, is likely to obscure his life, meanwhile allowing many just occasions for hazarding himself to escape him. And all the just ones are illustrious enough, since each man's conscience trumpets them sufficiently to himself. *Our glory is the testimony of our conscience* [II Corinthians]. Whoever is a good man only because people will know it, and because they will esteem him better for it after knowing it, whoever will do well only on condition that his virtue will come to the knowledge of men, that man is not one from whom one can derive much service.

> "Orlando the remaining winter spent,
> I think, in doing deeds deserving fame;
> But they've been hid since then to such extent
> That if I tell them not, I'm not to blame:
> For ever was Orlando more intent
> A noble deed to do, than to proclaim.
> Nor ever would his exploits have been told
> Save when some witness was there to behold."
>
> *Ariosto*

We must go to war out of duty, and expect this reward, which cannot fail for all noble actions, however hidden they be, and even for virtuous thoughts; the contentment that a well-regulated conscience receives in itself from well-doing. We must be valiant for ourselves and for the advantage we derive from having our courage firmly grounded, and secure against the assaults of fortune.

> "Virtue ignores the voice of the profane,
> And brightly shines with honors without stain;
> Nor takes, nor lays the fasces down
> For a plebeian cheer or frown."
>
> *Horace*

It is not for show that our soul must play its part, it is at home, within us, where no eyes penetrate but our own. There it protects us from the fear of death, of pain, and even of shame; there it makes us secure against the loss of our children, of our friends, and of our fortunes; and, when the opportunity presents itself, it also leads us on to the hazards of war. *Not for any profit, but for the beauty of merit itself* [Cicero]. This profit is much greater, and more worthy of being coveted and hoped for, than honor and glory, which is nothing but a favorable judgment that people make of us.

We have to pick a dozen men out of a whole nation to pass judgment about an acre of land; and the judgment of our inclinations and our actions, the most difficult and important matter there is, we refer to the voice of the common people and of the mob, the mother of ignorance, injustice, and inconsistency. Is it reasonable to make the life of a sage depend on the judgment of fools? *Can anything be more foolish than to think that those whom we despise individually amount to something collectively?* [Cicero]. Whoever aims to please them has never done; this is a shapeless and elusive target. *Nothing is so unaccountable as the mind of the multitude* [Livy].

Demetrius used to say comically about the voice of the people that he set no more store by that which issued from above than by that which issued from below. This man goes still further: *My opinion is this, that though a thing is not shameful in itself, still it is not free from shame when it is praised by the multitude* [Cicero].

No art, no suppleness of mind, could guide our steps in following so erratic and unregulated a guide. In that windy confusion of rumors, reports, and popular opinions that push us about, no worth-while road can be charted. Let us not set ourselves a goal so fluctuating and wavering: let us steadfastly follow reason. Let public approbation follow us there, if it will; and since it depends entirely on fortune, we have no reason to expect it, rather by any other way than by that one. Even if I should not follow the straight road because of its straightness, I would follow it because I have found by experience that when all is said and done it is generally the happiest and the most useful. *Providence has given this gift to man, that the honorable is the most profitable* [Quintilian]. The ancient mariner spoke thus to Neptune in a great tempest: "O God, you may save me if you will; you may destroy me if you will; but I shall still hold my rudder straight."

I have seen in my time a thousand supple, two-faced, equivocating men, who no one doubted were more worldly-wise than I, ruin themselves where I saved myself:

> "I laughed to see how wiles could fail."
> *Ovid*

Aemilius Paulus, setting out on his glorious expedition into Macedonia, warned the people of Rome above all to restrain their tongues concerning his actions during his absence. How great a disturber in great affairs is complete liberty of judgment! Inasmuch as not everyone has the firmness of Fabius in the face of universal, hostile, and abusive clamor; he preferred to let his authority be dismembered by the vain fancies of men, rather than earn a favorable reputation and popular approval by performing his charge less well.

There is I know not what natural sweetness in hearing oneself praised, but we make much too much of it.

> "I fear not praise, no heart of horn have I.
> But that the test of worth is in your cry
> 'Bravo! Well done!'—this I deny."
>
> > Persius

I do not care so much what I am to others as I care what I am to myself. I want to be rich by myself, not by borrowing. Strangers see only the results and outward appearances. Any man can put on a good face outside, while full of fever and fright within. They do not see my heart, they see only my countenance.

People are right to decry the hypocrisy that is found in war; for what is easier for a practical man than to dodge the dangers and play tough, when his heart is full of flabbiness? There are so many ways to avoid occasions for risking our individual lives that we can deceive the world a thousand times before engaging ourselves in a dangerous situation; and even then, finding ourselves stuck, we can perfectly well hide our game for the moment with a good face and a confident word, though our soul trembles within us. And if they had the use of the Platonic ring[10] which made whoever wore it invisible if it was given a turn toward the palm of the hand, plenty of people would often hide when they ought to show themselves the most, and would repent of being placed in so honorable a spot, where necessity makes them act assured.

> "Who craves false honor and fears calumny
> A liar and a hypocrite must be."
>
> > *Horace*

That is why all these judgments that are founded on external appearances are marvelously uncertain and doubtful; and there is no witness so sure as each man to himself.

---

10. The ring of Gyges, described in Plato's *Republic,* Book II.

On those occasions, how many servants do we not have associated in our glory? He who stands firm in an open trench, what does he do that fifty poor trench diggers have not done before him, who open the way for him and protect him with their bodies for five sous a day?

> "Whatever giddy Rome decide,
> Care not, nor struggle to correct or chide
> Her faulty scales. Seek not thyself outside."
>   *Persius*

We call it making our name great to spread and sow it in many mouths; we want it to be received there in good part, and to profit by this growth: that is the most excusable element in this urge. But the excess of this malady goes so far that many seek to be talked about no matter how. Trogus Pompeius says of Herostratus, and Livy of Manlius Capitolinus, that they were more desirous of a big than of a good reputation. This vice is common. We care more that people should speak of us than how they speak of us; and it is enough for us that our name should be current in men's mouths, no matter in what way it may be current. It seems that to be known is to have one's life and duration somehow in the keeping of others.

As for me, I hold that I exist only in myself; and as for that other life of mine that lies in the knowledge of my friends, considering it naked and simply in itself, I know very well that I feel no fruit or enjoyment from it except by the vanity of a fanciful opinion. And when I am dead, I shall feel it even less; and moreover I shall lose completely the use of the real benefits which sometimes accidentally come after it. I shall no longer have any grip by which to seize reputation, nor by which it can touch me or reach me.

Indeed as for expecting my name to receive it, in the first place I have no name that is sufficiently my own. Of two that I have, one is common to my whole race, and indeed to others also. There is a family in Paris and one in Montpellier named Montaigne, another in Brittany and in Saintonge called de la Montaigne. The change of a single syllable will tangle our threads so that I will share in their glory, and they, perhaps, in my shame. And moreover, mine were formerly surnamed Eyquem[11] a name which still is attached to a well-known family in England.

As for my other name, it belongs to whoever wants to take it. Thus I shall perhaps honor a porter instead of myself. And then, even if I had a particular mark for myself, what can it mark when I am no longer there? Can it designate and benefit nothingness?

---

11. Actually Montaigne was the first of his family to drop the surname Eyquem.

> "Now does his tomb weigh lighter on his bones?
> Posterity applauds. Out of these stones,
> Out of his ashes, from his departed spirit,
> Do violets spring?"
>
> *Persius*

But of this I have spoken elsewhere.[12]

Besides, in a whole battle in which ten thousand men are maimed or killed, there are not fifteen that are talked about. It must be some very eminent greatness, or some important consequence that fortune has attached to it, that gives prominence to an individual action, not only a musketeer's, but even a general's. For to kill a man, or two, or ten: to offer oneself courageously to death, that is indeed something for each one of us, for everything is at stake. But for the world these are things so ordinary, so many of them are seen every day, and so many of them are needed to produce one notable effect, that we cannot expect any particular commendation for them.

> "An incident well-known, trite, cheap,
> And taken from the midst of Fortune's heap."
>
> *Juvenal*

Of so many myriads of valiant men who have died sword in hand in the last fifteen hundred years in France, there are not a hundred who have come to our knowledge. The memory not only of the leaders, but of the battles and victories, is buried.

The fortunes of more than half the world, for lack of a record, do not stir from their place, and vanish without duration. If I had in my possession all the unknown events, I should think I could very easily supplant those that are known, in every kind of examples.

Why, even of the Romans and the Greeks, amid so many writers and witnesses of so many rare and noble exploits, how few have come down as far as our time!

> "The faint breath of its fame scarce reached our ears."
>
> *Virgil*

It will be a lot if a hundred years from now people remember in a general way that in our time there were civil wars in France.

The Lacedaemonians sacrificed to the Muses on going into battle, so that their deeds might be well and worthily written down, judging that it was a

---

12. In the chapter "Of Names" (I:46).

divine and uncommon favor that fine actions should find witnesses who could give them life and memory.

Do we think that at every harquebus shot that touches us, and at every risk that we run, there is promptly a clerk to record it? And besides that, a hundred clerks may write it down, whose commentaries will last only three days and will come to no one's sight. We have not the thousandth part of the writings of the ancients: it is Fortune that gives them life, longer or shorter according to her favor; and it is permissible to wonder whether what we have is not the worst, since we have not seen the rest. People do not write histories about such petty things. A man must have been the leader in conquering an empire or a kingdom; he must have won fifty-two pitched battles, always with weaker numbers, like Caesar. Ten thousand good comrades and many great captains died in his service, valiantly and courageously, whose names have endured only as long as their wives and children lived,

> "Whom dim rumor hides."
> *Virgil*

Even of those whom we see doing bravely, three months or three years after they have been left on the field, you hear no more talk than if they had never been. Whoever will consider, with just measure and proportion, of what sort of men and what sort of deeds the glory is maintained in the memory of books, will find that in our time there are very few actions and very few persons who can claim any right to such remembrance. How many valiant men we have seen to survive their own reputation, who have seen and suffered the extinction in their presence of the honor and glory most justly acquired in their early years! And for three years of this fanciful and imaginary life shall we go and lose our real and essential life and engage ourselves in perpetual death? The sages set themselves a fairer and juster end for so important an enterprise; *The reward of a good deed is to have done it* [Seneca]. *The fruit of a service is the service itself* [Cicero].

It might perhaps be excusable for a painter or another artisan, or even for a rhetorician or a grammarian, to toil to acquire a name by his works; but the actions of virtue are too noble in themselves to seek any other reward than from their own worth, and especially to seek it in the vanity of human judgments.

However, if this false opinion is of service to the public in keeping men within their duty; if the people are thereby roused to virtue; if princes are touched by seeing the world bless the memory of Trajan and abominate that of Nero; if it moves them to see the name of that great gallows bird, once so frightful and so dreaded, so freely cursed and reviled by the first schoolboy who deals with it, let it grow boldly and let it be fostered among us as much as possible.

And Plato, employing every means to make his citizens virtuous, advises them also not to despise the good repute and esteem of the people. And he says that it happens by some divine inspiration that even the wicked, in words as well as in thought, often know how to distinguish correctly good men from bad. This person and his teacher are marvelous and bold workmen at bringing in divine operations and revelations everywhere that human power fails: *as the tragic poets have recourse to a god when they cannot unravel the end of their plot* [Cicero]. Perhaps that is why Timon, by way of insult, called him "the great forger of miracles."

Since men, because of their inadequacy, cannot be sufficiently paid with good money, let false be employed too. This means has been practiced by all lawgivers, and there is no polity in which there is not some admixture either of empty ceremony or of lying opinion to serve as a curb to keep the people in their duty. That is why most of them have their fabulous origins and beginnings, enriched with supernatural mysteries. That is what has given credit to bastard religions and brought them into favor with men of understanding; and that is why Numa and Sertorius, to strengthen their peoples' belief, fed them with this stupid story, the one that the nymph Egeria, the other that his white hind, brought him from the gods all the decisions that he adopted.

And the authority that Numa gave to his laws by claiming the patronage of this goddess, Zoroaster, lawgiver of the Bactrians and the Persians, gave to his in the name of the god Oromazis; Trismegistus of the Egyptians, in the name of Mercury; Zamolxis of the Scythians, in the name of Vesta; Charondas of the Chalcidians, in the name of Saturn; Minos of the Candiots, in the name of Jupiter; Lycurgus of the Lacedaemonians, in the name of Apollo; Draco and Solon of the Athenians, in the name of Minerva. And every polity has a god at its head: falsely so the others, truly so the one that Moses set up for the people of Judea just out of Egypt.

The religion of the Bedouins, as Sire de Joinville tells us, held among other things that the soul of any one of them who died for his prince departed into another body happier, handsomer, and stronger than the first; on account of which they risked their lives much more willingly:

> "They rush on weapons, death they seem to crave;
> The life they will regain they scorn to save."
> *Lucan*

That is a very salutary belief, however empty it may be. Every nation has many such examples of its own. But this subject would deserve a treatise in itself.

To say one more word on my first topic, neither do I advise the ladies to call their duty honor. *In common parlance only that is called honorable which is glorious in popular opinion* [Cicero]. Their duty is the pith, their honor is only the rind. Nor do I advise them to give us this excuse for payment of their refusal. For I assume that their intentions, their desire, and their will, which are parts in which honor is not concerned, since nothing of them appears on the outside, are even better regulated than their acts:

> "She who does not, because forbidden, really does."
> *Ovid*

The offense, both toward God and in the conscience, would be as great in the desiring as in the doing. And then these are actions of themselves hidden and secret; it would be very easy for women to conceal one of them from the knowledge of others, on which honor depends, if they had no other respect for their duty and for the affection they bear to chastity for its own sake.

Any person of honor chooses rather to lose his honor than to lose his conscience.

Francis Bacon, "Of Great Place"

Francis Bacon (1561–1626) was an English statesman and man of letters. After studying at Trinity College, Cambridge, in which he enrolled at the age of twelve, he entered Gray's Inn to pursue a career as a lawyer. He was elected to Parliament in 1584 and subsequently held various positions in government, including solicitor-general and lord chancellor. He was knighted in 1603. Bacon's political career ended in scandal in 1621. Henceforth, he immersed himself in a life of science and writing. In his philosophical work, Bacon stressed the importance of freeing human thought from "idols" or erroneous thoughts in favor of scientific reason. Considered by some to be the father of modern science, Bacon sought to "restore" to man mastery over nature. His major works include his Essays, The New Atlantis, The Advancement of Learning, *and the* New Organon.

Men in great place are thrice servants: servants of the sovereign or state, servants of fame, and servants of business. So as they have no freedom, neither in their persons, nor in their actions, nor in their times. It is a strange desire to seek power and to lose liberty, or to seek power over others and to lose power over a man's self. The rising unto place is laborious, and by pains men come to greater pains; and it is sometimes base, and by indignities men come to dignities. The standing is slippery, and the regress is either a downfall or at least an eclipse, which is a melancholy thing. *Cum non sis qui fueris, non esse cur velis vivere.*[13] Nay, retire men cannot when they would, neither will they when it were reason,[14] but are impatient of privateness, even in age and sickness, which require the shadow;[15] like old townsmen, they will be still sitting at their street door, though thereby they offer age to scorn. Certainly great persons had need to borrow other men's opinions, to think themselves happy; for if they judge by their own feeling, they cannot find it, but if they think with themselves what other men think of them, and that other men would fain be as they are, then they are happy as it were by report, when perhaps they find the contrary within. For they are the first that find their own griefs, though they be the last that find their own faults. Certainly men in great fortunes are strangers to themselves, and while they are in the puzzle of business, they have no time to tend their health either of body or mind. *Illi mors gravis incubat, qui notus*

---

13. "When you are no longer what you were, there is no reason for wishing to live." Cicero, *Letters to his Friends*, VII.3.

14. Right, reasonable.

15. Retirement.

nimis omnibus, ignotus moritur sibi.[16] In place there is licence to do good and evil; whereof the latter is a curse, for in evil the best condition is not to will, the second not to can.[17] But power to do good is the true and lawful end of aspiring. For good thoughts (though God accept them) yet towards men are little better than good dreams, except they be put in act; and that cannot be without power and place as the vantage and commanding ground. Merit and good works is the end of man's motion, and conscience[18] of the same is the accomplishment of man's rest. For if a man can be partaker of God's theatre, he shall likewise be partaker of God's rest. *Et conversus Deus, ut aspiceret opera quae fecerunt manus suae, vidit quod omnia essent bona nimis,*[19] and then the Sabbath. In the discharge of thy place set before thee the best examples, for imitation is a globe[20] of precepts. And after a time set before thee thine own example, and examine thyself strictly whether thou didst not best at first. Neglect not also the examples of those that have carried themselves ill in the same place, not to set off thyself by taxing[21] their memory, but to direct thyself what to avoid. Reform, therefore, without bravery,[22] or scandal of former times and persons, but yet set it down to thyself as well to create good precedents as to follow them. Reduce[23] things to the first institution, and observe wherein and how they have degenerate; but yet ask counsel of both times, of the ancient time, what is best, and, of the latter time, what is fittest. Seek to make thy course regular that men may know beforehand what they may expect, but be not too positive and peremptory; and express thyself well when thou digressest from thy rule. Preserve the right of thy place, but stir not questions of jurisdiction, and rather assume thy right in silence and *de facto,* than voice it with claims and challenges. Preserve likewise the rights of inferior places, and think it more honour to direct in chief than to be busy in all. Embrace and invite helps and advices reaching the execution of thy place, and do not drive away such as bring thee information, as meddlers, but accept of them in good part. The vices of authority are chiefly four: delays, corruption, toughness, and facility. For[24] delays, give easy access; keep times appointed; go through with that which is in hand; and interlace[25] not business but of necessity. For corruption,

16. "Death falls heavily upon him who, well known to others, dies ignorant of himself." Seneca, *Thyestes,* 401.

17. I.e., be able.

18. Consciousness.

19. "And God turned to behold the works which His hands had made, and saw that they were all very good." Cf. Genesis 1:31.

20. Collection.

21. Censuring.

22. Ostentation.

23. Lead or take back again.

24. As regards.

25. Intermix.

do not only bind thine own hands or thy servants' hands from taking, but bind the hands of suitors also from offering. For integrity used doth the one, but integrity professed, and with a manifest detestation of bribery, doth the other. And avoid not only the fault, but the suspicion. Whosoever is found variable, and changeth manifestly without manifest cause giveth suspicion of corruption. Therefore always when thou changest thine opinion or course, profess it plainly, and declare it, together with the reasons that move thee to change, and do not think to steal it.[26] A servant or a favourite, if he be inward,[27] and no other apparent cause of esteem, is commonly thought but a by-way to close[28] corruption. For roughness, it is a needless cause of discontent; severity breedeth fear, but roughness breedeth hate. Even reproofs from authority ought to be grave, and not taunting. As for facility, it is worse than bribery. For bribes come but now and then, but if importunity or idle respects[29] lead a man, he shall never be without. As Solomon saith, *To respect persons is not good; for such a man will transgress for a piece of bread.*[30] It is most true that was anciently spoken, *A place showeth the man.*[31] And it showeth some to the better, and some to the worse. *Omniun consensu capax imperii, nisi imperasset*[32] saith Tacitus of Galba, but of Vespasian he saith *Solus imperantium, Vespasianus mutatus in melius,*[33] though the one was meant of sufficieny,[34] the other of manners and affection. It is an assured sign of a worthy and generous spirit, whom honour amends. For honour is, or should be, the place of virtue; and as in nature things move violently to their place and calmly in their place, so virtue in ambition is violent, in authority settled and calm. All rising to great place is by a winding stair, and if there be factions, it is good to side a man's self whilst he is in the rising, and to balance himself when he is placed. Use the memory of thy predecessor fairly and tenderly, for if thou dost not, it is a debt will sure be paid when thou art gone. If thou have colleagues, respect them, and rather call them when they look not for it, than exclude them when they have reason to look to be called. Be not too sensible or too remembering[35] of thy place in conversation and private answers to suitors, but let it rather be said, *When he sits in place he is another man.*

26. Do it by stealth.
27. Intimate.
28. Secret, hidden.
29. Considerations, preferences.
30. Proverbs 28:21.
31. Variously attributed to Solon, Bias, and Epaminondas.
32. "Even had he not been emperor, all would have pronounced him fit to rule." *Hist.*, I:49.
33. "Vespasian alone amongst the emperors changed for the better." *Hist.*, I:50.
34. Ability, capacity.
35. Mindful.

The Wisdom of Baltasar Gracián:
A Practical Manual for Good and Perilous Times

Baltasar Gracián (1601–1658) was a Spanish philosopher and Jesuit. Born in Belmonte de Calayatud, Spain, Gracián studied at Calayatud and Zaragoza. Upon completing his studies, he entered the Jesuit order. Gracián wrote philosophical tracts that attempted to advise people in the ethics of everyday life. His terse style, his sometimes shocking use of metaphor, and his pessimistic view of society have influenced philosophers of many generations, including Friedrich Nietzsche and Arthur Schopenhauer.

"Rejoice in what you do, but do not boast of it"

They who have done the least make the greatest to-do of what they have done! A quirk in their character venerates the simplest deed they perform, and everything is made to appear marvelous. Even when speaking of others, self-applause is apparent in the theme of the praises they sing. Conceit is always frowned upon, and those who crow like a rooster only succeed in aggravating the hearing of those whom they try to impress. Real achievement needs no such affectation. Rejoice in the fulfillment of what you do, and leave talk to others. Aspire to be heroic without calling for a heavenly choir to herald your accomplishments.

"Good finds good"

Search for the good in everything. There is nothing that does not hold some good if we but seek it. But the minds of some men are burdened with such unhappiness that, out of a thousand good points, they manage to strike upon a lone defect, and this they toss about like scavengers of men's minds and purposes. There is perverse joy for these collectors of refuse in compiling the sins of others so that they can feel superior. Avoid such grave diggers, for in time it is they who fall into the hollow opening. Be the man who, among a thousand evils, strikes upon the single good. Good finds good, but good that comes too late is as good as nothing.

"Only foolish men are upset by events they cannot control"

He who grows in wisdom grows in impatience, just as he who knows much is hard to satisfy. At times we suffer most impatience with those upon whom we most depend. But this is a game of fools, for only foolish men are upset by events they cannot control. Learning to keep a rein on impatience when our nature is impetuous prepares us for encountering misfortunes with perfect calm. It is the lessons of restraint that force us to set up a school of self-control. Let him who cannot control his impatience take refuge within himself and test his strength in putting up with himself.

"It is a wearying business to govern men"

If you have a desire to officiate, know what the office holds. Opportunities are in abundance for the man who volunteers to give of himself, but nothing calls for greater care in choice. Some offices demand courage, and others shrewdness. It is easy to manage in those establishments which call merely for honesty, but most difficult in those which call for skill. It is a wearying business to govern men, who often include the neurotic and fool; and double brains are needed to deal with those who have none.

"He knows who knows that he does not know"

It is only the fool who does not see that which others see. He dwells in a garden of roses oblivious to the thorns. Living in mystical reverie, he is like the frog in a well who sees the sky as a little patch of blue no larger than the roundness of his shelter. Small-minded and foreign to vision, he becomes the greatest fool because he does not see himself as one, while declaring all other such. For the wise man, it is not enough to appear wise. He must display characteristics that deliberately suggest there are things that he does not know. This act will gain approval from others and achieve for him large measures of respectability. His casual denial of complete wisdom will make him seem all the wiser in a world full of fools.

"A fertile mind, deep understanding, and a cultured taste lend flavor to all of life"

Three things make the superior man: a fertile mind, a deep understanding, and a cultured taste. There are minds that radiate light, like the eyes of the lynx, which in the greatest darkness see most clearly. Then there are those born for the occasion. Guided by uncanny understanding, they always strike upon what is most beneficial. And good taste lends flavor to all of life. A good imagination is another great advantage, but even greater is the ability to think clearly, for clear thinking is the sweet fruit of reason. We soon learn that we are ruled by our age. At twenty years desire rules us; at thirty, expediency; at forty, judgment; beyond, the experience of wisdom. The shoes of the superior man may not fit all, but all should make every attempt to walk in them.

"Know how to conduct a successful interview"

In seeking employment the man standing before you waiting to be interviewed is prepared for your interrogation. It is an undeclared battle of wits. Your alertness is matched by his reserve. The answers will not surface if the questions go unasked, for great judgment is required to take the measure of another. More important by far is to know the composition and the properties of men than to know those of minerals and vegetables. This is the most delicate of the occupations of life: for metals are known by their ring, and men by what they speak. Words reflect the mind of a man, and hint at the quality of his work. To know how to truly analyze a man calls for the clearest observation, the subtlest understanding, and the most critical judgment. The rewards are countless for the gifted who can analyze a man by dividing his complex whole into its parts or elements.

"With much at stake, few play fair"

When there is much at stake, there are few who play fair. Warring opponents are often the same men who lived in honor and peace as long as they had no ambitious emulators; rivalry exposes the flaws which courtesy has covered over. Know that every effort you make to outshine your opponent does some damage to your own reputation, for the true purpose of competition is to find a way to belittle your opponent in order to weaken him. The heat of combat brings to life personal issues long dead and digs up stenches long gone. Even the dust of forgetfulness is shaken from old scandals. As the combat intensifies, competition brings forth a manifesto of slander and calls to its aid whatever it can, and not what it should. There is much to be considered before the sword is drawn. Men of peace should project for themselves the final scene of the play before they step onto the stage of battle.

"Men of skillful diplomacy turn insult to humor, foul play to fair"

There are few among us who can master all the tools of diplomacy. There are men who intuitively know that even a scrap of an important man's time is not to be wasted, who have the conviction in their hearts that inspires straight talk. When a man's knowledge is deep, he speaks well of an enemy, and deals with him even better. Instead of seeking revenge, he extends unexpected generosity. In all matters, men of skillful policy turn insult into humor, turn foul play into accepted fair play, and astonish their adversaries who find no reason

not to trust them. They wait, and victory comes to them. Although merit at-
tains it, they let modesty conceal it. Such is the basis of the greatness of feeling,
and the feeling of greatness.

"It is a great feat to make a friend of a rival"

Foresee insult and defuse its sting, for it is less stressful to avoid insult than
to avenge it. It is a great feat to make a friend of one who wished to be a rival,
and to turn him into a protector of your honor when he had threatened its
injury. Place him under such obligation that the insult on the tip of his tongue
is turned into thanksgiving. The man who knows these secrets of life is able
to transform ill will into trust. This is an art well worth learning.

"Weigh words carefully"

People at cross-purposes create sparks; in the heat of an argument, when
reason does not function, there lies the danger of unquenchable fires. One second of rage can cause damage that cannot be corrected in a lifetime. The
craftiness of another may draw you into such a disagreement to discover where
you stand, or what you think. Match this game of wiliness with determined
self-restraint, especially when the argument explodes into fast repartee. Such
restraint will keep you from divulging what you cannot reverse. It is true that
he who knows the danger proceeds with caution. Angry words reveal little control, and words tossed out lightly can seem heavy to the one who catches them,
and weighs them in his mind.

"Know that there are no secrets"

It is the wise man who knows that he is always seen, or that he will be seen
one day. He knows that walls have ears, and that what is evil breaks its shackles
to be free. Even when he is alone he works as though the eyes of the world are
upon him, because he knows that everything comes to be known. He knows
that those who hear his thoughts today are witnesses and can be testifiers tomorrow. So he lives by the rules of private thoughts. He knows that when he gives
up the smallest part of a secret, the rest is no longer in his power. In this manner
he is well prepared for confrontation, and in control of what becomes public.

"The more said, the less heard"

The man versed in one topic, who pursues one line of reason, and makes
only one long speech, is apt to be boring. Brevity charms and accomplishes the
daily course of events; it makes up in manner what it lacks in measure. The

good, if short, is doubly good, and the bad, if brief, is only half as bad. As in wine, the essence is always stronger than the dregs. It is commonly perceived that the man long-winded in rhetoric is rarely wise. The more he says, the less is heard, for what is well said is said quickly. There are men who cannot refrain from making themselves a nuisance, even in the company of the most accomplished who are much occupied. They never learned that the time allotted to a great man is more precious than gold. To impose on such a man is unforgivable.

"The novelty of the new is short-lived"

There is a measure of excitement in the new, be it possessions or people. For as long as you are deemed new, you rate high. Novelty fares well because it is different, it refreshes the senses. At times brand-new mediocrity is more cherished than shopworn perfection. Even the best of things become boring. But note that the glory of the new is short-lived, and that in a matter of days or weeks all respect for it will fade. For when the fire of the new is spent, fervor cools, and the excitement for the young, or the new, will be exchanged for the comfort, sometimes the boredom, of the old. Believe then that everything has its day, and also that it passes.

"There is danger in complacency"

Self-satisfaction should not be displayed or voiced, for there is not joy in it for anyone else. On the other hand, to be unsatisfied with yourself implies a lack of courage. Self-complacency starts for the most part in witlessness and ends in a blissful ignorance which, even though soothing to the soul, does not inspire respect from others. Even if you are unable to equal the qualifications of great men, do not find reasons to live with mediocrity within yourself. It is always more useful and more intelligent to have misgivings about yourself, either for your better assurance that things will come off well, or for your better comfort if they come off badly. It is said that he cannot be surprised by mishaps, or by a turn of luck, who has already feared it. Complacency, unchecked, grows and grows, sowing seeds, and therein lies its danger.

"Avoid being a complainer"

The need to release frustration makes a perfectly pleasant man a lamentable bore. Never cry about your woes; it only discredits you. Because problems pass and people remember, it is less regrettable to be timid in the outpouring of complaints. In politics, many a man with his protest of past injustices has invited additional problems by crying for help or expecting pity. It is far better to praise the generosity of one than to complain about a score of others; this invites further generosities. Reciting the favors done for you by those who are absent extracts and identifies them from those who are present; this calls others' attention to the esteem in which you are held. And so a man of good sense will never make known to the world the slights or the wrongs he may have suffered, but only the honor in which he is held.

"Do not condemn what the crowd applauds"

Be careful in condemning what pleases many; it must contain some good to be so satisfying to the public, even though it cannot be explained to your satisfaction. The man who stands apart, out of stubbornness or ignorance, is watching opportunity passing by. His business acumen is suspect, and his judgment is discredited, and he is likely to be left alone in his poor taste. If you do not know how to profit from the good, conceal your blindness, and do not condemn in wholesale fashion. Bad choice is ordinarily the child of ignorance. What the masses embrace, be it trend or novel, is reality for the moment.

"Walk the middle road"

No one and nothing today is in agreement. Intelligent writers present profound essays which we praise, only to find ourselves at another time praising another belief on the same topic that is just as convincing. We emotionally respond to ideas that match our moods so that at times we are discontent when our fortune is at its best and content in our minds when our fortune couldn't be worse. Our pendulum of moods sometimes makes us unhappy with our lot, only to see joy in someone else's. And there are those who believe that the past is better, and glorify only the things of yesterday. Better to walk the middle road, for it is to be concluded that he is just as much a fool who laughs at everything as is he who weeps at everything.

"Exit gracefully"

Know how to make a triumph of your exit. The graceful exit at the propitious moment is a victory in itself. At times the sun herself, at its brightest, will retire behind a cloud so that she may not be seen, leaving us to wonder and long for her return. Do not wait until men turn their backs upon you, until they bury you, still alive in your feelings but dead in their estimation. The man of foresight puts his inferior horse in the stable early, and does not wait to see it create shock by falling in the middle of the race. The beautiful woman wisely cracks her mirror when it is yet early in her life, so as not to smash it with impatience later when it has disillusioned her. A maxim for the wise: Leave before being left.

"Never exhibit your work half-done"

As all beginnings are without form, and the image of this shapelessness endures in the imagination, undertakings are to be enjoyed only when complete. Early stages of work when viewed by others leaves a memory of imperfection. Later, the same memory transfers itself into the completed project. By having been divided into two images of reference, memory forbids the enjoyment of the magnificence in one gaze; it blurs the judgment of final details. Before an object is everything, it is nothing. In its inception, it is still very close to being nothing. Recognize that the sight of preparation of even the daintiest morsel may turn more people to disgust than to appetite. Whatever your creative work, see to it that it not be shown in embryo form. Learn from nature herself not to bring it forth until it is ready to be seen.

"Enjoy a little more, strive a little less"

Men driven by ambition often succeed outwardly and fail inwardly. Their outer resources multiply at the cost of their spiritual energy. Yet they go blindly forward with small consideration that happy leisure is worth more than drive; for nothing belongs to us except time. Precious existence is squandered in stupid drudgery. Overwork is the mother of greed and the substitute for boredom. Once entrapped, escape comes only with the slow collapse of body functions. So be not crushed under success, and be not crushed under envy! To be so is to trample upon life and to suffocate the spirit. Enjoy a little more, strive a little less. The wise man will extend his life's work to prolong his life.

"Test the wind"

Testing out the public temper and learning where you stand is essential in law, in industry, and in government, for it is not enough to be right if you have a malicious face and others bear you malice. In a new enterprise or innovation, know which way the wind is blowing. Early warning helps one discover how a matter will later be received. Whether you expect its success or sanction, you gain assurance of its final outcome by canvassing opinions, collecting hardfisted facts, and understanding the leaning of your own intuition. Then you will discover if you must go forward or turn back.

"Fit yourself to the framework of your world"

Live as best you can in the state of affairs that surrounds you. Wish for what is available, work at what is achievable. Yet do not always journey through life by the laws written to regulate you, even when such laws have the face of righteousness and goodness. Take small liberties and byways without bringing harm to yourself and to others. Do not indicate too precisely what alone will satisfy you, for tomorrow your words may have to be disregarded. Stay flexible and be alert as the days change and new opportunities arise. There are some so unreasonable that they would have every circumstance of life fit itself into their own framework when it should be the other way around. The man of wisdom knows better: he lives as best as he can in the state of affairs that surrounds him.

"If you would lead, let others take responsibility for errors"

It is the wise strategy of those who govern, in state or industry, to carry a shield against vicious ill will pledged against them. They must know how to let the responsibility for something amiss rest upon another. It is not a mark of weakness, as the envious think, but of greater strength to have on hand someone to bear the brunt for failure in order to continue to govern without hindrance. Weigh the situation at hand. It may be a wise business decision to let someone atone for your errors even though it cost you some of your pride. Self-preservation is at the heart of survival. Not everything can come off well, nor everyone be satisfied.

"Examine both sides of a disagreement"

Know that every man believes according to his own interests, and that he is filled with reasons and excuses for his stand. In most instances feeling overwhelms judgment and passion takes hold. Thus two opinions confront each other and each man believes that his is the side of reason. But reason, always fair, cannot be two-faced. The man of good sense treads cautiously in so delicate a situation. He allows the possibility of misgivings in his own mind to moderate his judgment regarding that of the other. At that moment he lets his imagination stray to the opposite position. There he can examine the arguments of both sides, seeing what is so puzzling and exasperating to two well-intended people, who may in addition be two misguided idealists.

"Make intelligence the foundation of your life"

Be the architect of your life. Know how to arrange it with intelligence, not as accident may dictate. Plant its foundation firmly, and develop it with foresight. Know that life is a difficult, fatiguing expedition without recreation, much like a long journey without inns in which to refresh and rejuvenate oneself. Intellectual stimulation mixes well with the dust and stones of the long road to eternity. We are born to know the world and to know ourselves, and the great books of truth make us into men. Therefore, spend a period of your life in the company of the venerated thinkers and writers of the past. But spend the mainstream of your life with the living in order to see and to note all the good that is upon this earth. Know that everything is not to be found in one region; the omnipotent Father has divinely divided His blessing and has, at times, adorned the ugliest in the richest coverlets. Let the remainder of your life be wholly your own. To live in the mind and explore the tributaries of philosophy is the ultimate good fortune of man.

"The natural man is always more pleasing"

Affectation is the act of taking on an attitude of behavior not natural to oneself. It is as distasteful to everybody else as it is painful to him who practices it, for he is constantly witnessing and agonizing over speech and conduct not natural to himself. The greater your qualifications, the less the need to affect any of them, since all that is natural is always more pleasing than the artificial. The man of confidence and discrimination never flaunts his strength, for it is through its very concealment that it awakens the interest of others. He is twice great who carries all his perfections within himself and avoids the characteristics of conceit.

Hans J. Morgenthau, "Love and Power"

Hans J. Morgenthau (1904–1980) was a political theorist who became a celebrated student of international politics. He expounded the doctrine of "political realism." Born in Coburg, Germany, Morgenthau earned a doctorate in jurisprudence from the University of Frankfurt. He immigrated to the United States in 1937. He taught at the University of Chicago from 1943 to 1974, and also directed for seventeen years the Center for the Study of American Foreign and Military Policy.

Morgenthau was critical of rationalistic and legalistic approaches to political studies. He believed that abstract theorizing should be tempered with an understanding of and responsiveness to political realities. Practical political circumstances are grasped, Morgenthau argued, not with scientific methods but with wisdom, insight, moral sense, and an awareness of the central role of power in the political realm.

The proposition that power and love are organically connected, growing as they do from the same root of loneliness, must appear to the modern mind paradoxical, if not completely absurd. For power as the domination of man by man, pleasurable to one and painful to the other, and love as the voluntary and pleasurable surrender of two human beings to each other, seem not only to have nothing in common but to be mutually exclusive. Where two human beings are in the relation of power, they cannot be, so it seems to the modern mind, in the relation of love. The inability of the modern mind to see this connection between love and power is the measure of its inability to understand the true dimensions of either love or power. As Paul Tillich put it in the introductory chapter to *Love, Power, and Justice,* "It is unusual to take the word 'confusion' into the title of a chapter. But if one has to write about love, power, and justice the unusual becomes natural."

The modern mind, both in its Marxist and non-Marxists expressions, sees in the power of man over man not an ineluctable outgrowth of human nature but only an ephemeral phenomenon, the product of a peculiar historic configuration, bound to disappear with the disappearance of that configuration. According to Marx, the lust for power and its political manifestations are a mere by-product of the class division of society. In the classless society, the domination of man by man will be replaced by the administration of things. In liberal thought, power politics is regarded as a kind of atavism, a residue from the less enlightened and civilized era of autocratic rule, which is destined to be superseded by the institutions and practices of liberal democracy.

While the modern mind denies the intrinsic relation between the lust for power and human nature, transcending all historic configurations, antedating them, as it were, and even determining them, it does not understand the nature of love at all. Love as the reunion of two souls and bodies which belong together or, in the Platonic mythology, once were united, is reduced in the modern understanding to sex and gregariousness, the togetherness of the sexes on dates, in marriage, and in other associations, tending to be of a more or less fleeting nature. What the modern understanding misses is the totality of the commitment that characterizes the pure phenomenon of love. It is aware only of surface phenomena which may or may not be manifestations of love, because it is unaware of that very element in man on which love is built; his soul. And it is unaware of that quality of human existence which is the root both of the lust for power and the longing for love: loneliness.

Of all creatures, only man is capable of loneliness because only he is in need of not being alone, without being able in the end to escape being alone. It is that striving to escape his loneliness which gives the impetus to both the lust for power and the longing for love, and it is the inability to escape that loneliness, either at all or for more than a moment, that creates the tension between longing and lack of achievement, which is the tragedy of both power and love. In that existential loneliness man's insufficiency manifests itself. He cannot fulfill himself, he cannot become what he is destined to be, by his own effort, in isolation from other beings. The awareness of that insufficiency drives him on in search of love and power. It drives him on to seek the extension of his self in offspring—the work of his body; in the manufacture of material things—the work of his hands; in philosophy and scholarship—the work of his mind; in art and literature—the work of his imagination; in religion—the work of his pure longing toward transcendence.

Love and power both try to overcome loneliness, and the sense of man's insufficiency stemming from this loneliness, through duplication of his individuality. Through love, man seeks another human being like himself, the Platonic other half of his soul, to form a union which will make him whole. Through power, man seeks to impose his will upon another man, so that the will of the object of his power mirrors his own. What love seeks to discover in another man as a gift of nature, power must create through the artifice of psychological manipulation. Love is reunion through spontaneous mutuality, power seeks to create a union through unilateral imposition.

It is the common quality of love and power that each contains an element of the other. Power points toward love as its fulfillment, as love starts from power and is always threatened with corruption by it. Power, in its ultimate consummation, is the same as love, albeit love is corrupted by an irreducible residue of power. Love, in its ultimate corruption, is the same as power, albeit power is redeemed by an irreducible residue of love.

Love is a psychological relationship which in its pure form is marked by complete and spontaneous mutuality. *A* surrenders himself to *B,* as *B* surrenders himself to *A;* and both do so spontaneously, in recognition of their belonging together. Both are lover and beloved; what *A* is, feels, and wants, *B* is, feels, and wants, too. Love is the most perfect union two human beings are capable of, without losing their respective individualities. Aristophanes has given in the *Symposium* the classic description of the nature of pure love:

> And when one of them meets with his other half, the actual half of himself . . . the pair are lost in an amazement of love and friendship and intimacy, and one will not be out of the other's sight, as I may say, even for a moment: these are the people who pass their whole lives together; yet they could not explain what they desire of one another. For the intense yearning which each of them has towards the other does not appear to be the desire of lover's intercourse, but of something else which the soul of either evidently desires and cannot tell, and of which she has only a dark and doubtful presentiment . . . this meeting and melting into one another, this becoming one instead of two, was the very expression of his ancient need. And the reason is that human nature was originally one and we were a whole, and the desire and pursuit of the whole is called love.

Love in its purest form is the rarest of experiences. It is given to few men to experience it at all, and those who experience it do so only in fleeting moments of exaltation. What makes love as commonly experienced fall short of its pure form is the element of power with which love begins in triumph and ends in defeat and which corrupts it throughout. Love typically begins with *A* trying to submit *B* to his will, that is, as a relationship of power, and frequently it does not progress beyond it. As Socrates puts it in the *Phaedrus:* "As wolves love lambs so lovers love their loves." And it is significant that Socrates, in his first speech in that dialogue, in parodying Lysias' conception of love, presents a picture of the love relation which is tantamount to what we would call a relationship of power.

What makes the lover behave like a master and the beloved like the object of the master's power, what makes, in other words, the love relationship similar to the power relationship is the inevitable frustration of love. For if love is a reunion of two human beings who belong together, that reunion can never be complete for any length of time. For, except in the *Liebestod,* which destroys the lovers by uniting them, it stops short of the complete merger of the individualities of the lovers. It is the paradox of love that it seeks the reunion of two individuals while leaving their individualities intact. *A* and *B* want to be one, yet they must want to preserve each other's individuality for the sake of their love for each other. So it is their very love that stands in the way of their love's consummation.

That inner contradiction that lovers endeavor to overcome by letting power do what love is unable to do by itself. Power tries to break down the barrier of individuality which love, because it is love, must leave intact. Yet in the measure that power tries to do the work love cannot do, it puts love in jeopardy. An irreducible element of power is requisite to make a stable relationship of love, which without it would be nothing more than a succession of precarious exaltations. Thus without power love cannot persist; but through power it is corrupted and threatened with destruction. That destruction becomes actual when *A* and *B,* by trying to reduce each other to an object of their respective wills, transform the spontaneous mutuality of the love relationship into the unilateral imposition of the relationship of power.

Thus the lust for power is, as it were, the twin of despairing love. Power becomes a substitute for love. What man cannot achieve for any length of time through love he tries to achieve through power: to fulfill himself, to make himself whole by overcoming his loneliness, his isolation. As Shakespeare's Richard III puts it:

> And this word "love," which greybeards call divine,
> Be resident in men like one another
> And not in me: I am myself alone. . . .
> And am I then a man to be belov'd?
> O, monstrous fault, to harbor such a thought!
> Then, since this earth affords no joy to me,
> But to command, to check, to o'erbear such
> As are of better person than myself,
> I'll make my heaven to dream upon the crown. . . .

Yet of what love can at least approximate and in a fleeting moment actually achieve, power can only give the illusion.

Power is a psychological relationship in which one man controls certain actions of another man through the influence he exerts over the latter's will. That influence derives from three sources: the expectation of benefits, the fear of disadvantages, the respect or love for men or institutions. It may be exerted through orders, threats, promises, persuasion, the authority or charisma of a man or of an office, or a combination of any of these.

It is in the very nature of the power relationship that the position of the two actors within it is ambivalent. *A* seeks to exert power over *B; B* tries to resist that power and seeks to exert power over *A*, which *A* resists. Thus the actor on the political stage is always at the same time a prospective master over others and a prospective object of power over him. While he seeks power over others, others seek power over him. Victory will fall to him who marshals the stronger weapons of influence with greater skill.

Yet a political victory won with the weapons of threats and promises is likely to be precarious; for the power relation thus established depends upon the continuing submissiveness of a recalcitrant will, generated and maintained by the master's continuing influence. The will of the subject reflects the will of the master but incompletely and tenuously as long as the will of the master is imposed upon the will of the subject from without and against the latter's resistance. How to overcome that resistance and make the will of the subject one with the will of the master is one of the crucial issues with which all political orders must come to terms. It is the issue of political stability. The political masters, actual and potential, and on all levels of social interaction from the family to the state, have sought to meet that issue by basing their power upon the spontaneous consent of the subject. If the subject can be made to duplicate spontaneously within himself the master's will so that what the master wills the subject wills, too, not through inducement from without but through spontaneous consent from within, then the will of the master and the will of the subject are one, and the power of the master is founded not upon the master's threats and promises but upon the subject's love for the master.

So it is not by accident that the political philosophies which emphasize the stability of power relationships, such as those of monarchies and autocracies make a point of appealing to the love of the subject for the ruler. The philosophy and ritual of absolute monarchy, in particular, are full of references to the love of the subject for the monarch as the foundation of the monarch's power. That foundation has perhaps nowhere been more clearly revealed than in a letter which John Durie, Scotch Presbyterian and worker for Protestant unity, wrote in 1632 to the British Ambassador, Thomas Roe, explaining the decline of the power of Gustavus Adophus of Sweden, then fighting for the Protestant cause in Germany:

> The increase of his authority is the ground of his abode; and love is the ground of his authority; it must be through love; for it cannot be through power; for his power is not in his own subjects but in strangers; not in his money, but in theirs; not in their good will, but in mere necessity as things stand now betwixt him and them; therefore if the necessity be not so urgent as it is; or if any other means be shown by God (who is able to do as much by another man as by him) to avoid this necessity; the money and the power and the assistance which it yieldeth unto

him will fall from him and so his authority is lost, and his abode will be no longer: for the love which was at first is gone. . . .

In recent times, the continuous references to "our beloved leader" in the literature and ritual of Naziism and Stalinism point to the same relationship between ruler and subject—in the case of Naziism in good measure as an actual fact, however corrupted by power and hate; in the case of Stalinism as something to be desired but unattainable.

Obviously, this transformation of the unilateral imposition of the power relationship into the mutuality of love is in the political sphere, at least in its modern secular form, an ideal rather than an attainable goal. Thus the great political masters, the Alexanders and Napoleons, while painfully aware of the love that is beyond their reach, seek to compensate for the love they must miss with an ever greater accumulation of power. From the subjection of ever more men to their will, they seem to expect the achievement of that communion which the lack of love withholds from them. Yet the acquisition of power only begets the desire for more; for the more men the master holds bound to his will, the more he is aware of his loneliness. His success in terms of power only serves to illuminate his failure in terms of love.

There is then in the great political masters a demoniac and frantic striving for ever more power—as there is in the misguided lovers, the Don Juans who mistake sex for love, a limitless and ever unsatiated compulsion toward more and more experiences of sex—which will be satisfied only with the last living man has been subjected to the master's will. " 'More! More!' " in the words of William Blake, "is the cry of the mistaken soul; less than all cannot satisfy man." Thus the heights of the master's power signal the depths of his despair. For the world conqueror can subject all inhabitants of the earth to his will, but he cannot compel a single one to love him. The master of all men is also the loneliest of all men; for his loneliness, in spite of the totality of his power, proves that it cannot be cured by power. That fruitless search for love through power leads in the most passionate of the seekers of power from a despair, impotent in the fullness of power, to a hate, destructive of the objects of their successful power and frustrated love. Thus the Genghis Khans, Hitlers, and Stalins lash out with unreasoning fury at their subjects whom they can dominate but whose love they cannot command and, hence, whom they cannot afford to love.

Yet while the subjects may not love the master and the master may impose his will with bloody tyranny, there is even in the crudest of power relationships an irreducible element of love. What both master and subject seek is that union which remedies the awareness of insufficiency born of loneliness and which only love can give. But they have chosen the wrong track of power and are doomed to failure. Thus they—master and subject—must search forever and in vain for that other human being to whom they could say, I love you, to hear the reply, I love you, too.

The power relationship is, then, in the last analysis, a frustrated relationship of love. Those who must use and suffer power would rather be united in love. Master and subject are at the bottom of their souls lovers who have gone astray. The hostility of their relationship carries a trace of that frustrated love which is at the root of a type of hate. Napoleon, in his conversations with De Las Cases on Saint Helena, and Hitler, in his harangues to his generals, have bemoaned their fate that in the fulness of their power they could trust nobody and found nobody worthy of their love. Many of the powerful have throughout history sought the illusion of love in the promiscuous enjoyment of sex. Beneath that artificial community which power builds as a substitute for, and a spite to, love, there remains at least a glimmer of an aspiration which longs for that reunion only love can give. It manifests itself in the sometimes sudden emergence of charity, pity, and forgiveness in the relations between master and subject. Nowhere has that kinship of power and love been expressed with simpler profundity than in the two words which Homer makes Achilles speak when he is about to slay Lykauos: "Die, friend."

The loneliness of man is, then, impervious to both love and power. Power can only unite through the unilateral imposition of subjection, which leaves the master's isolation intact. Behold that master whom the wills of millions obey and who cannot find a single soul with which to unite his own. Love can unite only in the fleeting moments when two souls and bodies merge in spontaneous mutuality. The lovers bear the dual burden of Adam and Eve and of Moses. They see the promised land in their longing's imagination and enter it only to be expelled from it. Behold the lovers who find in their embrace the illusion of complete union and in fleeting moments even its reality, only to awaken alone in the embrace of another lover.

Thus in the end, his wings seared, his heart-blood spend, his projects come to nought—despairing of power and thirsting for, and forsaken by, love—man peoples the heavens with gods and mothers and virgins and saints who love him and whom he can love and to whose power he can subject himself spontaneously because their power is the power of love. Yet whatever he expects of the other world, he must leave this world as he entered it: alone.

Part II

ON GREATNESS AND THE HEROIC

There are many ways of leading and many levels at which leadership may show itself. The readings that follow in this section reflect on leading at the highest, most comprehensive levels.

Homer's Achilles

Achilles' speech in the *Iliad* is unique in its thoughtfulness about the warrior's pursuit of glory, which requires sacrificing the serenity and productiveness of the domestic life. Achilles speaks eloquently, addressing Odysseus, the hero of the *Odyssey*. In his struggle after the Trojan War to return to his homeland of Ithaca, Odysseus will learn through experience what Achilles here reports briefly. Achilles confronts the fact of human mortality, recognizing that it is the common denominator of all human beings, the key to finding wisdom about the human condition.

If we do not confront this fact about ourselves we have not yet grasped the human predicament, which is prerequisite to true insight and judgment: "We are all held in a single honour, the brave with the weaklings. A man dies still if he has done nothing, as one who has done much." Achilles carries two destinies: he may either return home, losing glory but gaining long life, or stay to fight and, in losing life, gain glory. If there is a reason to seek glory it is not spelled out by Achilles. His destiny is a fact, but it is also a mystery.

Achilles chooses glory and a short life. We can understand, even if we do not have to confront, the need to choose between these two destinies. Having to choose between them is contingent upon the unpredictability of circumstances and the disposition of the human spirit. The greatness of Achilles rests

71

partly in this mysterious fact. Despite his uniqueness, he is emblematic of all of us. Can we be content with a choice for which there is little extrinsic rationale, which offers no progressive development of social life? In considering Achilles, we consider our own self-understanding.

St. Thomas Aquinas

St. Thomas Aquinas describes leadership in a context suffused with awareness of the spiritual destiny of humanity, very different from Achillean destiny. In both cases, our mortality is central, but the mystery is conceived differently. In the Christian tradition, "glory" emerges in the sacrifice of worldliness (glory as the world can see and understand it) for the sake of the eternal life which we cannot directly see in this world.

The Christian leader must be a servant of the people in detachment from the trappings of worldly success that go with ruling positions. At the same time, such leaders cannot extricate themselves from worldly involvement, since that is the price of political participation; they must seek to leaven the world without expecting to overcome or permanently transform the world. It is difficult to be "in the world, but not of it," and the possibilities of self-deception and misunderstanding are infinite.

At the same time, St. Thomas proposes that there is an order in nature which offers guidance to our ordering of ourselves as human beings and as leaders. God is the governor of the universe and his creation is orderly and rational. Human beings are part of and participate in this order. Yet human beings are also endowed with reason, in the image of God, and thus participate actively in creating order for themselves by their judgment of and response to their conditions as they understand them. Nature is supportive, but nature does not do for us the work we must do. We enhance nature by realizing possibilities latent within it which come to the fore only through the undertakings of human beings.

We are also by nature members of communities, and thus we are responsible to and for each other in the way we order ourselves. In order to discharge this responsibility, someone must exercise authority in a manner analogous to God's authority over the creation. The humanly organized communities are both natural and artificial: They are natural insofar as they coincide with the rational order of nature; artificial, insofar as a variety of orderings will appear in different communities as they respond to differing circumstances. Those who exercise authority are thus similar to each other in one way, and yet inevitably differ in the particulars of their situation. Properly realized, however, each particular order would be a valid version of the general requirements of order embedded in nature. The greatest responsibility of the leader, then, is to pursue justice vigorously but temper it with mercy and compassion for the contingencies and uncertainties of the human condition.

Leaders must assist those whom they govern toward their proper fulfillment and flourishing. Of course, individuals must take responsibility personally for pursuing their goals. But because we are communal beings as well as unique individuals, we must do this in each other's company and we must achieve the coordination of efforts, and reconciliation of aims, which is impossible without the exercise of competent authority.

Leading is both comprehensive and serious. Human fulfillment cannot be gained in earthly communities alone, but requires the attainment of a heavenly destiny. This is in God's hands, not in the hands of the authorities, but the latter can be a help or a hindrance in setting the conditions under which we each must seek our path to the common, final destination. The ordering of earthly life must be made as compatible as possible with the higher task of seeking the fulfillment of the spiritual life and the supernatural or heavenly end of our existence.

The governor's tasks are to provide for the security of the community and to assist in acquiring adequate material goods without which we cannot operate successfully, but also to remind us continually that these goods serve something higher. While it is the Church's task to articulate the spiritual life, it is the joint task of both the civil and ecclesiastical authorities to assist us in coordinating the natural and supernatural ends. St. Thomas's view of greatness separates the purpose of leadership from the pursuit of worldly glory, putting before us the thought of spiritual glory, and the prospect of this kind of fulfillment as realized, through leadership, in the community of individuals as a whole.

Machiavelli

Machiavelli's *The Prince* stands in sharp contrast to St. Thomas, and Machiavelli intended explicitly to distinguish his view from that of the Christian tradition. He makes this explicit in the famous opening paragraph of chapter 15, where he warns prospective leaders that success in the political life requires learning how not to be good when necessity demands it.

Machiavelli severs the supportive connection of nature, describing instead the unruly and chaotic conditions which obtain when gifted human beings do not unreservedly exercise power to impose order where there is none, or where it has been lost. While Machiavelli could agree with St. Thomas on the priority of ensuring the security and well-being of the community, he understands that conditions of achieving them are dark and dispiriting to those lacking will and stamina. His leader must have the capacity for ruthlessness and even dishonesty when security demands it, not because these are desirable qualities in themselves, but because they are unavoidably necessary.

Machiavelli forces us to think carefully both about what we might be called upon to do in political life if we are to succeed (even in service to noble and righteous causes), and about the moral ambiguities we cannot avoid if we are to pursue transforming actions. He wants to disabuse us of naive romanticism about the nobility of leadership, which he fears is inherent to the Christian understanding, while asserting that there are great achievements potentially in store for those who can accept the "vocation" of the prince. It is not surprising that Machiavelli reasserts the ancient virtues of "glory" and of "ambition" to gain perpetual memory in history, against the invisible, spiritual glory of Thomas Aquinas.

Hegel

Hegel was a great historian of philosophy as well as a profound philosopher. He absorbed the antagonistic alternatives of ancient, medieval, and early modern thinkers, such as Machiavelli. Hegel's method was to understand and reconcile the elements of truth in each position in order to arrive at a comprehensive grasp of the whole of human reality. Hegel saw this as a kind of philosophic heroism or quest for intellectual greatness. In his introduction to the philosophy of history, Hegel recognizes the fundamental political necessity to preserve the nation or state, and he insists on the joint involvement of all members in that endeavor. But he puts this task in the vast context of world history.

As Hegel sees it, there is an unfolding story of history in which nations in different historical periods contribute different but necessary elements to the completion of the story, which he reveals in developing his *philosophy* of world history. Each new era, carrying forward the unfolding story towards its conclusion, may only succeed by overcoming and replacing a preceding era as the latter exhausts all of its potential. This continuous process of transformation is unavoidable. Great individuals are those who somehow grasp the changes that must occur in their time and spur them on to realization. These are individuals who avoid the distractions of daily life and see further than most into what will be truly important.

Insofar as such individuals succeed in promoting historical changes (changes which must come to pass), they are seen as heroes: "they draw their inspiration from another source, from that hidden spirit whose hour is near but which still lies beneath the surface and seeks to break out without yet having attained an existence in the present. For this spirit, the present world is but a shell which contains the wrong kind of kernel."

Leadership at the world historical level is, therefore, destructive of what remains of a passing order, but also creative in bringing into being the elements out of which a new order will be made. Yet the course of history uses these heroic figures for purposes which they themselves intuitively grasp but cannot fully understand. Of course, at any historical moment there are many ideas and aspirations expressing themselves. But if they are inadequately attuned to what is unfolding historically they will, for that reason alone, fail to reach fulfillment and will fall by the wayside.

There is superficial leadership—celebrity without depth—and there is true leadership. There is, however, no formula to ensure that we can distinguish these, nor full knowledge of where history will move beyond our own time. We can see in retrospect why what has happened happened as it did. Thus, although one can gain insight into the character of heroic leadership and can see manifestations of it, one cannot be sure of what it will look like in the future, or how the present will finally play out. Hegel combines confidence in his understanding of how history works with scepticism about our ability to see where it is going.

In this way, Hegel combines the tragic reflection on glory of Achilles with the spiritual aspirations of Christianity and the demythologizing scepticism of Machiavelli. The human story is, for him, both spiritual and violent, destructive and creative, in our control and out of our control. The ability of the great leaders to live at the intersection of these antagonisms sets them apart from everyone else. They do not, Hegel asserts, seek happiness, but the attainment of destined ends. Happiness is a pursuit for the private life. Even honor and fame are secondary.

Those who insist that leaders are not happy, or that they seek only honor and fame, are judging by an inappropriate and superficial standard. The gaining of their ends is the fulfillment the heroic seek. In one way they personify the ends they seek, and yet in another they are absorbed into the tasks they take on, becoming identified with the work itself, which is all that matters.

On the other hand, as we are all implicated in the movement of the spirit of world history, what is vividly magnified in the leader is experienced in diminished degree in those who are led as they participate, with greater or lesser awareness, in the drama of which they are parts. Hegel distinguishes the envious, who begrudge the great their prominence, from the truly free who applaud greatness in others and thus show a spark of greatness themselves.

Burckhardt

Jacob Burckhardt's reflection on the great men of history shows Hegel's influence but also a distinct change of mood. The historical affirmation one might take from Hegel is met with a new kind of scepticism because Burckhardt, like other nineteenth-century thinkers, feared the leveling consequences of the democratic age. The democratic age, Burckhardt argues, brings with it a resentment of and resistance to greatness and the heroic. We should not confuse this with the commonplace adulation of celebrities and personalities in our time. Burckhardt himself was of the contemplative sort—not one of the great men of action moved by "a genuine will to master the situation"— and there is a degree of discouragement in his view as he considers the tendencies of the incipient world of mass society.

History shows that the great have "greatness of soul," which appears unpredictably because it always appears as an exception to normal standards. Lest we mistake what he means by soul, however, we must remember his apparently Machiavellian point: "no power has ever yet been founded without crime." This view is to be found also in the Augustinian tradition of Christianity. St. Augustine established the classic version of the doctrine of original sin, which teaches that all human accomplishments have, at their foundation, flaws which will eventually show themselves, and which human beings cannot successfully conceal from themselves or their enemies. In this vein, Burckhardt has no intention of exalting the state. Powerful governments are no less a threat to genius than is the leveling force of democracy. Governments are ruled by utility. The state in the democratic age combines with democracy to squeeze the genius and the potentially great. It is a major task in itself to remind the denizens of democracy of the possibility of greatness when their disposition is to deny or suppress it. Leadership requires a kind of critical friendship for democracy, acknowledging but not indulging it.

Homer, *Iliad*

The Iliad, *generally considered the earliest surviving work in Greek literature, is ascribed to Homer, the progenitor of Western literature. Homer
probably lived in the ninth or eighth century* B.C. *The* Iliad, *an epic poem,
was probably written down long after it was constructed orally and edited
in numerous recitations. Homer's literary work, regarded with awe by the
ancient Greeks, still retains its preeminence. His poems, the* Iliad *and the*
Odyssey, *had a profound influence on later literary figures such as Virgil,
Dante, William Shakespeare, and James Joyce.*

Homer's Iliad *tells the story of the wrath of Achilles (Achilleus) and its
consequences for the Greeks in their war with the Trojans. Agamemnon has
taken possession of Achilles' war prize, the young girl Briseis, daughter of
Briseus. A furious Achilles withdraws from the war to his tent. The inability
of the Greeks to defeat the Trojans compels Agamemnon to send emissaries
to placate Achilles and persuade him to rejoin the struggle. In the following
episode, the entreaty to Achilles elicits a response which brings to light that
he has reflected, uniquely among the warrior heroes in the* Iliad, *on glory
and the mortality of human things, and wondered about the meaning of
ambition and seeking recognition. Achilles eventually returns to the war to
revenge the death of his friend Patroklos.*

Thereupon the Gerenian horseman Nestor answered him:
'Son of Atreus, most lordly and king of men, Agamemnon,
none could scorn any longer these gifts you offer to Achilleus
the king. Come, let us choose and send some men, who in all speed
will go to the shelter of Achilleus, the son of Peleus;
or come, the men on whom my eye falls, let these take the duty.
First of all let Phoinix, beloved of Zeus, be their leader,
and after him take Aias the great, and brilliant Odysseus
and of the heralds let Odios and Eurybates go with them.
Bring also water for their hands, and bid them keep words of good omen,
so we may pray to Zeus, son of Kronos, if he will have pity.'
So he spoke, and the word he spoke was pleasing to all of them
And the heralds brought water at once, and poured it over
their hands, and the young men filled the mixing-bowl with pure wine
and passed it to all, pouring first a libation in goblets.
Then when they had poured out wine, and drunk as much as their hearts wished,
they set out from the shelter of Atreus' son, Agamemnon.

And the Gerenian horseman Nestor gave them much instruction,
looking eagerly at each, and most of all at Odysseus,
to try hard, so that they win over the blameless Peleion.
    So these two walked along the strand of the sea deep-thundering
with many prayers to the holder and shaker of the earth, that they
might readily persuade the great heart of Aiakides.
Now they came beside the shelters and ships of the Myrmidons
and they found Achilleus delighting his heart in a lyre, clear-sounding,
splendid and carefully wrought, with a bridge of silver upon it,
which he won out of the spoils when he ruined Eëtion's city.
With this he was pleasuring his heart, and singing of men's fame,
as Patroklos was sitting over against him, alone, in silence,
watching Aiakides and the time he would leave off singing.
Now these two came forward, as brilliant Odysseus led them,
and stood in his presence. Achilleus rose to his feet in amazement
holding the lyre as it was, leaving the place where he was sitting.
In the same way Patroklos, when he saw the men come, stood up.
And in greeting Achilleus the swift of foot spoke to them:
'Welcome. You are my friends who have come, all greatly I need you,
who even to this my anger are dearest of all the Achaians.'
    So brilliant Achilleus spoke. . . .
They put their hands to the good things that lay ready before them.
But when they had put aside their desire for eating and drinking,
Aias nodded to Phoinix, and brilliant Odysseus saw it,
and filled a cup with wine, and lifted it to Achilleus:
'Your health, Achilleus. You have no lack of your equal portion
either within the shelter of Atreus' son, Agamemnon,
nor here now on your own. We have good things in abundance
to feast on; here it is not the desirable feast we think of,
but a trouble all too great, beloved of Zeus, that we look on
and are afraid. There is doubt if we save our strong-benched vessels
or if they will be destroyed, unless you put on your war strength.
The Trojans in their pride, with their far-renowned companions,
have set up an encampment close by the ships and the rampart,
and lit many fires along their army, and think no longer
of being held, but rather to drive in upon the black ships.
And Zeus, son of Kronos, lightens upon their right hand, showing them
portents of good, while Hektor in the huge pride of his strength rages
irresistibly, reliant on Zeus, and gives way to no one
neither god nor man, but the strong fury has descended upon him.

He prays now that the divine Dawn will show most quickly,
since he threatens to shear the uttermost horns from the ship-sterns,
to light the ships themselves with ravening fire, and to cut down
the Achaians themselves as they stir from the smoke beside them.
All this I fear terribly in my heart, lest immortals
accomplish all these threats, and lest for us it be destiny
to die here in Troy, far away from horse-pasturing Argos.
Up, then! if you are minded, late though it be, to rescue
the inflicted sons of the Achaians from the Trojan onslaught.
It will be an affliction to you hereafter, there will be no remedy
found to heal the evil thing when it has been done. . . .
. . . Yet even now
stop, and give way from the anger that hurts the heart. Agamemnon
offers you worthy recompense if you change from your anger.
Come then, if you will, listen to me, while I count off for you
all the gifts in his shelter that Agamemnon has promised:
Seven unfired tripods; ten talents' weight of gold; twenty
shining cauldrons; and twelve horses, strong, race-competitors
who have won prizes in the speed of their feet. That man would not be
poor in possessions, to whom were given all these have won him,
nor be unpossessed of dearly honoured gold, were he given
all the prizes Agamemnon's horses won in their speed for him.
He will give you seven women of Lesbos, the work of whose hands
is blameless, whom when you yourself captured strong-founded Lesbos
he chose, and who in their beauty surpassed the races of women.
He will give you these, and with these shall go the one he took from you,
the daughter of Briseus. . . .
All these gifts shall be yours at once; but again, if hereafter
the gods grant that we storm and sack the great city of Priam,
you may go to your ship and load it deep as you please with
gold and bronze, when we Achaians divide the war spoils,
and you may choose for yourself twenty of the Trojan women,
who are the loveliest of all after Helen of Argos. . . .
All this he will bring to pass for you, if you change from your anger.
But if the son of Atreus is too much hated in your heart,
himself and his gifts, at least take pity on all the other
Achaians, who are afflicted along the host, and will honour you
as a god. You may win very great glory among them.
For now you might kill Hektor, since he would come very close to you
with the wicked fury upon him, since he thinks there is not his equal

among the rest of the Danaans the ships carried hither.'
    Then in answer to him spoke Achilleus of the swift feet:
'Son of Laertes and seed of Zeus, resourceful Odysseus:
without consideration for you I must make my answer,
the way I think, and the way it will be accomplished, that you may not
come one after another, and sit by me, and speak softly.
For as I detest the doorways of Death, I detest that man, who
hides one thing in the depths of his heart, and speaks forth another.
But I will speak to you the way it seems best to me: neither
do I think the son of Atreus, Agamemnon will persuade me,
nor the rest of the Danaans, since there was no gratitude given
for fighting incessantly forever against your enemies.
Fate is the same for the man who holds back, the same if he fights hard.
We are all held in a single honour, the brave with the weaklings.
A man dies still if he has done nothing, as one who has done much.
Nothing is won for me, now that my heart has gone through its afflictions
in forever setting my life on the hazard of battle.
For as to her unwinged young ones the mother bird brings back
morsels, wherever she can find them, but as for herself it is suffering,
such was I, as I lay through all the many nights unsleeping,
such as I wore through the bloody days of the fighting,
striving with warriors for the sake of these men's women.
But I say that I have stormed from my ships twelve cities
of men, and by land eleven more through the generous Troad.
From all these we took forth treasures, goodly and numerous,
and we would bring them back, and give them to Agamemnon,
Atreus' son; while he, waiting back beside the swift ships,
would take them, and distribute them little by little, and keep many.
All the other prizes of honour he gave the great men and the princes
are held fast by them, but from me alone of all the Achaians
he has taken and keeps the bride of my heart. Let him lie beside her
and be happy. Yet why must the Argives fight with the Trojans?
And why was it the son of Atreus assembled and led here
these people? Was it not for the sake of lovely-haired Helen?
Are the sons of Atreus alone among mortal men the ones
who love their wives? Since any who is a good man, and careful,
loves her who is his own and cares for her, even as I now
loved this one from my heart, though it was my spear that won her.
Now that he has deceived me and taken from my hands my prize of honour,
let him try me no more. I know him well. He will not persuade me.
Let him take counsel with you, Odysseus, and the rest of the princes

how to fight the ravening fire away from his vessels.
Indeed, there has been much hard work done even without me;
he has built himself a wall and driven a ditch about it,
making it great and wide, and fixed the sharp stakes inside it.
Yet even so he cannot hold the strength of manslaughtering
Hektor; and yet when I was fighting among the Achaians
Hektor would not drive his attack beyond the wall's shelter
but would come forth only so far as the Skaian gates and the oak tree.
There once he endured me alone, and barely escaped my onslaught.
But, now I am unwilling to fight against brilliant Hektor,
tomorrow, when I have sacrificed to Zeus and to all gods,
and loaded well my ships, and rowed out on to the salt water,
you will see, if you have a mind to it and if it concerns you,
my ships in the dawn at sea on the Hellespont where the fish swarm
and my men manning them with good will to row. If the glorious
shaker of the earth should grant us a favoring passage
on the third day thereafter we might raise generous Phthia.
I have many possessions there that I left behind when I came here
on this desperate venture, and from here there is more gold, and red bronze,
and fair-girdled women, and grey iron I will take back;
all that was allotted to me. But my prize: he who gave it,
powerful Agamemnon, son of Atreus, has taken it back again
outrageously. Go back and proclaim to him all that I tell you,
openly, so other Achaians may turn against him in anger
if he hopes yet one more time to swindle some other Danaan,
wrapped as he is forever in shamelessness; yet he would not,
bold as a dog though he be, dare look in my face any longer.
I will join with him in no counsel and in no action.
He cheated me and he did me hurt. Let him not beguile me
with words again. This is enough for him. Let him of his own will
be damned, since Zeus of the counsels has taken his wits away from him.
I hate his gifts. I hold him light as the strip of a splinter.
Not if he gave me ten times as much, and twenty times over
as he possesses now, not if more should come to him from elsewhere,
or gave all that is brought in to Orchomenos, all that is brought in
to Thebes of Egypt, where the greatest possessions lie up in the houses,
Thebes of the hundred gates, where through each of the gates two hundred
fighting men come forth to war with horses and chariots;
not if he gave me gifts as many as the sand or the dust is,
not even so would Agamemnon have his way with my spirit
until he had made good to me all this heartrending insolence.

Nor will I marry a daughter of Atreus' son, Agamemnon,
not if she challenged Aphrodite the golden for loveliness,
not if she matched the work of her hands with grey-eyed Athene;
not even so will I marry her; let him pick some other Achaian,
one who is to his liking and is kinglier than I am.
For if the gods will keep me alive, and I win homeward,
Peleus himself will presently arrange a wife for me.
There are many Archaian girls in the land of Hellas and Phthia,
daughters of great men who hold strong places in guard. And of these
any one that I please I might make my beloved lady.
And the great desire in my heart drives me rather in that place
to take a wedded wife in marriage, the bride of my fancy,
to enjoy with her the possessions won by aged Peleus. For not
worth the value of my life are all the possessions they fable
were won for Ilion, that strong-founded citadel, in the old days
when there was peace, before the coming of the sons of the Achaians
not all that the stone doorsill of the Archer holds fast within it,
of Phoibos Apollo in Pytho of the rocks. Of possessions
cattle and fat sheep are things to be had for the lifting,
and tripods can be won and the tawny high heads of horses,
but a man's life cannot come back again, it cannot be lifted
nor captured again by force, once it has crossed the teeth's barrier.
For my mother Thetis the goddess of the silver feet tells me
I carry two sorts of destiny toward the day of my death. Either,
if I stay here and fight beside the city of the Trojans
my return home is gone, but my glory shall be everlasting
but if I return home to the beloved land of my fathers,
the excellence of my glory is gone, but there will be a long life
for me, and my end in death will not come to me quickly.
And this would be my counsel to others also, to sail back
home again, since no longer shall you find any term set
on the sheer city of Ilion, since Zeus of the wide brows has strongly
held his own hand over it, and its people are made bold. . . .'

St. Thomas Aquinas,
"On Princely Government"

St. Thomas Aquinas (1224–1274), the celebrated scholastic philosopher and theologian, sought a synthesis of Aristotelian philosophy and Christian theology, a reconciliation of reason and revelation, that is one of the greatest monuments of Western thought. In the reading that follows, Aquinas applies his thought to the political community. Specifically, his analysis of the function of the ruler shows how we might understand the relationship between the civic life (in Aristotelian terms, the place where human beings can find the fullest flourishing of their natural lives) and their pursuit of their supernatural end (the end beyond nature) ordained by God. It is instructive to compare the Aristotelian/Thomistic view of the ruler and of political life with the Machiavellian view.

Chapter XII.—The Duties of a King: The Similarity between Royal Power and the Power of the Soul over the Body and of God over the Universe.

To complete what we have so far said it remains only to consider what is the duty of a king and how he should comport himself. And since art is but an imitation of nature, from which we come to learn how to act according to reason, it would seem best to deduce the duties of a king from the examples of government in nature. Now in nature there is to be found both a universal and a particular form of government. The universal is that by which all things find their place under the direction of God, who, by His providence, governs the universe. The particular is very similar to this divine control, and is found within man himself; who, for this reason, is called a microcosm, because he provides all examples of universal government. Just as the divine control is exercised over all created bodies and over all spiritual powers, so does the control of reason extend over the members of the body and the other facilities of the soul: so, in a certain sense, reason is to man what God is to the universe. But because, as we have shown above, man is by nature a social animal living in community, this similarity with divine rule is found among men, not only in the sense that a man is directed by his reason, but also in the fact that a community is ruled by one man's intelligence; for this is essentially the king's duty. A king, then, should realize that he has assumed the duty of being to his kingdom what the soul is to the body and what God is to the universe. If he thinks attentively upon this point he will, on the one hand, be fired with zeal for justice, seeing himself appointed to administer justice throughout his realm in the name of God, and, on the other hand, he will grow in mildness and clemency, looking upon the persons subject to his government, as the members of his own body.

Chapter XIV.—Comparison between the Priestly Power and That of a King.

We must first have in mind that to govern is to guide what is governed to its appointed end. So we say that a ship is under control when it is sailed on its right course to port by the skill of a sailor. Now when something is ordered to an end which lies outside itself, as a ship is to harbour, it is the ruler's duty not only to preserve its integrity, but also to see that it reaches its appointed destination. If there were anything with no end beyond itself, then the ruler's sole task would be to preserve it unharmed in all its perfection. But though there is no such example to be found in creation, apart from God who is the end of all things, care for higher aims is beset with many and varied difficulties. For it is very clear that there may be one person employed about the preservation of a thing in its present state, and another concerned with bringing it to higher perfection; as we see in the case of a ship, which we have used as an example of government. Just as it is the carpenter's task to repair any damage which may occur and the sailor's task to steer the ship to port, so also in man himself the same processes are at work. The doctor sets himself to preserve man's life and bodily health; the economist's task is to see that there is no lack of material goods; the learned see to it that he knows the truth; and the moralist that he should live according to reason. Thus, if man were not destined to some higher end, these attentions would suffice.

But there is a further destiny for man after this mortal life; that final blessedness and enjoyment of God which he awaits after death. For, as the Apostle says (*II Corinthians* V, 6): 'While we are in the body we are absent from God.' So it is that the Christian, for whom that blessedness was obtained by the blood of Christ, and who is led to it through the gift of the Holy Ghost, has need of another, spiritual, guide to lead him to the harbour of eternal salvation: such guidance is provided for the faithful by the ministers of the Church of Christ.

Our conclusion must be the same, whether we consider the destiny of one person or of a whole community. Consequently, if the end of man were to be found in any perfection existing in man himself, the final object of government in a community would lie in the acquisition of such perfection and in its preservation once acquired. So that if such an end, whether of an individual or of a community, were life and bodily health, doctors would govern. If, on the other hand, it were abundance of riches, the government of the community could safely be left in the hands of the economist. If it were knowledge of truth, the king, whose task it is to guide the community, would have the duties of a professor. But the object for which a community is gathered together is to live a virtuous life. For men consort together that they may thus attain a fullness of life which would not be possible to each living singly: and the full life is one which is lived according to virtue. Thus the object of human society is a virtuous life.

Chapter XV.—How to Attain the Aim of a Good Life in the Political Community.

Just as the good life of men on this earth is directed, as to its end, to the blessed life which is promised us in heaven, so also all those particular benefits which men can procure for themselves, such as riches, or gain, or health, or skill, or learning, must be directed to the good of the community. But, as we have said, he who has charge of supreme ends must take precedence over those who are concerned with aims subordinate to these ends, and, must guide them by his authority; it follows, therefore, that a king, though subject to that power and authority must, nevertheless, preside over all human activities, and direct them in virtue of his own power and authority. Now, whoever has a duty of completing some task, which is itself connected with some higher aim, must satisfy himself that his action is rightly directed towards that aim. Thus the smith forges a sword which is fit to fight with; and the builder must construct a house so that it is habitable. And because the aim of a good life on this earth is blessedness in heaven, it is the king's duty to promote the welfare of the community in such a way that it leads fittingly to the happiness of heaven; insisting upon the performance of all that leads thereto, and forbidding, as far as is possible, whatever is inconsistent with this end. The road to true blessedness and the obstacles which may be found along it, are learnt through the medium of the divine law; to teach which is the duty of priests, as we read in *Malachy* (Chapter II, 7): 'The lips of the priest shall keep knowledge, and they shall seek the law at his mouth.' So the Lord commands (*Deuteronomy* XVII, 18): 'But after he is raised to the throne of his kingdom, he shall copy out to himself the Deuteronomy of this law in a volume, taking the copy of the priests of the Levitical tribe, and he shall have it with him and shall read it all the days of his life, that he may learn to fear the Lord his God, and keep his words and ceremonies, that are commanded in the law.' A king then, being instructed in the divine law, must occupy himself particularly with directing the community subject to him to the good life. In this connection he has three tasks. He must first establish the welfare of the community he rules; secondly, he must ensure that nothing undermines the well-being thus established; and thirdly he must be at pains continually to extend this welfare.

For the well-being of the individual two things are necessary: the first and most essential is to act virtuously (it is through virtue, in fact, that we live a good life); the other, and secondary requirement, is rather a means, and lies in a sufficiency of material goods, such as are necessary to virtuous action. Now man is a natural unit, but the unity of a community, which is peace, must be brought into being by the skill of the ruler. To ensure the well-being of a community, therefore, three things are necessary. In the first place the community must be united in peaceful unity. In the second place the community, thus united, must be directed towards well-doing. For just as man could do no good if he were not an integral whole, so also a community of men which is disunited and at strife within itself, is hampered in well-doing. Thirdly and finally, it is necessary that there be, through the ruler's sagacity, a sufficiency of those material goods which are indispensable to well-being. Once the welfare of the community is thus ensured, it remains for the king to consider its preservation.

Now there are three things which are detrimental to the permanence of public welfare and one of these springs from the nature of things. For the common prosperity should not be for any limited period, but should endure, if possible, in perpetuity. But men, being mortal, cannot live for ever. Nor, even while they are still alive, have they always the same vigour; for human life is subject to many changes, and a man is not always capable of fulfilling the same tasks throughout the span of his lifetime. Another obstacle to the preservation of public welfare is one which arises from within, and lies in the perversity of the will; for many are inattentive in carrying out duties necessary to the community, or even harm the peace of the community by failing to observe justice and disturbing the peace of others. Then there is a third obstacle to the preservation of the community which comes from without; when peace is shattered by hostile invasion, and sometimes the kingdom or city itself is entirely destroyed. Corresponding to these three points, the task of a king has a threefold aspect. The first regards the succession and substitution of those who hold various offices: just as divine providence sees to it that corruptible things, which cannot remain unchanged for ever, are renewed through successive generations, and so conserves the integrity of the universe, it is the king's duty also to preserve the well-being of the community subject to him, by providing successors for those who are failing. Secondly he must, in governing, be concerned, by laws and by advice, by penalties and by rewards, to dissuade men from evil-doing and to induce them to do good; following thus the example of God, who gave to men a law, and rewards those who observe it but punishes those who transgress. Thirdly it is a king's duty to make sure that the community subject to him is made safe against its enemies. There is no point in guarding against internal dangers, when defence from enemies without is impossible.

So, for the right ordering of society there remains a third task for the king: he must be occupied with its development. This task is best fulfilled by keeping in mind the various points enumerated above; by attention to what may be a cause of disorder, by making good whatever is lacking and by perfecting whatever can be better done. Therefore the Apostle (*I Corinthians*, XII), warns the faithful always to prize the better gifts. . . .

Machiavelli, *The Prince*

"Anyone who picks up Machiavelli's The Prince *holds in his hands the most famous book on politics ever written." So writes Harvard University scholar Harvey C. Mansfield, Jr., whose English translation of* The Prince *by Niccolò Machiavelli (1469–1527) is the source for the selection below. The* Prince *is concerned with the means necessary for a prince to get and keep power. It offers advice regarding the manipulation, or channeling, of the energies of the masses in such a way as to preserve the ruler's power with a minimal use of violence. Machiavelli's candid advice was based in part on his practical experience as senior advisor to the Florentine Republic between the years 1498 and 1512, and on his subsequent treatment by the Medici, who overthrew the republic in 1512. After a year of imprisonment and torture at the hands of the Medici, Machiavelli retired and began work on his writings, including* The Prince, *which was completed in 1513, and* Discourses on the First Ten Books of Titus Livius, *which was completed between 1513 and 1521.*

In The Prince, *Machiavelli breaks with a long tradition of political theorists who concerned themselves with an ideal political system that would be the end of political action. Machiavelli revised the concept of "idealism" by insisting that political goals (such as unifying Italy as a great state) required study of military history and strategy, not Platonic philosophy or Christian spirituality. The pursuit of any lofty aim is constrained by iron necessities of the human condition.*

XV. Of Those Things for Which Men and Especially Princes Are Praised or Blamed

It remains now to see what the modes and government of a prince should be with subjects and with friends. And because I know that many have written of this, I fear that in writing of it again, I may be held presumptuous, especially since in disputing this matter I depart from the orders of others. But since my intent is to write something useful to whoever understands it, it has appeared to me more fitting to go directly to the effectual truth of the thing than to the imagination of it. And many have imagined republics and principalities that have never been seen or known to exist in truth; for it is so far from how one lives to how one should live that he who lets go of what is done for what should be done earns his ruin rather than his preservation. For a man who wants to make a profession of good in all regards must come to ruin among so many who are not good. Hence it is necessary to a prince, if he wants to maintain himself, to learn to be able not to be good, and to use this and not use it according to necessity.

Thus, leaving out what is imagined about a prince and discussing what is true, I say that all men, whenever one speaks of them, and especially princes, since they are placed higher, are noted for some of the qualities that bring them either blame or praise. And this is why someone is considered liberal, someone mean (using a Tuscan term because *avaro* [greedy] in our language is still one who desires to have something by violence, *misero* [mean] we call one who refrains too much from using what is his); someone is considered a giver, someone rapacious; someone cruel, someone merciful;[1] the one a breaker of faith, the other faithful; the one effeminate and pusillanimous, the other fierce and spirited; the one humane, the other proud; the one lascivious, the other chaste; the one honest, the other clever; the one hard, the other agreeable;[2] the one grave, the other light; the one religious, the other unbelieving, and the like. And I know that everyone will confess that it would be a very laudable thing to find in a prince all of the above-mentioned qualities that are held good. But because he cannot have them, nor wholly[3] observe them, since human conditions do not permit it, it is necessary for him to be so prudent as to know how to avoid the infamy of those vices that would take his state from him and to be on guard against those that do not, if that is possible; but if one cannot, one can let them go on with less hesitation. And furthermore one should not care about incurring the reputation[4] of those vices without which it is difficult to save one's state; for if one considers everything well, one will find something appears to be virtue, which if pursued would be one's ruin, and something else appears to be vice, which if pursued results in one's security and well-being.

XVI. Of Liberality and Parsimony

Beginning, then, with the first of the above-mentioned qualities, I say that it would be good to be held liberal; nonetheless, liberality, when used so that you may be held liberal, harms[5] you. For if it is used virtuously and as it should be used, it may not be recognized, and you will not escape the infamy of its contrary. And so, if one wants to maintain a name for liberality among men, it is necessary not to leave out any kind of lavish display, so that a prince who has done this will always consume all his resources in such deeds. In the

1. *Pietoso* has a connotation of "pious."
2. Lit.: easy.
3. Or honestly.
4. Lit.: fame; some manuscripts have *infamia*, "infamy."
5. Lit.: offends.

end it will be necessary, if he wants to maintain a name for liberality, to burden the people extraordinarily, to be rigorous with taxes, and to do all those
things that can be done to get money. This will begin to make him hated by
his subjects, and little esteemed by anyone as he becomes poor; so having
offended the many and rewarded the few with this liberality of his, he feels
every least hardship and runs into risk at every slight danger. When he recognizes this, and wants to draw back from it, he immediately incurs the infamy
of meanness . . .

XVII. Of Cruelty and Mercy,[6] and Whether It Is Better to Be Loved Than Feared, or the Contrary

Descending next to the other qualities set forth before, I say that each
prince should desire to be held merciful and not cruel; nonetheless he should
take care not to use this mercy badly. Cesare Borgia was held to be cruel; nonetheless his cruelty restored the Romagna, united it, and reduced it to peace
and to faith. If one considers this well, one will see that he was much more
merciful than the Florentine people, who so as to escape a name for cruelty,
allowed Pistoia to be destroyed.[7] A prince, therefore, so as to keep his subjects
united and faithful, should not care about the infamy of cruelty, because with
very few examples he will be more merciful than those who for the sake of too
much mercy allow disorders to continue, from which come killings or robber-
ies; for these customarily harm[8] a whole community . . .[9]

From this a dispute arises whether it is better to be loved than feared, or
the reverse. The answer is that one would want to be both the one and the
other; but because it is difficult to put them together, it is much safer to be
feared than loved, if one has to lack one of the two. For one can say this generally of men: that they are ungrateful, fickle, pretenders and dissemblers,
evaders of danger, eager for gain. While you do them good, they are yours,
offering you their blood, property, lives, and children, as I said above,[10] when
the need for them is far away; but, when it is close to you, they revolt. And that
prince who has founded himself entirely on their words, stripped of other
preparation, is ruined; for friendships that are acquired at a price and not with
greatness and nobility of spirit are bought, but they are not owned and when
the time comes they cannot be spent. And men have less hesitation to offend

6. Or piety, throughout *The Prince*.

7. From 1500 to 1502 Pistoia, a city subject to Florence, was torn by factional disputes and riots.
NM was there as representative of the Florentines on several occasions in 1501.

8. Lit.: offend.

9. Lit.: a whole universality.

10. See Chapter 9.

one who makes himself loved than one who makes himself feared; for love is held by a chain of obligation, which, because men are wicked, is broken at every opportunity for their own utility, but fear is held by a dread of punishment that never forsakes you.

I conclude, then, returning to being feared and loved, that since men love at their convenience and fear at the convenience of the prince, a wise prince should found himself on what is his, not on what is someone else's; he should only contrive to avoid hatred, as was said.

XVIII. In What Mode Faith Should Be Kept by Princes

How laudable it is for a prince to keep his faith, and to live with honesty and not by astuteness, everyone understands. Nonetheless one sees by experience in our times that the princes who have done great things are those who have taken little account of faith and have known how to get around men's brains with their astuteness; and in the end they have overcome those who have founded themselves on loyalty.

Thus, you[11] must know that there are two kinds of combat: one with laws, the other with force. The first is proper to man, the second to beasts; but because the first is often not enough, one must have recourse to the second. Therefore it is necessary for a prince to know well how to use the beast and the man. This role was taught covertly to princes by ancient writers, who wrote that Achilles, and many other ancient princes, were given to Chiron the centaur to be raised, so that he would look after them with his discipline. To have as teacher a half-beast, half-man means nothing other than that a prince needs to know how to use both natures; and the one without the other is not lasting.

Thus, since a prince is compelled of necessity to know well how to use the beast, he should pick the fox and the lion,[12] because the lion does not defend itself from snares and the fox does not defend itself from wolves. So one needs to be a fox to recognize snares and a lion to frighten the wolves. Those who stay simply with the lion do not understand this. A prudent lord, therefore, cannot observe faith, nor should he, when such observance turns against him, and the causes that made him promise have been eliminated. And if all men were good, this reaching would not be good; but because they are wicked and do not observe faith with you, you also do not have to observe it with them. Nor does a prince ever lack legitimate causes to color his failure to observe faith. One could give infinite modern examples of this, and show how many peace treaties and promises have been rendered invalid and vain through the

11. The formal or plural you.
12. A possible source for this: Cicero, *De Officiis* I.ii.34;13.41.

infidelity of princes; and the one who has known best how to use the fox has come out best. But it is necessary to know well how to color this nature, and to be a great pretender and dissembler; and men are so simple and so obedient to present necessities that he who deceives will always find someone who will let himself be deceived.

Thus, it is not necessary for a prince to have all the above-mentioned qualities in fact, but it is indeed necessary to appear to have them. Nay, I dare say this, that by having them and always observing them, they are harmful; and by appearing to have them, they are useful, as it is to appear merciful, faithful, humane, honest, and religious, and to be so; but to remain with a spirit built so that, if you need not to be those things, you are able and know how to change to the contrary. This has to be understood: that a prince, and especially a new prince, cannot observe all those things for which men are held good, since he is often under a necessity, to maintain his state, of acting against faith, against charity, against humanity, against religion. And so he needs to have a spirit disposed to change as the winds of fortune and variations of things command him, and as I said above, not depart from good, when possible, but know how to enter into evil, when forced by necessity.

A prince should thus take great care that nothing escape his mouth that is not full of the above-mentioned five qualities and that, to see him and hear him, he should appear all mercy, all faith, all honesty, all humanity, all religion. And nothing is more necessary to appear to have than this last quality. Men in general[13] judge more by their eyes than by their hands, because seeing is given[14] to everyone, touching to few. Everyone sees how you appear, few touch what you are; and these few dare not oppose the opinion of many, who have the majesty of the state to defend them; and in the actions of all men, and especially of princes, where there is no court to appeal to, one looks to the end. So let a prince win and maintain his state: the means will always be judged honorable, and will be praised by everyone. For the vulgar are taken in by the appearance and the outcome of a thing and in the world there is no one but the vulgar; the few have a place there[15] when the many have somewhere to lean on. A certain prince of present times, whom it is not well to name,[16] never preaches anything but peace and faith, and is very hostile to both. If he had observed both, he would have had either his reputation or his state taken from him many times.

13. Lit.: universally.
14. Lit.: touches.
15. One manuscript says "the few have no place there . . . "; and the authorities have divided, Casella, Russo, and Sasso accepting "no place," Chabod and Bertelli "a place."
16. Apparently Ferdinand the Catholic, whom NM unhesitatingly names in Chapter 21.

Georg Wilhelm Friedrich Hegel, "Reason in History"

German idealist philosopher Georg Wilhelm Friedrich Hegel (1770–1831) has influenced nearly every aspect of modern philosophical thought. A theologian by training, Hegel served as a tutor, then lecturer, then a professor and headmaster. He was, according to University of Chicago political theorist Allan Bloom, "arguably the greatest university man there ever was." Hegel argued that the historical process is inherently rational and that men are unconsciously instruments of a plan which is greater than they are and which may or may not coincide with their own personal and political aims. It is through the "cunning of reason" that the actions of men through history serve this greater plan.

One of the essential moments in history is the preservation of the individual nation or state and the preservation of the ordered departments of its life. And the activity of individuals consists in participating in the common cause and helping to further it in all its particular aspects; for it is by this means, that ethical life is preserved. But the second moment in history is that the further existence of the national spirit is interrupted (inasmuch as it has exhausted itself and worked itself out to its conclusion) in order that world history and the world spirit may continue in their course. Neither the position of individuals within the ethical whole nor their moral attitudes and duties need be discussed here, for we are concerned only with the development, progress, and ascetic of the spirit towards a higher concept of itself. But this is accompanied by the debasement, fragmentation, and destruction of the preceding mode of reality which had already developed its concept to the full. All this takes place to some extent automatically through the inner development of the Idea; yet, on the other hand, the Idea is itself the product of factors outside itself, and it is implemented and brought to its realisation by the actions of individuals. It is precisely at this point that we encounter those great collisions between established and acknowledged duties, laws, and rights on the one hand, and new possibilities which conflict with the existing system and violate it or even destroy its very foundations and continued existence, on the other (although their content may well appear equally good and for the most part propitious, essential and necessary). These new possibilities then become part of history. They incorporate a universal of a different order from that on which the continued existence of a nation or state is based. For the universal they embody is a moment of the productive Idea itself, of that truth which works its way on to its own realisation.

The great individuals of world history, therefore, are those who seize upon this higher universal and make it their own end. It is they who realise the end appropriate to the higher concept of the spirit. To this extent, they may be called heroes. They do not find their aims and vocation in the calm and regular system of the present, in the hallowed order of things as they are. Indeed, their justification does not lie in the prevailing situation, for they draw their inspiration from another source, from that hidden spirit whose hour is near but which still lies beneath the surface and seeks to break out without yet having attained an existence in the present. For this spirit, the present world is but a shell which contains the wrong kind of kernel. It might, however, be objected that everything which deviates from the established order—whether intentions, aims, opinions, or so-called ideals—is likewise different from what is already there. Adventures of all kinds have such ideals, and their activities are based on attitudes which conflict with the present circumstances. But the fact that all such attitudes, sound reasons, or general principles differ from existing ones does not mean to say that they are justified. The only true ends are those whose content has been produced by the absolute power of the inner spirit itself in the course of its development, and world-historical individuals are those who have willed and accomplished not just the ends of their own imagination or personal opinions, but only those which were appropriate and necessary. Such individuals know what is necessary and timely, and have an inner vision of what it is.

It is possible to distinguish between the insight of such individuals and the realisation that even such manifestations of the spirit as this are no more than moments within the universal Idea. To understand this is the prerogative of philosophy. World-historical individuals have no need to do so, as they are men of practice. They do, however, know and will their own enterprise, because the time is ripe for it, and it is already inwardly present. Their business is to know this universal principle, which is the necessary and culminating stage in the development of their world, to make it their end, and to devote their energy, to its realisation. They derive the universal principle whose realisation they accomplish from within themselves: it is not, however, their own invention, but is eternally present and is merely put into practice by them and honoured in their persons. But since they draw it from within themselves, from a source which was not previously available, they appear to derive it from themselves alone; and the new world order and the deeds they accomplish appear to be their own achievement, their personal interest and creation. But right is on their side, for they are the far-sighted ones: they have discerned what is true in their world and in their age, and have recognised the concept, the next universal to emerge. And the others, as already remarked, flock to their standard, for it is they who express what the age requires. They are the most far-sighted among their contemporaries; they know best what issues are involved, and whatever they do is right. The others feel that this is so, and therefore have to obey them. Their words and deeds are the best that could be said and done in their time. Thus, the great individuals of history can only be understood within their own context; and they are admirable simply because they have made themselves the instruments of the substantial spirit. This is the true relationship between the individual and his universal substance. For this substance is the source of everything, the sole aim, the sole power, and the sole end which is willed by such individuals; it seeks its satisfaction through them and is accomplished by them. It is this which gives them their power in the world, and only in so far as their ends are compatible with that of the spirit which has being in and for itself do they have absolute right on their side— although it is a right of a wholly peculiar kind.

The state of the world is not yet fully known, and the aim is to give it reality. This is the object of world-historical individuals, and it is through its attainment that they find satisfaction. They can discern the weakness of what still appears to exist in the present, although it possesses only a semblance of reality. The spirit's inward development has outgrown the world it inhabits, and it is about to progress beyond it. Its self-consciousness no longer finds satisfaction in the present, but its dissatisfaction has not yet enabled it to discover what it wants, for the latter is not yet positively present; its status is accordingly negative. The world-historical individuals are those who were the first to formulate the desires of their fellows explicitly. It is not easy for us to know what we want; indeed, we may well want something, yet still remain in a negative position, a position of dissatisfaction, for we may as yet be unconscious of the positive factor. But the individuals in question knew what they wanted, and what they wanted was of a positive nature. They do not at first create satisfaction, however, and the aim of their actions is not that of satisfying others in any case. If this were so, they would certainly have plenty to do, because their fellows do not know what the age requires or even what they themselves desire. But to try to resist these world-historical individuals is a futile undertaking, for they are irresistibly driven on to fulfil their task. Their course is the correct one, and even if the others do not believe that it corresponds to their own desires, they nevertheless adopt it or acquiesce in it. There is a power within them which is stronger than they are, even if it appears to them as something external and alien and runs counter to what they consciously believe they want. For the spirit in its further evolution is the inner soul of all individuals, although it remains in a state of unconsciousness until great men call it to life. It is the true object of all men's desires, and it is for this reason that it exerts a power over them to which they surrender even at the price of denying their conscious will; they follow these leaders of souls because they feel the irresistible power of their own inner spirit pulling them in the same direction.

If we go on to examine the fate of these world-historical individuals, we see that they had the good fortune [to be] the executors of an end which marked a stage in the advance of the universal spirit. But as individual subjects, they also have an existence distinct from that of the universal substance, an existence in which they cannot be said to have enjoyed what is commonly called happiness. They did not wish to be happy in any case, but only to attain their end, and they succeeded in doing so only by dint of arduous labours. They knew how to obtain satisfaction and to accomplish their end, which is the universal end. With so great an end before them, they boldly resolved to challenge all the beliefs of their fellows. Thus it was not happiness that they chose, but exertion, conflict, and labour in the service of their end. And even when they reached their goal, peaceful enjoyment and happiness were not their lot. Their actions are their entire being and their whole nature and character are determined by their ruling passion. When their end is attained, they fall aside like empty husks. They may have undergone great difficulties in order to accomplish their purpose, but as soon as they have done so, they die early like Alexander, are murdered like Caesar, or deported like Napoleon. One may well ask what they gained for themselves. What they gained was that concept or end which they succeeded in realising. Other kinds of gain, such as peaceful enjoyment, were denied them. The fearful consolation that the great men of history did not enjoy what is called happiness—which is possible only in private life, albeit under all kinds of different external circumstances—this consolation can be found in history by those who are in need of it. It is needed by the envious, who resent all that is great and outstanding and who accordingly try to belittle it and to find fault with it. The existence of such outstanding figures only becomes bearable to them because they know that such men did not enjoy happiness. In this knowledge, envy sees a means of restoring the balance between itself and those whom it envies. Thus, it has often enough been demonstrated even in our own times that princes are never happy on their thrones; this enables men not to grudge them their thrones, and to accept the fact that it is the princes rather than they themselves who sit upon them. The free man, however, is not envious, for he readily acknowledges and rejoices in the greatness of others.

But such great men are fastened upon by a whole crowd of envious spirits who hold up their passions as weaknesses. It is indeed possible to interpret their lives in terms of passion, and to put the emphasis on moral judgements by declaring that it was their passions which motivated them. Of course, they were men of passion, for they were passionately dedicated to their ends, which they served with their whole character, genius, and nature. In such individuals, then, that which is necessary in and for itself assumes the form of passion. Great men of this kind admittedly do seem to follow only the dictates of their passions and of their own free will, but the object of their will is universal, and it is this which constitutes their pathos. Passion is simply the energy of their ego, and without this, they could not have accomplished anything.

In this respect, the aim of passion and that of the Idea are one and the same; passion is the absolute unity of individual character and the universal. The way in which the spirit in its subjective individuality here coincides exactly with the Idea has an almost animal quality about it.

A man who accomplishes something excellent puts his whole energy into the task; he is not sufficiently dispassionate to vary the objects of his will or to dissipate his energy in following various separate ends, but is entirely dedicated to the one great end to which he truly aspires. His passion is the energy of the end itself and the determinate aspect of his will. That a man can thus devote his whole energy to a particular cause suggests a kind of instinct of an almost animal quality. We also describe such passions as zeal or enthusiasm, but we only use the term enthusiasm when the ends in question are of a more ideal and universal nature. The man of politics is not an enthusiast, for he must possess that clear circumspection which we do not normally attribute to enthusiasts. Passion is the prerequisite of all human excellence, and there is accordingly nothing immoral about it. And if such zeal is genuine, it remains cool and reflecting; the theoretical faculty retains a clear view of the means by which its true ends can be realised.

We must further note that, in fulfilling their grand designs as necessitated by the universal spirit, such world-historical individuals not only attained personal satisfaction but also acquired new external characteristics in the process. The end they achieved was also their own end, and the hero himself is inseparable from the cause he promoted, for both of these were satisfied. One may however, attempt to distinguish the hero's self-satisfaction from the success of the cause itself and to show that the great men in question were really pursuing their own ends, and then conclude that it was only their own ends which they were pursuing. Such men did indeed win fame and honour, and were recognized both by their contemporaries and by posterity—at least so long as the latter has not succumbed to the temptations of criticism, and of envy in particular. But it is absurd to believe that anyone can do anything without wishing to obtain satisfaction from doing so. Nevertheless, since the subjective factor

is of a purely particular character, and since its ends are purely finite and individual, it must necessarily subordinate itself to the universal. But in so far as
it implements the Idea, it must also help to sustain the underlying substance.

To make a distinction of this kind, however, is simply psychological
pedantry. Those who indulge in it label every passion as a lust, and thereby
cast doubt on the morality of the individuals in question. In so doing, they
present the results of such individuals' actions as their actual ends, and reduce
the deeds themselves to the position of means, declaring that those concerned
acted solely out of lust for fame, lust for conquest, and the like. Thus the aspirations of Alexander, for example, are characterised as lust for conquest,
which lends them a subjective colouring and presents them in an unfavourable
light. This so-called psychological approach contrives to trace all actions to the
heart and to interpret them subjectively, with the result that their authors appear to have done everything because of some greater or lesser passion or lust,
and, on account of such passions and lusts, cannot have been moral men.
Alexander of Macedonia partly conquered Greece, and then Asia; therefore he
was filled with a lust for conquest. He acted from a lust for fame and conquest,
and the proof that these were his motives is that his actions brought him fame.
What schoolmaster has not demonstrated of Alexander the Great or Julius
Caesar that they were impelled by such passions and were therefore immoral
characters—from which it at once follows that the schoolmaster himself is a
more admirable man than they were, because he does not have such passions
(the proof being that he does not conquer Asia or vanquish Darius and Porus,
but simply lives and lets live). These psychologists are particularly apt to dwell
on the private idiosyncrasies of the great figures of history. Man must eat and
drink; he has relationships with friends and acquaintances, and has feelings
and momentary outbursts of emotion. The great men of history also had such
idiosyncrasies; they ate and drank, and preferred this course to another and
that wine to another (or to water). 'No man is a hero to his valet de chambre'
is a well known saying. I have added—and Goethe repeated it two years later—
'not because the former is not a hero, but because the latter is a valet.' The valet
takes off the hero's boots, helps him into bed, knows that he prefers cham-
pagne, etc. The hero as such does not exist for the valet, but for the world, for
reality, and for history. Historical personages who are waited upon in the history books by such psychological valets certainly come off badly enough; they
are reduced to the same level of morality as these fine connoisseurs of humanity, or rather to a level several degrees below theirs. Homer's Thersites, the
critic of kings, is a stock figure in all ages. Admittedly, not every age belabours
him—in the sense of thrashing him with a stout cudgel—as happened to him
in Homer's time, but his envy and obstinacy are the thorn which he carries in

his flesh, and the undying worm which eats at him is the tormenting knowledge that all his excellent intentions and criticisms have no effect whatsoever upon the world. We may even derive a malicious satisfaction from the fate of Thersites and his kind.

Besides, psychological pedantry of this variety is not even internally consistent. It depicts the honour and fame of great men as faults, as if honour and fame had been the objects they aimed for. Yet, on the other hand, we are told that the designs of great men must have the assent of others, that is, that their subjective will should be respected by their fellows. But the very fact that they rose to honour and fame implies that they did meet with this required assent and that their aims were recognised by others as correct. The ends which world-historical individuals set themselves in fact correspond to what is already the inner will of mankind. Yet the assent which they are supposed to receive from others is treated as a fault after they have received it, and they are accused of having coveted the honour and fame they achieved. To this we may reply that they were not at all concerned with honour and fame, for the ordinary and superficial appearances which had previously been revered are precisely what they would have treated with derision. And only by so doing were they able to fulfil their task, for otherwise they would have remained within the ordinary channels of human existence, and someone else would have accomplished the will of the spirit.

Jacob Burckhardt, *Force and Freedom:*
An Interpretation of History

Swiss historian Jacob Burckhardt (1818–1897) wrote extensively on art and social history and was one of the first historians to stress the importance of culture to an understanding of history. Burckhardt, in his masterful The Civilization of the Renaissance in Italy *(1860), was the first to categorize the Renaissance as a distinct period in history. Burckhardt conceptualized this period as one in which individualism was born.* Force and Freedom, *which is excerpted below, emerged from a series of lectures Burckhardt gave at the University of Basel.*

Finally, the great men of the rest of the world movement in history.

History tends at times to become suddenly concentrated in one man, who is then obeyed by the world.

These great individuals represent the coincidence of the general and the particular, of the static and the dynamic, in one personality. They subsume States, religions, cultures and crises. . . .

In crises, the old and the new (the revolution) culminate together in the great men, whose nature is one of the true mysteries of world history. Their relationship to their time is a "sacred marriage." Such a union can only be consummated in times of terror, which provide the one supreme standard of greatness and are also unique in their need of great men.

It is true that, at the onset of a crisis, there is always a superfluity of men regarded as great, since those who happen to be party-leaders—often men of genuine talent and initiative—are indulgently regarded as such. A judgment of this kind is based on the naive assumption that a movement must find from the outset the man who will permanently and completely represent it. In actual fact, it is soon involved in transformations of which there was no inkling in its initial stage . . .

Men as a whole are unsure of themselves, confused in mind and glad to run with the herd, or else they are envious or totally indifferent. What then will be the qualities or deeds which turn the admiration of a man's immediate entourage, which has long existed in a latent state, into open and general admiration?

If the point at issue here is the nature of greatness, we must, first and foremost, be on our guard against the idea that what we have to describe is a moral ideal, for in history the great individual is not set up as an example, but as an exception. For our present purpose, we may sketch the following outline of greatness: The great man's faculties unfold naturally and completely, keeping pace with the growth of his self-confidence and the tasks before him. It is not only that he appears complete in every situation, but every situation at once seems to cramp him. He does not merely fill it. He may shatter it.

It is doubtful how long he will be able to keep himself in hand and be pardoned for the greatness of his nature.

Further, he has the natural faculty of concentrating at will on one issue, and then passing on to concentrate on another. Hence things appear to him simple, while to us they seem highly complicated, perpetually throwing each other out of gear. Where we grow confused, he begins to see really clearly.

The great individual sees every connection as a whole and masters every detail according to cause and effect. That is an inevitable function of his brain. He sees even small connections for the simple reason that by multiplication they become great, while he can dispense with the knowledge of small individuals.

Two main things he beholds with perfect clarity: first and foremost, the true situation and the means at his command, and he will neither allow appearances to blind him nor any momentary clamor to deafen him. From the very outset he knows what can be the foundations of his future power. Confronted with parliaments, senates, assemblies, press, public opinion, he knows at any moment how far they are real or only imaginary, and makes frank use of them accordingly. Afterwards they may wonder at having been mere means even while they conceived themselves to be ends.

Secondly, he knows in advance the moment when to act, while we first read about events afterwards in the papers. With that moment in view, he will curb his impatience and know no flinching (like Napoleon in 1797). He looks at everything from the standpoint of its utilizable strength, and there no study is too toilsome for him.

Mere contemplation is incompatible with such a nature. It is moved primarily by a genuine will to master the situation and at the same time by an exceptional strength of will, which creates an atmosphere of fascination, attracts to itself every element of power and rule, and subjects them to its own ends. Yet the great man is not confused by the breadth of his view and his memory, but manipulates the elements of power in their due co-ordination and subordination, as though they had always been his. . . .

Finally, as the most characteristic and necessary complement to all these things, comes the strength of soul which is alone able, and therefore alone loves, to ride the storm. This is not merely the passive aspect of strength of will. It is a different thing.

The fate of peoples and States, the trends of whole civilizations, may depend on the power of one exceptional individual to endure certain acute stresses at certain times.

The fact that Frederick the Great possessed that power in a supreme degree from 1759 to 1763 has determined the course of all subsequent European history.

No sum of ordinary minds and hearts can replace that power.

In the endurance of great and perpetual menaces, such as the constant threat of assassination, even while his mind is strained to the utmost, the great man obviously fulfils a purpose going far beyond his earthly existence. . . .

The rarest thing of all in men who have made history is greatness of soul. It resides in the power to forego benefits in the name of morality, in voluntary self-denial, not merely from motives of prudence but from goodness of heart, while the political great man must be an egoist, out to exploit every advantage. Greatness of soul cannot be demanded *a priori* because, as we have already seen, the great individual is set up as an exception, and not as an example. The great man of history, however, regards it as his prime duty to stand his ground and increase his power, and power never yet improved a man. . . .

Here we become aware of the great man's strange exemption from the ordinary moral code. Since that exemption is allowed by convention to nations and other great communities, it is, by an inevitable logic, also granted to those individuals who act for the community. Now, in actual fact, no power has ever yet been founded without crime, yet the most vital spiritual and material possessions of the nations can only grow when existence is safeguarded by power. The "man after God's heart" then appears—a David, a Constantine, a Clovis; his utter ruthlessness is generally condoned for the sake of some service rendered to religion, but also where there has been none. Richard III, it is true, met with no such indulgence, for all his crimes were mere simplifications of his personal situation.

The crimes of the man, therefore, who bestows on a community greatness, power and glory, are condoned, in particular breach of forced political treaties, since the advantage of the whole, the State or the people, is absolutely inalienable and may not be permanently prejudiced by anything whatever; but he must then continue to be great and realize that he will bequeath to his successors a fateful legacy, the necessity of genius, if what has been won by force is to be preserved until the world regards it as a right.

Here everything depends on success. The same man, endowed with the same personality, would find no such condonation for crimes which entailed no such results. Only because he has achieved great things does he find indulgence even for his private crimes . . .

A secondary justification for the crimes of great men seems to lie in the fact that by them an end is put to the crimes of countless others. When crime is thus monopolized by a communal criminal in the seat of government, the security of the community may prosper greatly. Before he came on to the scene, the powers of a brilliantly gifted nation may have been employed in a permanent and internecine war of destruction, which prevented the rise of everything which can flourish only in peace and security. The great individual, however, destroys, domesticates or employs unbridled individual egoisms. They suddenly gather into a power which continues to serve his purpose. In such cases—we might think of Ferdinand and Isabella—we are sometimes astonished by the rapid and brilliant bloom of culture till then retarded. Later it bears the name of the great man—the age of so-and-so ...

In our own day, we must first eliminate a class of men who declare themselves and the age emancipated from the need of great men. They declare that the present wants to look after its own affairs, and imagine that with no great men to commit great crimes the reign of virtue will set in. As if little men did not turn evil at the slightest opposition, not to speak of their greed and mutual envy!

Others actually achieve that emancipation (*N.B.* as a rule in the intellectual sphere only) by a general guarantee of mediocrity, the insurance of second-rate talents and false reputations, recognizable as such by the speed and noise of their rise. Such reputations, however, are very quickly exploded. The rest is done by the official suppression of all splendid spontaneity. Powerful governments have a repugnance to genius. In the State, it is hardly of use except by supreme compromise, for in the life of the State every thing is judged by its "utility." Even in the other walks of life, men prefer great talents, i.e., the capacity for making the most of what is to hand, to the great, i.e., the new.

From time to time, however, there is an outcry for great men, and that mainly in the State, because in all countries matters have taken such a turn that ordinary dynasts and higher officials no longer suffice. Great men should be there. (Prussia, for instance, to maintain her position and increase her power, could do with a whole series of Frederick the Greats.)

Yet even though the great man should come and survive his beginnings, the question still remains whether he would not be talked out of existence or overcome by contempt. Our age has a great power of attrition.

On the other hand, our age is very apt to be imposed upon now and again by adventurers and visionaries.

We can still remember how, in 1848, Europe sighed for a great man, and who was later accepted as such.

Not every age finds its great man, and not every great endowment finds its time. There may now exist great men for things that do not exist. In any case, the dominating feeling of our age, the desire of the masses for a higher standard of living, cannot possibly become concentrated in one great figure. What we see before us is a general leveling down, and we might declare the rise of great individuals an impossibility if our prophetic souls did not warn us that the crisis may suddenly pass from the contemptible field of "property and gain" on to quite another and that then the "right man" may appear overnight—and all the world will follow in his train.

For great men are necessary to our life in order that the movement of history may periodically wrest itself free from antiquated forms of life and empty argument.

And for the thinking man, reviewing the whole course of history hitherto, one of the few certain premises of a higher spiritual happiness is an open mind for all greatness.

Part III

DEMOCRACY AND LEADERSHIP

A. Leadership and the Advent of Democracy

The three readings from Benjamin Constant, Alexis de Tocqueville, and Søren Kierkegaard which are included in this section help to illuminate the way in which the advent of the democratic era affected the understanding of leadership.

Benjamin Constant

Constant argues that there is an ancient and a modern form of liberty. Ancient liberty was "political liberty"; one enjoyed liberty if one were a citizen with the privilege of participating in the political life of the society. To be excluded from participation was to be deprived of full freedom. Modern liberty is "individual liberty"; one's enjoyment of liberty derives from the right to go one's own way, even to elect not to participate when one has the privilege of doing so.

For the former, the public life is highest, for the latter, the private life. For the former, personal independence is subordinate to the authority of the community. For the latter, the authority of the community is contingent upon acknowledging and respecting personal independence.

This change in the concept of liberty is explained, in part, by the vast territorial range and population size of the modern state compared to the ancient city. People today do not live so compactly and they are far more mobile. With the expansion of commerce, meaningful relations are extended over long distances, often conferring greater importance on those far away than on those who are neighbors. Slavery, an essential and virtually universal feature of ancient societies, is in principle ended in a modern world committed to the idea of universal individual dignity. Each of us must take care of ourselves in numerous ways, and few can attain the leisure necessary to immerse ourselves in the public life. The possibilities for individual fulfillment are now, for many, prerequisite to pursuing happiness.

Constant worried, nevertheless, that a severe decline in the practice of political liberty would be a source of the corruption of the public well-being. This concern Constant shared with virtually every political thinker in Europe and North America who has reflected on the implications of the democratic era. Tocqueville follows Constant in this respect explicitly. The need for participation does not disappear merely because it is demoted in the thinking of many modern people.

Constant thus argued for the importance of education in civic responsibility in order to inculcate in modern individuals a commitment to public service. The modern emphasis on the indispensability of education is one consequence of this. In the United States, where modern liberty has shown itself most powerfully, it has been understood from the beginning that the education of the citizenry is essential to the health of the republican form of government. Thus, while Americans demand limited government and constrained exercise of political power, they recognize that an educated and responsible citizenry is equally necessary to maintain efficient and responsible government. The new needs of leadership may be found significantly in the educative function. The importance of teachers in the era of modern liberty is thus assumed to be very great. This is a kind of leading which is not always seen for what it is.

According to Constant, there are those, of course, who do not accept this historic emergence of modern, individual liberty. They seek to reestablish the participatory forms of the ancient city as superior to the individuality and personal freedom which define modern liberty; they seek a collectivity which cannot fail to be in tension with the dominant modern outlook. This attempt, Constant argues, cannot succeed, for it tries to fit an ancient form to modern substance. The proper modern form is the rule of law and limited government, which provides procedural constraints and rules for individuals to follow in relating themselves to each other voluntarily according to their own views of their best interests. Such persons can associate but cannot collectivize.

These conditions must affect leadership. Leadership becomes representation, and leading involves the effort to create a voluntary consensus from a wide range of differing interests and aspirations. Leaders cannot expect, apart from the massive use of compulsion, to create a collective identity. And, even if some say they want such a thing, as soon as it is attempted they will begin to resist it. Moreover, a compelled unity is inherently unstable and will crumble as soon as the coercive power sustaining it weakens. These are conditions which define the modern situation and cannot be removed. Leaders will often seem more like managers, convenors, or facilitators. The judgment of such leaders is subjected to continuing questions, to review and criticism, to second-guessing, and to charges of arbitrariness or unfairness. Procedures of assessment and accountability inevitably multiply. The desire for leadership is not eradicated, but deference to actual exercises of leadership and authority is diluted. In a world where all have the right to speak and, in principle at least, to be recognized, many will insist on exercising that right. Those in positions of leadership must become listeners and often counselors as much as directors or shapers. Yet in becoming counselors and listeners, leaders also indirectly, often by stealth, seek to shape and direct the groups, organizations, and polities for which they are responsible. They can hardly help it (whether they admit it or not). The character of leadership becomes more ambiguous.

Alexis de Tocqueville

Tocqueville is widely regarded as the most astute student of American democracy. His great work, *Democracy in America,* still stands as an indispensable source for reflection on the meaning of the American experiment in creating the first modern democratic society, a society not organized in terms of traditional aristocracies. Tocqueville foresaw that democracy would be the dominant form of the modern world, and he accepted that. But he also saw that all orders have their strengths and weaknesses. Tocqueville compared the advantages and disadvantages of democratic and aristocratic orders, among other reasons in order to understand better the perils of democracy and to discern what might protect a democracy from realizing its worst tendencies.

Like Constant, Tocqueville recognized that some of the strengths of the old orders would still be needed in the new, democratic orders. His analysis of the situation is of great value to those who would understand the nature and function of leadership in democratic societies. Tocqueville emphasized the fundamental impact of the idea of equality on all democratic institutions and personalities. Tocqueville argued that the modern liberty of individuality Constant emphasizes is threatened by the demand for equality, which represses individual expression insofar as it sets people apart or lends them distinctiveness. He feared the advent of the "mass age," in which a new kind of tyranny— the "tyranny of the majority"—would become more repressive than the old forms of tyranny. In the old forms of tyranny it was sufficient to maintain control of people's external conduct, but in the tyranny of the majority, the control of one's thought by public opinion controls the soul or consciousness.

In the present reading, Tocqueville tells us that high ambition is powerfully present when the new democratic order is being established; but when democracy becomes the norm, high ambition disappears. In the world of equality, ambition of a different and lower sort does not disappear, but, on the contrary, becomes universal: the ambition for personal betterment. Since the resources of a democratic society are widely distributed, especially by comparison to any of the societies preceding democracy, ambition shows itself on a limited and local scale. Ambition is "eager and constant" but "not very high." Even those who achieve great wealth are careful to downplay it and to insist that they remain like everyone else. Also, because no one is born to high position, the time needed to reach high positions is considerable and the contingencies that could derail advancement are numerous. The petty tests imposed by a democratic people on individuals of talent and aspiration eventually limit their imagination and creativity, and perhaps inhibit their self-confidence and sense of free action. They must indeed resemble those whom they would lead and not stray very far from what is generally thought to be acceptable. Thus the danger of the tyranny of the majority is that it will undermine the opportunities afforded by the new individuality and the prosperity that is widely shared.

Success is confined to the present; the long-term is insignificant. To live for the ages is an undemocratic sentiment. It is appropriate for a democracy, Tocqueville urges, to put limits on the exercise of leadership, but it would be a blunder to try to eliminate it. The greater danger in democratic societies is not would-be tyrants but those who exalt the trivial and the paltry. Democratic people have a kind of humility in which they take a great deal of pride. This is certainly not all bad, but it cuts down the prospects for heroism, magnificence, and greatness of spirit. In the readings that follow, we shall see modern and contemporary responses to this predicament.

Søren Kierkegaard

Kierkegaard, the great nineteenth-century Danish theologian and philosopher, in his reflections on "the present age," parallels Tocqueville when he remarks that the modern emphasis on equality mistakenly is translated into "leveling" people. Leveling is a negative relationship in which resentment and envy of others lurks. While Constant emphasizes the prominence of "individual liberty," Kierkegaard fears the loss of the individual in the mass. The right to opt out of public participation does not mean that one has the capacity to opt out of the prevailing opinions, which seep in at every crack.

Moreover, the individual dignity inherent in the idea that every human being has unique importance in God's sight is lost in an age of secularization and massness. Under these conditions, no one in particular is responsible for what happens and many cannot see the threat to individuality. If anyone actually does see what is happening and attempts to oppose it, there will be immediate resistance on the part of many. They cannot see that it is to their benefit to acknowledge what the solitary individual is telling them.

In one sense, then, the individual is free because equal, but in another, unfree because isolated, enjoying few means to express overtly and effectively any individuality. No leader can alter this course of events, Kierkegaard insists, because of its ineluctable dominance and because "the age of chivalry is gone." All of our forms of association and our procedures support the leveling process. Leveling succeeds because it is impersonal—the concern is not for particular persons but rather that there should be a common condition of all persons. In place of individuals we find the abstraction, "the public."

Kierkegaard asserts the possibility of a religious response to this condition: to cultivate an inward strength and self-sufficiency that gives up the felt need for external manifestation. The religious individual is content to be equal in the mass with respect to outward existence. To the degree that public service, though widely praised, is service to an abstraction (since there is no fixed meaning to the "public"), it will be diffuse in its meaning and confused in its direction. In fact, the religious person will gain from living in these conditions insofar as the conditions reveal the limitations of worldliness, and will thus perhaps be moved to seek more directly the eternal and transcendent. This is a kind of secret leadership—not, certainly, what most people could mean by leadership, nor measurable in terms the world recognizes—insofar as it makes positive the otherwise destructive, unavoidable conditions of the "present age." The age of equality is, then, a peculiar dispensation which allows for a public form of leading which is misleading, and a private form of meditation which, in abandoning ordinary ideas of leading, invisibly exalts.

Benjamin Constant, "The Liberty of the Ancients Compared with That of the Moderns"

Benjamin Constant (1767–1830) was born in Switzerland. He enrolled in the University of Erlangen in Bavaria at the age of fourteen and transferred to the University of Edinburgh in Scotland the following year at his father's request. Following his university education Constant lived what might best be described as a reckless life, gambling and roving his way through Paris, Switzerland, and England before obtaining (through his father's intervention) a government post in Germany in 1788. In 1795, Constant returned to Paris with his lover, Mme. de Stael, and took up journalism. Caught up in the excitement of the French Revolution, Constant turned his attention to politics, producing several notable political pamphlets. He became a citizen of France and unsuccessfully made a bid for political office in 1799. Later he secured a seat in the Tribunate, where he and some others led an opposition to the reforms of Napoleon, an action which led to their expulsion from the Tribunate in 1802. Constant subsequently withdrew from politics but began work on several major works, including his Principes de politique, *published in 1815, and his famous novel* Adolphe, *published in 1816. In 1815, Constant returned to political life as a constitutional adviser to Napoleon. That he had been at once an opponent of Bonaparte's and then later in the emperor's employ has resulted in an ambiguous legacy, according to scholar Biancamaria Fontana. Indeed, Constant's role in French political thought was contested vigorously throughout the nineteenth century, and many of his writings were banned to the general readership. Constant spent the last decade of his life serving in various government posts and writing.*

Gentlemen, I wish to submit for your attention a few distinctions, still rather new, between two kinds of liberty; these differences have thus far remained unnoticed, or at least insufficiently remarked. The first is the liberty the exercise of which was so dear to the ancient peoples; the second the one the enjoyment of which is especially precious to the modern nations. If I am right, this investigation will prove interesting from two different angles.

Firstly, the confusion of these two kinds of liberty has been amongst us, in the all too famous days of our revolution, the cause of many an evil. France was exhausted by useless experiments, the authors of which, irritated by their poor success, sought to force her to enjoy the good she did not want, and denied her the good which she did want.

Secondly, called as we are by our happy revolution (I call it happy, despite its excesses, because I concentrate my attention on its results) to enjoy the benefits of representative government, it is curious and interesting to discover why this form of government, the only one in the shelter of which we could find some freedom and peace today, was totally unknown to the free nations of antiquity. . . .

First ask yourselves, Gentlemen, what an Englishman, A Frenchman, and a citizen of the United States of America understand today by the word "liberty."

For each of them it is the right to be subjected only to the laws, and to be neither arrested, detained, put to death or maltreated in any way by the arbitrary will of one or more individuals. It is the right of everyone to express their opinion, choose a profession and practise it, to dispose of property, and even to abuse it; to come and go without permission, and without having to account for their motives or undertakings. It is everyone's right to associate with other individuals, either to discuss their interests, or to profess the religion which they and their associates prefer, or even simply to occupy their days or hours in a way which is most compatible with their inclinations or whims. Finally it is everyone's right to exercise some influence on the administration of the government, either by electing all or particular officials, or through representations, petitions, demands to which the authorities are more or less compelled to pay heed. Now compare this liberty with that of the ancients.

The latter consisted in exercising collectively, but directly, several parts of the complete sovereignty; in deliberating, in the public square, over war and peace; in forming alliances with foreign governments; in voting laws, in pronouncing judgements; in examining the accounts, the acts, the stewardship of the magistrates; in calling them to appear in front of the assembled people, in accusing, condemning or absolving them. But if this was what the ancients called liberty, they admitted as compatible with this collective freedom the complete subjection of the individual to the authority of the community. You find among them almost none of the enjoyments which we have just seen form part of the liberty of the moderns. All private actions were submitted to a severe surveillance. No importance was given to individual independence, neither in relation to opinions, nor to labour, nor, above all, to religion. The right to choose one's own religious affiliation, a right which we regard as one of the most precious, would have seemed to the ancients a crime and a sacrilege. . . .

Thus among the ancients the individual, almost always sovereign in public affairs, was a slave in all his private relations. As a citizen, he decided on peace and war; as a private individual, he was constrained, watched and repressed in all his movements; as a member of the collective body, he interrogated, dismissed, condemned, beggared, exiled, or sentenced to death his magistrates

and superiors; as a subject of the collective body he could himself be deprived
of his status, stripped of his privileges, banished, put to death, by the discretionary will of the whole to which he belonged. Among the moderns, on the
contrary, the individual, independent in his private life, is, even in the freest of
states, sovereign only in appearance. His sovereignty is restricted and almost
always suspended. If, at fixed and rare intervals, in which he is again surrounded
by precautions and obstacles, he exercises this sovereignty, it is always only to
renounce it.

I must at this point, Gentlemen, pause for a moment to anticipate an ob-
jection which may be addressed to me. There was in antiquity a republic where
the enslavement of individual existence to the collective body was not as complete as I have described it. This republic was the most famous of all; you will
guess that I am speaking of Athens. I shall return to it later, and in subscribing
to the truth of this fact, I shall also indicate its cause. We shall see why, of all
the ancient states, Athens was the one which most resembles the modern ones.
Everywhere else social jurisdiction was unlimited. The ancients, as Condorcet
says, had no notion of individual rights. Men were, so to speak, merely ma-
chines, whose gears and cog-wheels were regulated by the law. The same subjection characterized the golden centuries of the Roman republic; the individual was in some way lost in the nation, the citizen in the city.

We shall now trace this essential difference between the ancients and ourselves back to its source.

All ancient republics were restricted to a narrow territory. The most popu-
lous, the most powerful, the most substantial among them, was not equal in
extension to the smallest of modern states. As an inevitable consequence of
their narrow territory, the spirit of these republics was bellicose; each people
incessantly attacked their neighbours or was attacked by them. Thus driven by
necessity against one another, they fought or threatened each other constantly.
Those who had no ambition to be conquerors, could still not lay down their
weapons, lest they should themselves be conquered. All had to buy their security, their independence, their whole existence at the price of war. This was the
constant interest, the almost habitual occupation of the free states of antiquity.
Finally, by an equally necessary result of this way of being, all these states had
slaves. The mechanical professions and even, among some nations, the industrial ones, were committed to people in chains.

The modern world offers us a completely opposing view. The smallest
states of our day are incomparably larger than Sparta or than Rome was over
five centuries. Even the division of Europe into several states is, thanks to the
progress of enlightenment, more apparent than real. While each people, in the
past, formed an isolated family, the born enemy of other families, a mass of

human beings now exists, that under different names and under different forms of social organization are essentially homogeneous in their nature. This mass is strong enough to have nothing to fear from barbarian hordes. It is sufficiently civilized to find war a burden. Its uniform tendency is towards peace.

This difference leads to another one. War precedes commerce. War and commerce are only two different means of achieving the same end, that of getting what one wants. Commerce is simply a tribute paid to the strength of the possessor by the aspirant to possession. It is an attempt to conquer, by mutual agreement, what one can no longer hope to obtain through violence. A man who was always the stronger would never conceive the idea of commerce. It is experience, by proving to him that war, that is the use of his strength against the strength of others, exposes him to a variety of obstacles and defeats, that leads him to resort to commerce, that is to a milder and surer means of engaging the interest of others to agree to what suits his own. War is all impulse, commerce, calculation. Hence it follows that an age must come in which commerce replaces war. We have reached this age.

I do not mean that amongst the ancients there were no trading peoples. But these peoples were to some degree an exception to the general rule. . . .

Finally, thanks to commerce, to religion, to the moral and intellectual progress of the human race, there are no longer slaves among the European nations. Free men must exercise all professions, provide for all the needs of society.

It is easy to see, Gentlemen, the inevitable outcome of these differences.

Firstly, the size of a country causes a corresponding decrease of the political importance allotted to each individual. The most obscure republican of Sparta or Rome had power. The same is not true of the simple citizen of Britain or of the United States. His personal influence is an imperceptible part of the social will which impresses on the government its direction.

Secondly, the abolition of slavery has deprived the free population of all the leisure which resulted from the fact that slaves took care of most of the work. Without the slave population of Athens, 20,000 Athenians could never have spent every day at the public square in discussions.

Thirdly, commerce does not, like war, leave in men's lives intervals of inactivity. The constant exercise of political rights, the daily discussion of the affairs of the state, disagreements, confabulations, the whole entourage and movement of factions, necessary agitations, the compulsory filing, if I may use the term, of the life of the peoples of antiquity, who, without this resource would have languished under the weight of painful inaction, would only cause trouble and fatigue to modern nations, where each individual, occupied with his speculations, his enterprises, the pleasures he obtains or hopes for, does not wish to be distracted from them other than momentarily, and as little as possible.

Finally, commerce inspires in men a vivid love of individual independence. Commerce supplies their needs, satisfies their desires, without the intervention of the authorities. This intervention is almost always—and I do not know why I say almost—this intervention is indeed always a trouble and an embarrassment. Every time collective power wishes to meddle with private speculations, it harasses the speculators. Every time governments pretend to do our own business, they do it more incompetently and expensively than we would. . . .

It follows from what I have just indicated that we can no longer enjoy the liberty of the ancients, which consisted in an active and constant participation in collective power. Our freedom must consist of peaceful enjoyment and private independence. The share which in antiquity everyone held in national sovereignty was by no means an abstract presumption as it is in our own day. The will of each individual had real influence; the exercise of this will was a vivid and repeated pleasure. Consequently the ancients were ready to make many a sacrifice to preserve their political rights and their share in the administration of the state. Everybody, feeling with pride all that his suffrage was worth, found in this awareness of his personal importance a great compensation.

This compensation no longer exists for us today. Lost in the multitude, the individual can almost never perceive the influence he exercises. Never does his will impress itself upon the whole; nothing confirms in his eyes his own co-operation.

The exercise of political rights, therefore, offers us but a part of the pleasures that the ancients found in it, while at the same time the progress of civilization, the commercial tendency of the age, the communication amongst peoples, have infinitely multiplied and varied the means of personal happiness.

It follows that we must be far more attached than the ancients to our individual independence. For the ancients when they sacrificed that independence to their political rights, sacrificed less to obtain more; while in making the same sacrifice, we would give more to obtain less.

The aim of the ancients was the sharing of social power among the citizens of the same fatherland; this is what they called liberty. The aim of the moderns is the enjoyment of security in private pleasures; and they call liberty the guarantees accorded by institutions to these pleasures. . . .

Through their failure to perceive these differences, otherwise well-intentioned men caused infinite evils during our long and stormy revolution. God forbid that I should reproach them too harshly. Their error itself was excusable. . . . The aim of our reformers was noble and generous. Who among us did not feel his heart beat with hope at the outset of the course which they seemed to open up? And shame, even today, on whoever does not feel the need to declare that acknowledging a few errors committed by our first guides does not mean blighting their memory or disowning the opinions which the friends of mankind have professed throughout the ages.

But those men had derived several of their theories from the works of two philosophers who had themselves failed to recognize the changes brought by two thousand years in the dispositions of mankind. I shall perhaps at some point examine the system of the most illustrious of these philosophers, of Jean-Jacques Rousseau, and I shall show that, by transposing into our modern age an extent of social power, of collective sovereignty, which belonged to other centuries, this sublime genius, animated by the purest love of liberty, has nevertheless furnished deadly pretexts for more than one kind of tyranny. . . .

Moreover, as we shall see, it is not to Rousseau that we must chiefly attribute the error against which I am going to argue; this is to be imputed much more to one of his successors, less eloquent but no less austere and a hundred times more exaggerated. The latter, the abbé de Mably, can be regarded as the representative of the system according to which the individual should be enslaved for the people to be free. . . .

Montesquieu, who had a less excitable and therefore more observant mind, did not fall into quite the same errors. He was struck by the differences which I have related; but he did not discover their true cause. The Greek politicians who lived under the popular government did not recognize, he argues, any other power but virtue. Politicians of today talk only of manufactures, of commerce, of finances, of wealth and even of luxury.[1] He attributes this difference to the republic and the monarchy. It ought instead to be attributed to the opposed spirit of ancient and modern times. . . .

The men who were brought by events to the head of our revolution were, by a necessary consequence of the education they had received, steeped in ancient views which are no longer valid, which the philosophers whom I mentioned above had made fashionable. . . . They wished to exercise public power as they had learnt from their guides it had once been exercised in the free states. They believed that everything should give way before collective will, and that all restrictions on individual rights would be amply compensated by participation in social power.

We all know, Gentlemen, what has come of it. Free institutions, resting upon the knowledge of the spirit of the age, could have survived. The restored edifice of the ancients collapsed, notwithstanding many efforts and many heroic acts which call for our admiration. The fact is that social power injured individual independence in every possible way, without destroying the need for it. The nation did not find that an ideal share in an abstract sovereignty was

1. The Duke of Richelieu.

worth the sacrifices required from her.[2] She was vainly assured, on Rousseau's authority, that the laws of liberty are a thousand times more austere than the yoke of tyrants. She had no desire for those austere laws, and believed sometimes that the yoke of tyrants would be preferable to them. Experience has come to undeceive her. She has seen that the arbitrary power of men was even worse than the worst of laws. But laws too must have their limits.

If I have succeeded, Gentlemen, in making you share the persuasion which in my opinion these facts must produce, you will acknowledge with me the truth of the following principles.

Individual independence is the first need of the moderns; consequently one must never require from them any sacrifices to establish political liberty.

It follows that none of the numerous and too highly praised institutions which in the ancient republics hindered individual liberty is any longer admissible in the modern times.

You may, in the first place, think, Gentlemen, that it is superfluous to establish this truth. Several governments of our days do not seem in the least inclined to imitate the republics of antiquity. However, little as they may like republican institutions, there are certain republican usages for which they feel a certain affection. It is disturbing that they should be precisely those which allow them to banish, to exile, or to despoil. I remember that in 1802, they slipped into the law on special tribunals an article which introduced into France Greek ostracism;[3] and God knows how many eloquent speakers, in order to have this article approved, talked to us about the freedom of Athens and all the sacrifices that individuals must make to preserve this freedom! Similarly, in much more recent times, when fearful authorities attempted, with a timid hand, to rig the elections, a journal which can hardly be suspected of republicanism proposed to revive Roman censorship to eliminate all dangerous candidates.

I do not think therefore that I am engaging in a useless discussion if, to support my assertion, I say a few words about these two much vaunted institutions.

Ostracism in Athens rested upon the assumption that society had complete authority over its members. On this assumption it could be justified; and

---

2. In the 1806 draft, Constant commented: "All legislation which exacts the sacrifice of these enjoyments is incompatible with the present conditions of the human race. From this viewpoint, nothing is more curious to observe than the rhetoric of French demagogues. The most intelligent among them, St. Just, made all his speeches in short sentences, calculated to arouse tired minds. Thus while he seemed to suppose the nation capable of the most painful sacrifices, he acknowledged her, by his style, incapable even of paying attention. E. Hofmann (ed.), Les "Principes de Politique," vol. 2, p. 432.

3. The law of 23 Floréal, Year X (13 May 1802) which extended the functions and powers of special tribunals.

in a small state, where the influence of a single individual, strong in his credit, his clients, his glory, often balanced the power of the mass, ostracism may appear useful. But amongst us individuals have rights which society must respect, and individual interests are, as I have already observed, so lost in a multitude of equal or superior influences, that any oppression motivated by the need to diminish this influence is useless and consequently unjust.[4] No-one has the right to exile a citizen, if he is not condemned by a regular tribunal, according to a formal law which attaches the penalty of exile to the action of which he is guilty. No-one has the right to tear the citizen from his country, the owner away from his possessions, the merchant away from his trade, the husband from his wife, the father from his children, the writer from his studious meditations, the old man from his accustomed way of life.

All political exile is a political abuse. All exile pronounced by an assembly for alleged reasons of public safety is a crime which the assembly itself commits against public safety, which resides only in respect for the laws, in the observance of forms, and in the maintenance of safeguards.

Roman censorship implied, like ostracism, a discretionary power. In a republic where all the citizens, kept by poverty to an extremely simple moral code, lived in the same town, exercised no profession which might distract their attention from the affairs of the state, and thus constantly found themselves the spectators and judges of the usage of public power, censorship could on the one hand have greater influence; while on the other, the arbitrary power of the censors was restrained by a kind of moral surveillance exercised over them. But as soon as the size of the republic, the complexity of social relations and the refinements of civilization deprived this institution of what at the same time served as its basis and its limit, censorship degenerated even in Rome. It was not censorship which had created good morals; it was the simplicity of those morals which constituted the power and efficacy of censorship.

In France, an institution as arbitrary as censorship would be at once ineffective and intolerable. In the present conditions of society, morals are formed by subtle, fluctuating, elusive nuances, which would be distorted in a thousand ways if one attempted to define them more precisely. Public opinion alone can reach them; public opinion alone can judge them, because it is of the same nature. It would rebel against any positive authority which wanted to give it greater precision. If the government of a modern people wanted, like the censors in Rome, to censure a citizen arbitrarily, the entire nation would protest against this arrest by refusing to ratify the decisions of the authority.

---

4. The large states have created in our day a new guarantee; obscurity. This guarantee diminishes the dependence of individuals on the nation. E. Hofmann (ed.). Les "Principes de Politique," vol. 2, p. 421.

What I have just said of the revival of censorship in modern times applies also to many other aspects of social organization, in relation to which antiquity is cited even more frequently and with greater emphasis. As for example, education; what do we not hear of the need to allow the government to take possession of new generations to shape them to its pleasure, and how many erudite quotations are employed to support this theory! The Persians, the Egyptians, Gaul, Greece, and Italy are one after another set before us. Yet, Gentlemen, we are neither Persians subjected to a despot, nor Egyptians subjugated by priests, nor Gauls who can be sacrificed by the druids, nor, finally, Greeks or Romans, whose share in social authority consoled them for their private enslavement. We are modern men, who wish each to enjoy our own rights, each to develop our own faculties as we like best, without harming anyone; to watch over the development of these faculties in the children whom nature entrusts to our affection, the more enlightened as it is more vivid; and needing the authorities only to give us the general means of instruction which they can supply, as travellers accept from them the main roads without being told by them which route to take.

Religion is also exposed to these memories of bygone ages. Some brave defenders of the unity of doctrine cite the laws of the ancients against foreign gods, and sustain the rights of the Catholic church by the example of the Athenians, who killed Socrates for having undermined polytheism, and that of Augustus, who wanted the people to remain faithful to the cult of their fathers; with the result, shortly afterwards, that the first Christians were delivered to the lions.

Let us mistrust, Gentlemen, this admiration for certain ancient memories. Since we live in modern times, I want a liberty suited to modern times; and since we live under monarchies, I humbly beg these monarchies not to borrow from the ancient republics the means to oppress us.

Individual liberty, I repeat, is the true modern liberty. Political liberty is its guarantee, consequently political liberty is indispensable. But to ask the peoples of our day to sacrifice, like those of the past, the whole of their individual liberty to political liberty, is the surest means of detaching them from the former and, once this result has been achieved, it would be only too easy to deprive them of the latter. . . .

Let power therefore resign itself: we must have liberty and we shall have it. But since the liberty we need is different from that of the ancients, it needs a different organization from the one which would suit ancient liberty. In the latter, the more time and energy man dedicated to the exercise of his political rights, the freer he thought himself; on the other hand, in the kind of liberty of which we are capable, the more the exercise of political rights leaves us the time for our private interests, the more precious will liberty be to us.

Hence, Sirs, the need for the representative system. The representative system is nothing but an organization by means of which a nation charges a few individuals to do what it cannot or does not wish to do herself. Poor men look after their own business; rich men hire stewards.[5]

This is the history of ancient and modern nations. The representative system is a proxy given to a certain number of men by the mass of the people who wish their interests to be defended and who nevertheless do not have the time to defend them themselves. But, unless they are idiots, rich men who employ stewards keep a close watch on whether these stewards are doing their duty, lest they should prove negligent, corruptible, or incapable; and, in order to judge the management of these proxies, the landowners, if they are prudent, keep themselves well-informed about affairs, the management of which they entrust to them. Similarly, the people who, in order to enjoy the liberty which suits them, resort to the representative system, must exercise an active and constant surveillance over their representatives, and reserve for themselves, at times which should not be separated by too lengthy intervals, the right to discard them if they betray their trust, and to revoke the powers which they might have abused.

For from the fact that modern liberty differs from ancient liberty, it follows that it is also threatened by a different sort of danger.

The danger of ancient liberty was that men, exclusively concerned with securing their share of social power, might attach too little value to individual rights and enjoyments.

The danger of modern liberty is that, absorbed in the enjoyment of our private independence, and in the pursuit of our particular interests, we should surrender our right to share in political power too easily.

The holders of authority are only too anxious to encourage us to do so. They are so ready to spare us all sort of troubles, except those of obeying and paying! They will say to us: what, in the end, is the aim of your efforts, the motive of your labours, the object of all your hopes? Is it not happiness? Well, leave this happiness to us and we shall give it to you. No, Sirs, we must not leave it to them. No matter how touching such a tender commitment may be, let us ask the authorities to keep within their limits. Let them confine themselves to being just. We shall assume the responsibility of being happy for ourselves.

5. This concept is derived from Sieyès.

Alexis de Tocqueville, "Why There Are So Many Men of Ambition in the United States But So Few Lofty Ambitions"

Alexis de Tocqueville (1805–1859) was born in Paris. After studying law, Tocqueville served as juge auditeur *in the courts at Versailles. In 1831 he traveled to the United States with his colleague and friend Gustave de Beaumont to conduct a study of prison systems in America. This study culminated in the publication of a tract on the appointed subject, but it also resulted in Tocqueville's thorough and impressive study of American democracy. The first part of Tocqueville's* Democracy in America *was published in 1835; the second part in 1840. His other major writings include his* Recollections *and* The Old Regime and the French Revolution.

The first thing that strikes one in the United States is the innumerable crowd of those striving to escape from their original social condition; and the second is the rarity, in a land where all are actively ambitious, of any lofty ambitions. Every American is eaten up with longing to rise, but hardly any of them seem to entertain very great hopes or to aim very high. All are constantly bent on gaining property, reputation, and power, but few conceive such things on a grand scale. That, at first sight, is surprising, since there is no obvious impediment in the mores or laws of America to put a limit to ambition or to prevent its taking wing in every direction.

Equality of conditions hardly seems a sufficient explanation of this strange state of affairs. For when this same equality was first established in France, it gave birth at once to almost unlimited ambitions. Nevertheless, I think that we may find the chief reason for this in the social conditions and democratic manners of the Americans.

Every revolution increases men's ambition, and that is particularly true of a revolution which overthrows an aristocracy.

When the barriers that formerly kept the multitude from fame and power are suddenly thrown down, there is an impetuous universal movement toward those long-envied heights of power which can at last be enjoyed. In this first triumphant exaltation nothing seems impossible to anybody. Not only is there no limit to desires, but the power to satisfy them also seems almost unlimited. Amid this general and sudden change of customs and of laws, when all men and all rules share one vast confusion, when citizens rise and fall at such an unthought-of rate, and when power passes so quickly from hand to hand, no one need despair of snatching it in his turn.

It is also important to remember that those who destroy an aristocracy once lived under its laws; they have seen its splendors and have unconsciously imbibed the feelings and ideas which it conceived. At the moment, therefore, of the dissolution of an aristocracy, its spirit still hovers over the masses, and its instincts are preserved long after it has been conquered.

Thus ambitions are on the grand scale while the democratic revolution lasts; that will no longer be true some considerable time after it has finished.

Men do not in one day forget the memory of extraordinary events which they have witnessed; and the passions roused by revolution by no means vanish at its close. A sense of instability is perpetuated amid order. The hope of easy success lives on after the strange turns of fortune which gave it birth. Longings on a vast scale remain, though the means to satisfy them become daily less. The taste for huge fortunes persists, though such fortunes in fact become rare, and on all sides there are those who eat out their hearts in secret, consumed by inordinate and frustrated ambition.

But little by little the last races of the battle are wiped out and the relics of aristocracy finally vanish. The great events which accompanied its fall are forgotten. Peace follows war, and order again prevails in a new world. Longings once more become proportionate to the available means. Wants, ideas, and feelings again learn their limits. Men find their level, and democratic society is finally firmly established.

When we come to take stock of a democratic people which has reached this enduring and normal state, it appears very different from the scene we have been contemplating. And we easily come to the conclusion that although high ambitions swell while conditions are in process of equalization, that characteristic is lost when equality is a fact.

When great fortunes have been divided up and education has spread, no one is absolutely deprived of either education or property. When both the privileges and the disqualifications of class have been abolished and men have shattered the bonds which once held them immobile, the idea of progress comes naturally into each man's mind; the desire to rise swells in every heart at once, and all men want to quit their former social position. Ambition becomes a universal feeling.

But equality, though it gives every citizen some resources, prevents any from enjoying resources of great extent, and for this reason desires must of necessity be confined within fairly narrow limits. Hence in democracies ambition is both eager and constant, but in general it does not look very high. For the most part life is spent in eagerly coveting small prizes within reach.

It is not so much the small scale of their wealth as the constant and strenuous efforts requisite to increase it which chiefly diverts men in democracies from high ambitions. They strain their faculties to the utmost to achieve paltry results, and this quickly and inevitably limits their range of vision and circumscribes their powers. They could well be much poorer and yet be more magnanimous.

The few opulent citizens of a democracy constitute no exception to this rule. A man who raises himself gradually to wealth and power contracts in the course of this patient ascent habits of prudence and restraint which he cannot afterward shake off. A mind cannot be gradually enlarged, like a house.

Much the same applies to the sons of such a man. They may, it is true, have been born into a high position, but their parents were humble. They have grown up among feelings and ideas from which it is difficult later to escape. One may suppose that they inherit their father's instincts together with his property.

On the other hand, one may find some poor offshoot of a powerful aristocracy whose ambition is vast, for the opinions traditional to his race and the whole spirit of his caste for some time yet buoy him up above his actual fortune.

Another impediment making it far from easy for men of democratic ages to launch on great ambitions is the length of time that must elapse before they are in a position to undertake any such matter. "It is a great advantage," says Pascal, "to be a man of quality, for it brings one man forward at eighteen or twenty, whereas another must wait till he is fifty, which is a clear gain of thirty years." Ambitious men in democracies generally have to do without those thirty years. Equality, while it allows any man to reach any height, prevents his doing so fast.

In a democratic society, as elsewhere, there are only a few great fortunes to be made. As the careers leading thereto are open without discrimination to every citizen, each man's progress is bound to be slow. When all candidates seem more or less alike and it is difficult to make any choice between them without violating the principle of equality which is the supreme law of democratic societies, the first idea which comes to mind is to make them all go forward at the same rate and submit to the same tests.

Therefore, as men become more alike and the principle of equality has quietly penetrated deep into the institutions and manners of the country, the rules of advancement become more inflexible and advancement itself slower. It becomes ever more difficult to reach a position of some importance quickly.

From hatred of privilege and embarrassment in choosing, all men, whatever their capacities, are finally forced through the same sieve, and all without discrimination are made to pass a host of petty preliminary tests, wasting their youth and suffocating their imagination. So they come to despair of ever fully enjoying the good things proffered, and when at last they reach a position in which they could do something out of the ordinary, the taste for it has left them.

In China, where equality has for a very long time been carried to great lengths, no man graduates from one public office to another without passing an examination. He has to face this test at every stage of his career, and the idea is now so deeply rooted in the manners of the people that I remember reading a Chinese novel in which the hero, after many ups and downs, succeeds at last in touching his mistress' heart by passing an examination well. Lofty ambition can hardly breathe in such an atmosphere.

What has been said about politics applies to everything else. Equality produces the same results everywhere. Even where no law regulates and holds back advancement, competition has this effect.

Hence great and rapid promotion is rare in a well-established democracy. Such events are exceptions to the general rule. Their very singularity makes men forget how seldom they occur.

The inhabitants of democracies do in the end get a glimpse of all these truths. They do at length appreciate that while the law opens an unlimited field before them, and while all can make some easy progress there, no one can flatter himself that his advance is swift. They see a multitude of little intermediate obstacles, all of which have to be negotiated slowly, between them and the great object of their ultimate desires. The very anticipation of this prospect tires ambition and discourages it. They therefore discard such distant and doubtful hopes, preferring to seek delights less lofty but easier to reach. No law limits their horizons, but they do so for themselves.

I have said that high ambitions were rarer in democratic ages than under aristocracies. I must add that when, despite all natural obstacles, they do appear, they wear another face.

Under aristocracies the career open to ambition is often wide, but it does have fixed limits. In democratic countries its field of action is usually very narrow, but once those narrow bounds are passed, there is nothing left to stop it. As men are weak, isolated, and changeable, and as precedents have little force and laws do not last long, resistance to innovation is half-hearted, and the fabric of society never stands up quite straight or firm. As a result, when ambitious men have once seized power, they think they can dare to do anything. When power slips from their grasp, their thoughts at once turn to overturning the state in order to get it again.

This gives a violent and revolutionary character to great political ambitions, a thing which is seldom seen, to the same extent, in aristocratic societies.

A multitude of petty, very reasonable desires from which occasionally a few higher and ill-controlled ambitions will break out—such is the usual state of affairs in democratic nations. In them one hardly ever finds ambition which is proportionate, moderate, and yet vast.

I have shown elsewhere by what secret means equality makes the passion for physical pleasures and an exclusive interest in immediate delights predominate in the human heart. These instincts of different origin mingle with ambition, and it takes its color from them.

I think that ambitious men in democracies are less concerned than those in any other lands for the interests and judgment of posterity. The actual moment completely occupies and absorbs them. They carry through great undertakings quickly in preference to erecting long-lasting monuments. They are much more in love with success than with glory. What they especially ask from men is obedience. What they most desire is power. Their manners almost always lag behind the rise in their social position. As a result, very vulgar tastes often go with their enjoyment of extraordinary prosperity, and it would seem that their only object in rising to supreme power was to gratify trivial and coarse appetites more easily.

I think that nowadays it is necessary to purge ambition, to control it and keep it in proportion, but that it would be very dangerous if we tried to starve it or confine it beyond reason. The task should be to put, in advance, limits beyond which it would not be allowed to break. But we should be very careful not to hamper its free energy within the permitted limits.

I confess that I believe democratic society to have much less to fear from boldness than from paltriness of aim. What frightens me most is the danger that, amid all the constant trivial preoccupations of private life, ambition may lose both its force and its greatness, that human passions may grow gentler and at the same time baser, with the result that the progress of the body social may become daily quieter and less aspiring.

I therefore think that the leaders of the new societies would do wrong if they tried to send the citizens to sleep in a state of happiness too uniform and peaceful, but that they should sometimes give them difficult and dangerous problems to face, to rouse ambition and give it a field of action.

Moralists are constantly complaining that the pet vice of our age is pride.

There is a sense in which that is true; everyone thinks himself better than his neighbor and dislikes obeying a superior. But there is another sense in which it is very far from the truth, for the same man who is unable to put up with either subordination or equality has nonetheless so poor an opinion of himself that he thinks he is born for nothing but the enjoyment of vulgar pleasures. Of his own free will he limits himself to paltry desires and dares not face any lofty enterprise; indeed, he can scarcely imagine such a possibility.

Thus, far from thinking that we should council humility to our contemporaries, I wish men would try to give them a higher idea of themselves and of humanity; humility is far from healthy for them; what they most lack, in my view, is pride. I would gladly surrender several of our petty virtues for that one vice.

Søren Kierkegaard, *The Present Age,*
"The Individual and 'the Public'"

Scholar H. A. Reinhold has called Søren Kierkegaard "the profoundest in-
terpreter of the psychology of the religious life . . . since Augustine." Born in
Denmark in 1813 and brought up in a Lutheran household, Kierkegaard
studied philosophy and theology at the University of Copenhagen. Reacting
against Hegel's philosophy of pure or universal reason, Kierkegaard moved
in the direction of a belief that truth resides in the individual, a philosophy
later known as existentialism. Early in his life Kierkegaard began a search
for one true idea for which "I can live and die." That one idea for him was
Christianity. Kierkegaard believed that the highest level of human existence
is the acknowledged need for religion, a choice that moves an individual be-
yond mere self-satisfaction or the observance of social norms. Those who
accept Christianity simply because they understand it are not true believers,
Kierkegaard argued, because belief requires suspension of understanding
and a "leap of faith." Kierkegaard died in 1855. The first complete transla-
tion of his works into English was published some eighty years later.

The dialect of antiquity tended towards *leadership* (the great individual and
the masses—the free man and the slaves); so far the dialectic of Christendom
tends toward *representation* (the majority sees itself in its representative and is
set free by the consciousness that it is the majority which is represented, in a sort
of self-consciousness); the dialectic of the present age tends toward *equality,*
and its most logical—though mistaken—fulfillment is leveling, as the negative
relationship of the particular units to one another.

It must be obvious to everyone that the profound significance of the leveling process lies in the fact that it means the predominance of the category
"generation" over the category "individuality." In antiquity the total number
of the individuals was there to express, as it were, the value of the outstanding
individual. . . . The individual in the masses had no importance whatsoever;
the outstanding individual signified them all. The present age tends toward a
mathematical equality in which it takes so and so many to make one individual. Formerly the outstanding individual could allow himself everything
and the individual in the masses nothing at all. Now everyone knows that so
and so many make an individual, and quite consistently people add themselves
together (it is called joining together, but that is only a polite euphemism) for
the most trivial purposes. Simply in order to put a passing whim into practice
a few people add themselves together, and the thing is done—then they dare

do it. For that reason not even a preeminently gifted man can free himself from reflection[6], because he very soon becomes conscious of himself as a fractional part in some trivial matter, and so fails to achieve the infinite freedom of religion.

The fact that several people united together have the courage to meet death does not nowadays mean that each, individually, has the courage, for even more than death the individual fears the judgment and protest of reflection upon his wishing to risk something on his own. The individual no longer belongs to God, to himself, to his beloved, to his art or to his science; he is conscious of belonging in all things to an abstraction to which he is subjected by reflection, just as a serf belongs to an estate. That is why people band together in cases where it is an absolute contradiction to be more than one. The apotheosis of the positive principle of association is nowadays the devouring and demoralizing principle which in slavery of reflection makes even virtues into *vitia splendida*. There is no other reason for this than that eternal responsibility and the religious singling out of the individual before God is ignored. When corruption sets in at that point, people seek consolation in company, and so reflection catches the individual for life. And those who do not realize even the beginning of this crisis are engulfed without further ado in the reflective relationship.

The leveling process is not the action of an individual, but the work of reflection in the hands of an abstract power. It is therefore possible to calculate the law governing it in the same way that one calculates the diagonal in a parallelogram of forces. The individual who levels down is himself engulfed in the process, . . . and while he seems to know selfishly what he is doing, one can only say of people *en masse* that they know not what they do; for just as collective enthusiasm produces a surplus which does not come from the individual, there is also a surplus in this case. A demon is called up over whom no individual has any power, and though the very abstraction of leveling gives the individual a momentary, selfish kind of enjoyment, he is at the same time signing the warrant for his own doom. Enthusiasm *may* end in disaster, but leveling is *eo ipso* the destruction of the individual. No age, and therefore not the present age, can bring the skepticism of that process to a stop, for as soon as it tries to stop it, the law of the leveling process is again called into action. It can therefore only be stopped by the individual's attaining the religious courage which springs from his individual religious isolation.

I was once the witness of a street fight in which three men most shamefully set upon a fourth. The crowd stood and watched them with indignation; expressions of disgust began to enliven the scene; then several of the onlookers

6. I.e., from viewing himself as reflected in a collective entity of some sort.

set on one of the three assailants and knocked him down and beat him. The avengers, had, in fact, applied precisely the same rules as the offenders. . . . I went up to one of the avengers and tried by argument to explain to him how illogical his behavior was; but it seemed quite impossible for him to discuss the question: he could only repeat that such a rascal richly deserved to have three people against him. The humor of the situation would have been even more apparent to someone who had not seen the beginning of the brawl and so simply heard one man saying of another (who was alone) that he was three against one, and heard the remark just when the very reverse was the case— when they were three to one against him. In the first place it was humorous because of the contradiction which it involved, as when the policeman told a man standing in the street "to kindly disperse." Secondly it had all the humor of self-contradiction. But what I learned from it was that I had better give up all hope of putting a stop to that skepticism, lest it should turn upon me.

No single individual (I mean no outstanding individual—in the sense of leadership and conceived according to the dialectical category "fate") will be able to arrest the abstract process of leveling, for it is negatively something higher, and the age of chivalry is gone. No society or association can arrest that abstract power, simply because an association is itself in the service of the leveling process. Not even the individuality of the different nationalities can arrest it, for on a higher plane the abstract process of leveling is a negative representation of *humanity pure and unalloyed.* The abstract leveling process, that self-combustion of the human race, produced by the friction which arises when the individual ceases to exist as singled out by religion, is bound to continue, like a trade wind, and consume everything. But through it each individual for himself may receive once more a religious education and, in the highest sense, be helped by the *examen rigorosum* of the leveling process to an essentially religious attitude. For the younger men who, however strongly they personally may cling to what they admire as eminent, realize from the beginning that the leveling process is evil in both the selfish individual and in the selfish generation, but that it can also, if they desire it honestly and before God, become the starting-point for the highest life—for them it will indeed be an education to live in the age of leveling. Their age will, in the very highest sense, develop them religiously and at the same time educate them aesthetically and intellectually, because in this way the comic will receive its absolute expression. The highest form of the comic arises precisely when the individual comes directly under the infinite abstraction of "pure humanity," without any of those intermediary qualifications which temper the humor of man's position and strengthen its pathos, without any of the concrete particulars of organization which the leveling process destroys. But that again is only another expression of the fact that man's only salvation lies in the reality of religion for each individual.

And it will add fuel to their enthusiasm to understand that it is in fact through error that the individual is given access to the highest, if he courageously desires it. But the leveling process will have to continue and must be completed, just as scandal had to come into the world, though woe to them by whom it comes.

It has often been said that a reformation should begin with each man reforming himself. That, however, is not what actually happened, for the Reformation produced a hero who paid God high enough for this position as hero. By joining up with him directly people buy cheap, indeed at bargain prices, what he had paid for so dearly; but they do not buy the highest of all things. The abstract principle of leveling, on the contrary, like the biting east wind, has no personal relation to any individual, but has only an abstract relationship which is the same for everyone. There no hero suffers for others, or helps them; the taskmaster of all alike is the leveling process, which itself takes on their education. And the man who learns most from the leveling and himself becomes greatest does not become an outstanding man or a hero—that would only impede the leveling process, which is rigidly consistent to the end; he himself prevents that from happening because he has understood the meaning of leveling: he becomes a man and nothing else, in the complete equalitarian sense. That is the idea of religion. But, under those conditions, the equalitarian order is severe and the profit is seemingly very small; seemingly, for unless the individual learns in the reality of religion and before God to be content with himself, and learns, instead of dominating others, to dominate himself, content as priest to be his own audience, and as author his own reader—if he will not learn to be satisfied with that as the highest, because it is the expression of the equality of all men before God and of our likeness to others, then he will not escape from reflection. It may be that for one deceptive moment it will seem to him, in relation to his gifts, as though he were leveling, but in the end he will sink down beneath the leveling process. There is no good calling upon a Holger Danske or a Martin Luther; their day is over, and at bottom it is only the individual's laziness which makes a man long to have them back, a worldly impatience which prefers to buy something cheap, second-hand, rather than to buy the highest of all things very dear and first-hand. It is worse than useless to found society after society, because negatively speaking there is something above them, even though the short-sighted member of the society cannot see it.

The principle of individuality in its immediate and beautiful formation symbolizes the generation in the outstanding and eminent individual; it groups subordinate individualities around the representative. This principle of individuality, in its eternal truth, uses the abstraction and equality of the generation to level down, and in that way co-operates in developing the individual religiously into a real man. For the leveling process is as powerful where temporary things are concerned as it is impotent where eternal things are concerned. Reflection is a snare in which one is caught, but, once the "leap" of enthusiasm has been taken, the relation is a different one and it becomes a noose which drags one into eternity. Reflection is and remains the hardest creditor in existence; hitherto it has cunningly bought up all the possible views of life, but it cannot buy the essentially religious and eternal view of life; on the other hand, it can tempt people astray with its dazzling brilliance and dishearten them by reminding them of all the past. But, by leaping into the depths, one learns to help oneself, learns to love others as much as oneself, even though one is accused of arrogance and pride—because one will not accept help—or of selfishness, because one will not cunningly deceive people by healing them, i.e., by helping them to escape their higher destiny. . . .

Throughout many changes the tendency in modern times has remained a leveling one. These changes themselves have not, however, all of them been leveling, for they are none of them abstract enough, each having a certain concrete reality. To some extent it is true that the leveling process goes on when one great man attacks another, so that both are weakened, or when one is neutralized by the other, or when an association of people, in themselves weak, grow stronger than the eminent. Leveling can also be accomplished by one particular caste, e.g. the clergy, the bourgeois, the peasants, or by the people themselves. But all that is only the first movement of an abstract power within the concreteness of individuality.

In order that everything should be reduced to the same level, it is first of all necessary to procure a phantom, a spirit, a monstrous abstraction, an all-embracing something which is nothing, a mirage—and that phantom is the public. It is only in an age which is without passion, yet reflective, that such a phantom can develop itself with the help of the Press which itself has become an abstraction. In times of passion and tumult and enthusiasm, even when a people desire to realize a fruitless idea and lay waste and destroy everything—even then there is no such thing as a public. There are parties and they are concrete. The Press, in times such as those, takes on a concrete character according to the division of parties. But just as sedentary professional people are the first to take up any fantastic illusion which comes their way, so a passionless, sedentary, reflective age, in which only the Press exhibits a vague sort of life, fosters this phantom. The public is, in fact, the real leveling master rather than the actual leveler, for whenever leveling is only approximately accomplished it is done by something, but the public is a monstrous nothing. The public is a concept which could not have occurred in antiquity because the people *en masse, in corpore,* took part in any situation which arose and were responsible for the actions of the individual, and, moreover, the individual was personally present and had to submit at once to applause or disapproval for his decision. Only when the sense of association in society is no longer strong enough to give life to concrete realities is the Press able to create that abstraction, "the public," consisting of unreal individuals who never are and never can be united in an actual situation or organization—and yet are held together as a whole.

The public is a host, more numerous than all the peoples together, but it is a body which can never be reviewed; it cannot even be represented, because it is an abstraction. Nevertheless, when the age is reflective and passionless and destroys everything concrete, the public becomes everything and is supposed to include everything. And that again shows how the individual is thrown back upon himself.

The real moment in time and the real situation of being simultaneous with real people, each of whom is something—that is what helps to sustain the individual. But the existence of a public produces neither a situation nor simultaneity. The individual reader of the Press is not the public, and even though little by little a number of individuals or even all of them should read it, the simultaneity is lacking. Years might be spent gathering the public together, and still it would not be there. This abstraction, which the individuals so illogically form, quite rightly repulses the individual instead of coming to his help. The man who has no opinion of an event at the actual moment accepts the opinion of the majority or, if he is quarrelsome, of the minority. But it must be remembered that both majority and minority are real people, and that is why the individual is assisted by adhering to them. A public, on the contrary, is an abstraction. To adopt the opinions of this or that man means that one knows that they will be subjected to the same dangers as oneself, that they will go astray with one if the opinion goes astray. But to adopt the same opinions as the public is a deceptive consolation, because the public is only there in abstraction. Whilst, therefore, no majority has ever been so certain of being right and victorious as the public, that is not much consolation to the individual, for a public is a phantom which forbids all personal contact. And if a man adopts public opinion today and is hissed tomorrow, he is hissed by the public.

A generation, a people, an assembly of the people, a meeting or a man are responsible for what they are and can be made ashamed if they are inconstant and unfaithful; but a public remains a public. A people, an assembly or a man can change to such an extent that one may say: they are no longer the same; a public on the other hand can become the very opposite and still be the same—a public. But it is precisely by means of this abstraction and this abstract discipline that the individual will be formed (insofar as the individual is not already formed by his inner life), if he does not succumb in the process: taught to be content, in the highest religious sense, with himself and his relation to God, to be at one with himself instead of being in agreement with a public which destroys everything that is relative, concrete and particular in life; educated to find peace within himself and with God, instead of counting hands; and the absolute difference between the modern world and antiquity will be: that the totality is not concrete and is therefore unable to support the individual, or to educate him as the concrete should (though without developing him absolutely), but is an abstraction which by its abstract equality repels him and thus helps him to be educated absolutely—unless he succumbs in the process. The *taedium vitae* so constant in antiquity was due to the fact that the outstanding individual was what others *could not be;* the inspiration of modern times will be that any man who finds himself, religiously speaking, has only achieved what *everyone can achieve.*

A public is neither a nation, nor a generation, nor a community, nor a society, nor these particular men, for all these are only what they are through the concrete. No single person who belongs to the public makes a real commitment; for some hours of the day, perhaps, he belongs to the public—at moments when he is nothing else, since when he really is what he is, he does not form part of the public. Made up of such individuals, of individuals at the moments when they are nothing, a public is a kind of gigantic something, an abstract and deserted void which is everything and nothing. But on this basis anyone can arrogate to himself a public, and just as the Roman Church chimerically extended its frontiers by appointing bishops *in partibus infidelium,* so a public is something which everyone can claim, and even a drunken sailor exhibiting a "peep show" has dialectically absolutely the same right to a public as the greatest man; he has just as logical a right to put all those many noughts *in front* of his single number.

A public is everything and nothing, the most dangerous of all powers and the most insignificant: one can speak to a whole nation in the name of the public and still the public will be less than a single real man, however unimportant. The qualification "public" is produced by the deceptive juggling of an age of reflection, which makes it appear flattering to the individual, who in this way can arrogate to himself his monster in comparison with which concrete realities seem poor. The public is the fairy story of an age of understanding, which in imagination makes the individual into something even greater than a king above his people; but the public is also a gruesome abstraction through which the individual will receive his religious formation—or sink.

     . . . More and more individuals, owing to their bloodless indolence, will aspire to be nothing at all in order to become the public, that abstract whole formed in the most ludicrous way, by all participants becoming a third party (an onlooker). This indolent mass which understands nothing and does nothing itself, this gallery, is on the look-out for distraction and soon abandons itself to the idea that everything that anyone does is done in order to give it (the public) something to gossip about. That indolent mass sits with its legs crossed, wearing an air of superiority, and anyone who tries to work, whether king, official, school teacher or the better type of journalist, the poet or the artist, has to struggle to drag the public along with it, while the public thinks in its own superior way that it is the horse.

If I tried to imagine the public as a particular person . . . I should perhaps think of one of the Roman emperors, a large well-fed figure, suffering from boredom, looking only for the sensual intoxication of laughter, since the divine gift of wit is not earthly enough. And so for a change he wanders about, indolent rather than bad, but with a negative desire to dominate. Everyone who has read the classical authors knows how many things a Caesar could try out in order to kill time. In the same way the public keeps a dog to amuse it. That dog is literary scum.[7] If there is some one superior to the rest, perhaps even a great man, the dog is set on him and the fun begins. The dog goes for him, snapping and tearing at his coat-tails, allowing itself every possible ill-mannered familiarity—until the public tires, and says it may stop. That is an example of how the public levels. Their betters and superiors in strength are mishandled and the dog remains a dog which even the public despises. The leveling is therefore done by a third party; a non-existent public leveling with the help of a third party which in its insignificance is less than nothing, being already more than leveled. And so the public is unrepentant, for it was after all not the public that acted, but the dog; just as one says to children—the cat's mother did it. The public is unrepentant—it was not really belittling anyone; it just wanted a little amusement. . . .

The public is unrepentant, for it is not they who own the dog—they only subscribe. They neither set the dog on anyone, nor whistle it off—directly. If asked, they would answer: the dog is not mine, it has no master. And if the dog had to be killed, they would say: it was really a good thing that bad-tempered dog was put away, everyone wanted it killed—even the subscribers.

Perhaps someone, familiarizing himself with such a case, and inclined to fix his attention upon the outstanding individual who suffered at the hands of the public, may be of the opinion that such an ordeal is a great misfortune. I cannot at all agree with such an opinion, for anyone who really wishes to be helped to attain the highest is in fact benefited by undergoing such a misfortune, and must rather desire it, even though people may be led to revolt. The really terrible thing is the thought of the many lives that are or easily may be wasted. I will not even mention those who are lost, or at any rate led completely astray—those who play the part of the dog for money—but the many who are helpless, thoughtless and sensual, who live superior lazy lives and

7. E.g., *The Corsair.*

never receive any deeper impression of existence than this meaningless grin, and all those bad people who are led into further temptation because in their stupidity they even become self-important by commiserating with the one who is attacked, without even understanding that in such a position the person attacked is always the stronger, without understanding that in this case the terrible and ironical truth applies: Weep not over him, but over yourselves.[8]

That is the leveling process at its lowest, for it always equates itself to the divisor by means of which everyone is reduced to a common denominator. Eternal life is also a sort of leveling, and yet that is not so, because the unity is that everyone should really and essentially be a man in a religious sense. . . .

And so when the generation, which itself desired to level and to be emancipated, to destroy authority and at the same time itself, has, through the skepticism of the principle "association," started the hopeless forest fire of abstraction; when as a result of leveling with this skepticism, the generation has rid itself of the individual and of everything organic and concrete, and put in its place "humanity" and the numerical equality of man and man; when the generation has, for a moment, delighted in this unlimited panorama of abstract infinity, unrelieved by even the smallest eminence, undisturbed by even the slightest interest, a sea of desert: then the time has come for work to begin, for every individual must work for himself, each for himself. No longer can the individual, as in former times, turn to the great for help when he grows confused. That is past; he is either lost in the dizziness of unending abstraction or saved forever in the reality of religion. . . .

For the development is, in spite of everything, a progress, because all the individuals who are saved will receive the specific weight of religion, its essence at first hand, from God himself. Then it will be said: "Behold, all is in readiness: see how the cruelty of abstraction makes the true form of worldliness only too evident, the abyss of eternity opens before you, the sharp scythe of the leveler makes it possible for every one individually to leap over the blade—and behold, it is God who waits. Leap, then, into the arms of God."

8. Luke 23:28.

B. Leadership in Practice in a Democratic Era

Three of the greatest American presidents speak directly to us in this section of the readings, exemplifying American leadership at three crucial historical moments. Only a tiny handful of people will ever be in leadership positions of the magnitude of national office. However, a democratic republic encourages active civic participation of all citizens. Our beliefs about, and memories of, major leaders influence how we understand the responsibilities of leading. Figures of such prominence disseminate their legacy and their personae across entire populations, and their legacy is assimilated into the thinking of countless individuals in innumerable ways.

There is another handful of people who never held official positions of national leadership but whose thought, eloquence, and style also changed this nation's self-understanding. Frederick Douglass and Martin Luther King, Jr., represent this powerful form of leadership in the readings in this section.

It has often been remarked that America is an idea as much as it is a country. From the founding to the present there has been an incessant dialogue and debate of many voices bound together, despite profound disagreements, by a common appeal to the American idea and ideal. All of the voices presented in these readings contributed in their time, and still contribute today, to the quest for American self-understanding. The leadership with the greatest impact in America has always been marked by a substantial contribution to the debate over the meaning of America and of its role in the world. At every level of society, this debate goes on and is implied in virtually everything Americans say and do. This restlessness and dynamism uniquely characterizes American life and society, and makes roles of leadership both exciting, complex, and often indeterminate. In this sense, American leadership is only incidentally about solving specific policy questions; at a deeper level, it is this quest for self-understanding which demands reflective and creative leadership, a kind of leadership which always sees itself as moving forward into the future while harking back to what the informing principles of the American republic are understood to be. Think of the readings that follow, then, as a continuing dialogue of voices each of which, in a distinctive way, speaks to the common concern to know ourselves.

George Washington

George Washington, traditionally known as "the father of the country," has always been the chief symbol and embodiment of the founding of the new

American Republic. George Washington's Farewell Address begins by explaining his refusal of a third term as the first President of the United States. His acceptance of his first two terms he calls a "sacrifice of inclination to the opinion of duty." Reluctant acceptance of public duty is a characteristic of Washington's persona, illustrating one salient feature of what is meant by republican virtue. Washington reveals his preference for the pursuits best undertaken in the private life, while acknowledging that citizens must serve their country. Washington admits his duty while making it clear he has no lust for power or prominence. This establishes his suitability to governing in a polity where the vigorous exercise of power may be required but where, in addition to institutional safeguards such as the separation of powers, the temptation to the corrupt use of power must be combated by strength of character and by clarity about serving the well-being of a republican people.

Washington both asserts the importance of his office and chastens the understanding of it. He thereby encourages seeking political office with a certain sobriety and sense of self-limitation (a pattern not broken until Franklin Roosevelt sought a third term in 1940). He speaks of the "fallibility" of his judgment, of the "inferiority" of his qualifications, and of a certain "diffidence" (lack of confidence) about himself. Prudence, he says, dictates it is time for him to retire, while "patriotism does not forbid it." Washington thus seeks to balance patriotic duty with prudent self-examination. One could say that Washington is setting out for us the method of reflection incumbent upon a public servant in a democratic society.

All of this is the prelude to his setting forth to the people for "solemn contemplation" what he finds, upon "much reflection" and "no inconsiderable observation," to be guides to the nation's "permanent felicity." The message of his Farewell Address is justified by its thoughtfulness, but also by its source in a republican character from which will emerge principles compatible with the society for which they are intended. In this way, Washington both describes the requirements of leadership and puts them into practice in his address.

Frederick Douglass, Abraham Lincoln, and Martin Luther King, Jr.

For many, Abraham Lincoln is the greatest American president because he preserved the union in its moment of greatest peril in the Civil War. He is often described as the country's second founder.

The issue of slavery was central to the preservation of the Union. The compromises over slavery, first necessary to the original ratification of the Constitution, were a continuous source of tension between North and South from the 1780s until the Civil War. Lincoln emerged as the central figure in the debate over slavery in the 1850s and as the focus of conflict between North and

South when his election to the presidency in 1860 precipitated the secession of the South. Lincoln had made it clear that slavery was wrong, but he had also made it clear that the preservation of the Union was his highest duty.

But the preservation of the Union came to take on both the literal meaning of preventing secession and also the rededication of the country in a "new birth of freedom." Lincoln envisioned aligning the Constitution with the principle of the Declaration of Independence, that "all men are created equal." The speeches of Lincoln presented here show Lincoln's understanding of his task as a leader responsible to the fundamental principles by which American society defined itself.

Frederick Douglass understood it to be his task to hold Americans accountable for their national commitment to the principles of individual liberty. His eloquent 1852 speech, delivered before the Lincoln speeches here, was typical of Douglass's works. Richly detailed, beautifully crafted, and sharply critical, it demonstrates Douglass's awareness that leadership is all too often endowed not with the power of office but with the power of persuasion. More than a hundred years after Douglass, Martin Luther King, Jr., continued to challenge the American conscience. Like Douglass, King never held an official position of national leadership, but his eloquence and style changed a nation's understanding of itself, reinforcing the power of words to effect change.

Woodrow Wilson

Woodrow Wilson transformed and expanded the role of the president as a leader and not merely an executor of the laws passed by Congress (an expansion implicit in Lincoln's presidency). In Wilson's time, America emerged fully onto the world stage as one of the chief powers of the twentieth century. More than any other president, Wilson approached the question of national leadership explicitly and intellectually. Wilson shaped the understanding of the president as popular leader which has dominated the office throughout the 20th century. We have the benefit here not only of Wilson's commentary on the character of leadership in his time, but of his interpretation of Lincoln's leadership.

We read first Woodrow Wilson reflecting on Lincoln as a man of the people. Although, Wilson says, Lincoln had no special talent, "he seems to stand unique and singular and complete in himself . . . he contained a world within himself," and this universal capacity showed forth in the greatest crisis of the country. Lincoln was studious without depending on "theories," and he was a frontiersman who was born and grew up simultaneously with the westward expansion of America. But Wilson lived at the end of the frontier era, and he wonders if we can have Lincolns anymore.

This is pressing for Wilson because he believes the tensions of American society will impose upon us crisis after crisis and that we will continue to need leaders like Lincoln, whether the environment is conducive to producing them or not. "Lincoln was of the mass, but he was so lifted and big that all men could look upon him." A great nation requires, Wilson tells us, a leader who is both "of the people" and yet who can articulate "a new principle for a new age." The leaders we require will be generalists whose vision is not narrowed by the abstractions of any theory, the confines of a profession, or the biases of membership in a particular class, but who can see the whole plainly and directly. Such leaders will combine the capacity for action with an ability to resist immediate response. They will have the capacity to survey the scene with detachment even in the midst of struggle. Moreover, not only leaders but all of us should live as if each day is the day "upon which America was born to be remade." For Wilson, Lincoln, as a man of the people, magnifies what is potentially in all of us. He is a man of the people because, in transcending the mass, he nevertheless exemplifies the latent power for good within it. Wilson's own conception of leading was to mobilize the latent power of the people towards good ends and to bring to the fore Lincolnian powers of leadership in a post-Lincolnian age.

In his speech on "Leaders of Men," Wilson shows that to be a leader means to be girded for action. Ideas are important but in action they lose their refinement and appear more crudely and without subtlety. The thinker's ideas will be present in actions taken under the influence of those ideas, but the thinker is not the leader; without the leader, who is not restrained by qualifications and caution, the thought will never succeed in practice. Because of this, there is an inevitable antagonism between the literary and the political: the "men who write" love proportion, the "men who act" neglect proportion. Those who contemplate cannot be at ease with the majority.

Contemplatives look at things in themselves, leaders look upon others as resources to be used in the most productive manner. Possessing information does not guarantee one's persuasiveness with the people; "persuasion is accomplished by creeping into the confidence of those you would lead." The people must be able to see "at once" what one has to say. They are citizens, not pupils. According to Wilson, the hundred years prior to his time have produced a revolution in leadership which demands, whether intellectuals like it or not, a closeness of leadership to the prevailing thought of the people. Leading requires the articulation of what is possible within the constraints of democratic opinion. Leaders must mobilize opinion, but in so doing they also must pay attention to its possibilities and limitations. At the same time, leadership must be distinguished from demagoguery. According to Wilson, this means distinguishing "popular thought" from the "popular mood" or mere "transitory

passion." To the "literary temperament" (exhibited in those we today call intellectuals) there is no distinction to be made, because both the statesman and
the demagogue appear, from that perspective, to have sullied the purity of ideas.

Democratic leaders must accept the pervasive requirement of compromise
among contested views: "Uncompromising thought is the luxury of the closeted recluse." The democratic leader is one who gathers together in his vision
the contested elements and sees a way for them to become a whole. There is,
for Wilson, no higher task.

If we take what Wilson says of Lincoln together with his discourse on
leadership, we realize that Wilson was articulating a possible idea of greatness
for a democratic era, one in which, as Tocqueville and Kierkegaard warned us,
greatness may be longed for but is inevitably an object of suspicion.

George Washington, "Farewell Address to Americans, 1796"

George Washington (1732–1799) was commander in chief of the Continental army during the American Revolution and the first president of the United States. Born in Westmoreland County, Virginia, Washington moved to Mount Vernon to live with his half-brother Lawrence upon the death of Washington's father in 1743. Under Lawrence's tutelage, Washington received a broad liberal education, eventually specializing in surveying. In 1753, a year after Lawrence's death of tuberculosis, Washington was recruited into service by Gov. Robert Dinwiddie in an unsuccessful attempt to convince the French to halt encroachment upon territorial claims of the British. During the ensuing Great War for Empire (French and Indian War), Washington was promoted rapidly through the military ranks, becoming lieutenant colonel at the age of twenty-two and colonel at the age of twenty-three. In 1755 he was appointed commander in chief of the Virginia militia.

Washington returned to Mount Vernon, which he had inherited from Lawrence, in 1759. That same year he entered political life via the Virginia House of Burgesses, in which he served until 1774. An opponent of Britain's colonial policies, Washington served as a delegate to the First and Second Continental Congress. In 1775, Congress unanimously chose him to serve as commander in chief of the Continental army. By the close of the Revolutionary War, Washington's popularity and his regard among the elite made him a natural candidate for the United States' first executive office. Although he had serious reservations about accepting this office, he was elected and became president in 1789, serving until 1797. Washington embodied the spirit of republican government, emphasizing civic responsibility without glorifying government.

United States, September 19, 1796

Friends, and Fellow-Citizens: The period for a new election of a Citizen, to Administer the Executive government of the United States, being not far distant, and the time actually arrived, when your thoughts must be employed in designating the person, who is to be cloathed with that important trust, it appears to me proper, especially as it may conduce to a more distinct expression of the public voice, that I should now apprise you of the resolution I have formed, to decline being considered among the number of those, out of whom a choice is to be made. . . .

The acceptance of, and continuance hitherto in, the office to which your Suffrages have twice called me, have been a uniform sacrifice of inclination to the opinion of duty, and to a deference for what appeared to be your desire. I constantly hoped, that it would have been much earlier in my power, consistently with motives, which I was not at liberty to disregard, to return to that retirement, from which I had been reluctantly drawn. The strength of my inclination to do this, previous to the last Election, had even led to the preparation of an address to declare it to you; but mature reflection on the then perplexed and critical posture of our Affairs with foreign Nations, and the unanimous advice of persons entitled to my confidence, impelled me to abandon the idea.

I rejoice, that the state of your concerns, external as well as internal, no longer renders the pursuit of inclination incompatible with the sentiment of duty, or propriety; and am persuaded whatever partiality may be retained for my services, that in the present circumstances of our country, you will not disapprove my determination to retire.

The impressions, with which I first undertook the arduous trust, were explained on the proper occasion. In the discharge of this trust, I will only say, that I have, with good intentions, contributed towards the Organization and Administration of the government, the best exertions of which a very fallible judgment was capable. Not unconscious, in the outset, of the inferiority of my qualifications, experience in my own eyes, perhaps still more in the eyes of others, has strengthned the motives to diffidence of myself; and every day the encreasing weight of years admonishes me more and more, that the shade of retirement is as necessary to me as it will be welcome. Satisfied that if any circumstances have given peculiar value to my services, they were temporary, I have the consolation to believe, that while choice and prudence invite me to quit the political scene, patriotism does not forbid it.

In looking forward to the moment, which is intended to terminate the career of my public life, my feelings do not permit me to suspend the deep acknowledgment of that debt of gratitude wch. I owe to my beloved country, for the many honors it has conferred upon me; still more for the stedfast confidence with which it has supported me; and for the opportunities I have thence enjoyed of manifesting my inviolable attachment, by services faithful and persevering, though in usefulness unequal to my zeal. If benefits have resulted to our country from these services, let it always be remembered to your praise, and as an instructive example in our annals, that . . . the constancy of your support was the essential prop of the efforts, and a guarantee of the plans by which they were effected. Profoundly penetrated with this idea, I shall carry it with me to my grave, as a strong incitement to beneficence; that your Union and brotherly affection may be perpetual; that the free constitution, which is the work of your hands, may be sacredly maintained; that its Administration in every department may be stamped with wisdom and Virtue; that, in fine, the happiness of the people of these States, under the auspices of liberty, may be made complete. . . .

Here, perhaps, I ought to stop. But a solicitude for your welfare, which cannot end but with my life, and the apprehension of danger, natural to that solicitude, urge me on an occasion like the present, to offer to you solemn contemplation, and to recommend to your frequent review, some sentiments; which are the result of much reflection, of no inconsiderable observation, and which appear to me all important to the permanency of your felicity as a People. . . .

The Unity of Government which constitutes you one people is also now dear to you. It is justly so; for it is a main Pillar in the Edifice of your real independence, the support of your tranquility at home; your peace abroad; of your safety; of your prosperity; of that very Liberty which you so highly prize. But as it is easy to foresee, that from different causes and from different quarters, much pains will be taken, many artifices employed, to weaken in your minds the conviction of this truth; as this is the point in your political fortress against which the batteries of internal and external enemies will be most constantly and actively (though often covertly and insidiously) directed, it is of infinite moment, that you should properly estimate the immense value of your national Union to your collective and individual happiness; that you should cherish a cordial, habitual and immoveable attachment to it; accustoming yourselves to think and speak of it as of the Palladium [protection] of your political safety and prosperity; watching for its preservation with jealous anxiety; discountenancing whatever may suggest even a suspicion that it can in any event be abandoned, and indignantly frowning upon the first dawning of every attempt to alienate any portion of our Country from the rest, or to enfeeble the sacred ties which now link together the various parts.

For this you have every inducement of sympathy and interest. Citizens by birth or choice, of a common country, that country has a right to concentrate your affections. The name of AMERICAN, which belongs to you, in your national capacity, must always exalt the just pride of Patriotism, more than any appellation derived from local discriminations. With slight shades of difference, you have the same Religeon, Manners, Habits and political Principles. You have in a common cause fought and triumphed together. The independence and liberty to possess are the work of joint councils, and joint efforts; of common dangers, sufferings and successes.

But these considerations, however powerfully they address themselves to your sensibility are greatly outweighed by those which apply more immediately to your Interest. Here every portion of our country finds the most commanding motives for carefully guarding and preserving the Union of the whole.

The North, in an unrestrained intercourse with the South, protected by the equal Laws of a common government, finds in the productions of the latter, great additional resources of Maritime and commercial enterprise and precious materials of manufacturing industry. The South in the same Intercourse, benefitting by the Agency of the North, sees its agriculture grow and its commerce expand. Turning partly into its own channels the seamen of the North, it finds its particular navigation envigorated; and while it contributes, in different ways, to nourish and increase the general mass of the National navigation, it looks forward to the protection of a Maritime strength, to which itself is unequally adapted. The East, in a like intercourse with the West, already finds, and in the progressive improvement of interior communications, by land and water, will more and more find a valuable vent for the commodities which it brings from abroad, or manufactures at home. The West derives from the East supplies requisite to its growth and comfort, and what is perhaps of still greater consequence, it must of necessity owe the secure enjoyment of indispensable outlets for its own productions to the weight, influence, and the future Maritime strength of the Atlantic side of the Union, directed by an indissoluble community of Interest as one Nation. Any other tenure by which the West can hold this essential advantage, whether derived from its own separate strength, or from an apostate and unnatural connection with any foreign Power, must be intrinsically precarious.

While then every part of our country thus feels an immediate and particular Interest in Union, all the parts combined cannot fail to find in the united mass of means and efforts greater strength, greater resource, proportionably greater security from external danger, a less frequent interruption of their Peace by foreign Nations; and, what is of inestimable value! they must derive from Union an exemption from those broils and Wars between themselves, which so frequently afflict neighbouring countries, not tied together by the same government; which their own rivalships alone would be sufficient to produce, but which opposite foreign alliances, attachments and intriegues would stimulate and imbitter. Hence likewise they will avoid the necessity of those overgrown Military establishments, which under any form of Government are inauspicious to liberty, and which are to be regarded as particularly hostile to Republican Liberty: In this sense it is, that your Union ought to be considered as a main prop of your liberty, and that the love of the one ought to endear to you the preservation of the other.

These considerations speak a persuasive language to every reflecting and virtuous mind, and exhibit the continuance of the Union as a primary object of Patriotic desire. Is there a doubt, whether a common government can embrace so large a sphere? Let experience solve it. To listen to mere speculation in such a case were criminal. We are authorized to hope that a proper organization of the whole, with the auxiliary agency of governments for the respective Sub divisions, will afford a happy issue to the experiment. 'Tis well worth a fair and full experiment. With such powerful and obvious motives to Union, affecting all parts of our country, while experience shall not have demonstrated its impracticability, there will always be reason, to distrust the patriotism of those, who in any quarter may endeavor to weaken its bands.

In contemplating the causes wch. may disturb our Union, it occurs as matter of serious concern, that any ground should have been furnished for characterizing parties by Geographical discriminations: Northern and Southern; Atlantic and Western; whence designing men may endeavour to excite a belief that there is a real difference of local interests and views. One of the expedients of Party to acquire influence, within particular districts, is to misrepresent the opinions and aims of other Districts. You cannot shield yourselves too much against the jealousies and heart burnings which spring from these misrepresentations. They tend to render Alien to each other those who ought to be bound together by fraternal affection. . . .

To the efficacy and permanency of Your Union, a Government for the whole is indispensable. . . . Sensible of this momentous truth, you have improved upon your first essay, by the adoption of a Constitution of Government, better calculated than your former for an intimate Union, and for the efficacious management of your common concerns. This government, the offspring of our own choice uninfluenced and unawed, adopted upon full investigation and mature deliberation, completely free in its principles, in the distribution of its powers, uniting security with energy, and containing within itself a provision for its own amendment, has a just claim to your confidence and your support. Respect for its authority, compliance with its Laws, acquiescence in its measures, are duties enjoined by the fundamental maxims of true Liberty. The basis of our political systems is the right of the people to make and to alter their Constitutions of Government. But the Constitution which at any time exists, 'till changed by an explicit and authentic act of the whole People, is sacredly obligatory upon all. The very idea of the power and the right of the People to establish Government presupposes the duty of every Individual to obey the established Government.

All obstructions to the execution of the Laws, all combinations and Associations, under whatever plausible character, with the real design to direct, controul, counteract, or awe the regular deliberation and action of the Constituted authorities are distructive of this fundamental principle and of fatal tendency. They serve to organize faction, to give it an artificial and extraordinary force; to put in the place of the delegated will of the Nation, the will of a party; often a small but artful and enterprizing minority of the Community; and, according to the alternative triumphs of different parties, to make the public administration the Mirror of the ill concerted and incongruous projects of faction, rather than the organ of consistent and wholesome plans digested by common councils and modefied by mutual interest. However combinations of Associations of the above description may now and then answer popular ends, they are likely, in the course of time and things, to become potent engines, by which cunning, ambitious and unprincipled men will be enabled to subvert the Power of the People, and to usurp for themselves the reins of Government; destroying afterwards the very engines which have lifted them to unjust dominion.

Towards the preservation of your Government and the permanency of your present happy state, it is requisite, not only that you steadily discountenance irregular oppositions to its acknowledged authority, but also that you resist with care the spirit of innovation upon its principles however specious the pretexts. . . .

I have already intimated to you the danger of Parties in the State, with particular reference to the founding of them on Geographical discriminations. Let me now take a more comprehensive view, and warn you in the most solemn manner against the baneful effects of the Spirit of Party, generally.

This spirit, unfortunately, is inseparable from our nature, having its root in the strongest passions of the human Mind. It exists under different shapes in all Governments, more or less stifled, controuled, or repressed; but, in those of the popular form it is seen in its greatest rankness and is truly their worst enemy.

The alternate domination of one faction over another, sharpened by the spirit of revenge natural to party dissention, which in different ages and countries has perpetrated the most horrid enormities, is itself a frightful despotism. But this leads at length to a more formal and permanent despotism. The disorders and miseries, which result, gradually incline the minds of men to seek security and repose in the absolute power of an Individual: and sooner or later the chief of some prevailing faction more able or more fortunate than his competitors, turns this disposition to the purposes of his own elevation, on the ruins of Public Liberty.

Without looking forward to an extremity of this kind (which nevertheless ought not to be entirely out of sight) the common and continual mischiefs of the spirit of Party are sufficient to make it the interest and the duty of a wise People to discourage and restrain it.

It serves always to distract the Public Councils and enfeeble the Public administration. It agitates the Community with ill founded jealousies and false alarms, kindles the animosity of one part against another, foments occasionally riot and insurrection. It opens the door to foreign influence and corruption, which find a facilitated access to the government itself through the channels of party passions. Thus the policy and . . . the will of one country, are subjected to the policy and will of another. . . .

It is important, likewise, that the habits of thinking in a free Country should inspire caution in those entrusted with its administration, to confine themselves within their respective Constitutional spheres; avoiding in the exercises of the Powers of one department to encroach upon another. The spirit of encroachment tends to consolidate the powers of all the departments in one, and thus to create whatever the form of government, a real despotism. A just estimate of that love of power, and proneness to abuse it, which predominates in the human heart is sufficient to satisfy us of the truth of this position. The necessity of reciprocal checks in the exercise of political power; by dividing and distributing it into different depositories, and constituting each the Guardian of the Public Weal against invasion by the others, has been evinced by experiments ancient and modern; some of them in our country and under our own eyes. To preserve them must be as necessary as to institute them. If in the opinion of the People, the distribution or modification of the Constitutional powers be in any particular wrong, let it be corrected by an amendment in the way which the Constitution designates. But let there be no change by usurpation; for though this, in one instance, may be the instrument of good, it is the customary weapon by which free governments are destroyed. The precedent must always greatly overbalance in permanent evil any partial or transient benefit which the use can at any time yield.

Of all the dispositions and habits which lead to political prosperity, Religion and morality are indispensable supports. . . . Reason and experience both forbid us to expect that National morality can prevail in exclusion of religious principle.

'Tis substantially true, that virtue or morality is a necessary spring of popular government. The rule indeed extends with more or less force to every species of free Government. Who that is a sincere friend to it, can look with indifference upon attempts to shake the foundation of the fabric.

Promote then as an object of primary importance, Institutions for the general diffusion of knowledge. In proportion as the structure of a government gives force to public opinion, it is essential that public opinion should be enlightened.

As a very important source of strength and security, cherish public credit. One method of preserving it is to use it as sparingly as possible; avoiding occasions of expence by cultivating peace, but remembering also that timely disbursements to prepare for danger frequently prevent much greater disbursements to repel it; avoiding likewise the accumulation of debt, not only by shunning occasions of expence, but by vigorous exertions in time of Peace to discharge the Debts which unavoidable wars may have occasioned, not ungenerously throwing upon posterity the burthen which we ourselves ought to bear. The execution of these maxims belongs to your Representatives, but it is necessary that public opinion should cooperate. To facilitate to them the performance of their duty, it is essential that you should practically bear in mind, that towards the payment of debts there must be Revenue; that to have Revenue there must be taxes; that no taxes can be devised which are not more or less inconvenient and unpleasant. . . .

Observe good faith and justice towds. all Nations. Cultivate peace and harmony with all. Religion and morality enjoin this conduct; and can it be that good policy does not equally enjoin it? It will be worthy of a free, enlightened, and, at no distant period, a great Nation, to give to mankind the magnanimous and too novel example of a People always guided by an exalted justice and benevolence. Who can doubt that in the course of time and things the fruits of such a plan would richly repay any temporary advantages wch. might be lost by a steady adherence to it? Can it be, that Providence has not connected the permanent felicity of a Nation with its virtue? . . .

In the execution of such a plan nothing is more essential than that permanent, inveterate antipathies against particular Nations and passionate attachments for others should be excluded; and that in place of them just and amicable feelings towards all should be cultivated. The Nation, which indulges towards another an habitual hatred, or an habitual fondness, is in some degree a slave. It is a slave to its animosity or to its affection, either of which is sufficient to lead it astray from its duty and its interest. . . . The peace often, sometimes perhaps the Liberty, of Nations has been the victim. . . .

Frederick Douglass, "Fourth of July Oration, 1852"

Frederick Douglass (1818–1895) was an anti-slavery activist, newspaper founder, political leader, and diplomat. Born in Talbot County, Maryland, the young Douglass, a slave then surnamed Bailey after his mother, Harriet Bailey, was relocated into the service of Hugh Auld in Baltimore. There Douglass was exposed to many opportunities and ideas he might not have encountered on the Lloyd plantation. Sophie Auld, against her husband's wishes, taught Douglass the rudiments of reading; Douglass learned to read the newspapers, learning therein the meaning of the word "abolition" and discovering that black people escaped slavery by fleeing to the free states of the North. In 1838 Douglass disguised himself as a freeman, caught a train out of Baltimore, and by ferry reached New York where he gained liberty. He married, moved to Massachusetts, and assumed the surname Douglass.

Douglass' intellectual depth, his passion, and his demeanor combined to make him an enormously successful lecturer at the abolitionist meetings and conventions he began attending upon his arrival in New Bedford. By 1841 Douglass had secured a paid position as lecturer for the Massachusetts Anti-Slavery Society. He traveled for several years delivering anti-slavery speeches in numerous free states. His orations were profoundly persuasive. In 1845 Douglass published his autobiographical Narrative of the Life of Frederick Douglass, An American Slave. *After publication of the* Narrative, *Douglass founded several abolitionist newspapers, took on several advisory and diplomatic tasks for the Republican party, and continued delivering speeches denouncing slavery and racial discrimination. In this Fourth of July oration, delivered in fact on July 5, 1852, and generally regarded as Douglass's most influential speech, Douglass hotly denied a common perception that the U.S. Constitution was pro-slavery. "In that instrument," he said, "I hold there is no warrant, license, nor sanction of the hateful thing; but, interpreted as it ought to be interpreted, the Constitution is a* GLORIOUS LIBERTY DOCUMENT."

Mr. President, Friends and Fellow Citizens: . . . This, for the purpose of this celebration, is the Fourth of July. It is the birthday of your National Independence, and of your political freedom. This, to you, is what the Passover was to the emancipated people of God. It carries your minds back to the day, and to the act of your great deliverance; and to the signs, and to the wonders, associated with that act, and that day. This celebration also marks the beginning of another year of your national life; and reminds you that the Republic of

America is now 76 years old. I am glad, fellow-citizens, that your nation is so young. Seventy-six years, though a good old age for a man, is but a mere speck in the life of a nation. Three score years and ten is the allotted time for individual men; but nations number their years by thousands. According to this fact, you are, even now, only in the beginning of your national career, still lingering in the period of childhood. I repeat, I am glad this is so. There is hope in the thought, and hope is much needed, under the dark clouds which lower above the horizon. The eye of the reformer is met with angry flashes, portending disastrous times; but his heart may well beat lighter at the thought that America is young, and that she is still in the impressible stage of her existence. May he not hope that high lessons of wisdom, of justice and of truth, will yet give direction to her destiny? Were the nation older, the patriot's heart might be sadder, and the reformer's brow heavier. Its future might be shrouded in gloom, and the hope of its prophets go out in sorrow. There is consolation in the thought that America is young—Great streams are not easily turned from channels, worn deep in the course of ages. They may sometimes rise in quiet and stately majesty, and inundate the land, refreshing and fertilizing the earth with their mysterious properties. They may also rise in wrath and fury, and bear away, on their angry waves, the accumulated wealth of years of toil and hardship. They, however, gradually flow back to the same old channel, and flow on as serenely as ever. But, while the river may not be turned aside, it may dry up, and leave nothing behind but the withered branch, and the unsightly rock, to howl in the abyss-sweeping wind, the sad tale of departed glory. As with rivers so with nations.

Fellow-citizens, I shall not presume to dwell at length on the associations that cluster about this day. The simple story of it is, that 76 years ago, the people of this country were British subjects. The style and title of your "sovereign people" (in which you now glory) was not then born. You were under the British Crown. Your fathers esteemed the English Government as the home government; and England as the fatherland. This home government, you know, although a considerable distance from your home, did, in the exercise of its parental prerogatives, impose upon its colonial children, such restraints, burdens and limitations, as, in its mature judgment, it deemed wise, right and proper.

But your fathers, who had not adopted the fashionable idea of this day, of the infallibility of government, and the absolute character of its acts, presumed to differ from the home government in respect to the wisdom and the justice of some of those burdens and restraints. They went so far in their excitement as to pronounce the measures of government unjust, unreasonable, and oppressive, and altogether such as ought not to be quietly submitted to. I scarcely need say, fellow-citizens, that my opinion of those measures fully accords with that of your fathers. Such a declaration of agreement on my part would not be worth much to anybody. It would certainly proved nothing as to what part I might have taken had I lived during the great controversy of 1776. To say now that America was right, and England wrong, is exceedingly easy. Everybody can say it; the dastard, not less than the noble brave, can flippantly descant on the tyranny of England towards the American Colonies. It is fashionable to do so; but there was a time when, to pronounce against England, and in favor of the cause of the colonies, tried men's souls. They who did so were accounted in their day plotters of mischief, agitators and rebels, dangerous men. To side with the right against the wrong, with the weak against the strong, and with the oppressed against the oppressor! here lies the merit, and the one which, of all others, seems unfashionable in our day. The cause of liberty may be stabbed by the men who glory in the deeds of your fathers. But, to proceed.

Feeling themselves harshly and unjustly treated, by the home government, your fathers, like men of honesty, and men of spirit, earnestly sought redress. They petitioned and remonstrated; they did so in a decorous, respectful, and loyal manner. Their conduct was wholly unexceptional. This, however, did not answer the purpose. They saw themselves treated with sovereign indifference, coldness and scorn. Yet they persevered. They were not the men to look back. . . .

With brave men there is always a remedy for oppression. Just here, the idea of a total separation of the colonies from the crown was born! It was a startling idea, much more so than we, at this distance of time, regard it. The timid and the prudent (as has been intimated) of that day were, of course, shocked and alarmed by it. . . .

On the 2d of July, 1776, the old Continental Congress, to the dismay of the lovers of ease, and the worshipers of property, clothed that dreadful idea with all the authority of national sanction. They did so in the form of a resolution; and as we seldom hit upon resolutions, drawn up in our day, whose transparency is at all equal to this, it may refresh your minds and help my story if I read it.

"Resolved, That these united colonies are, and of right, ought to be free and Independent States; that they are absolved from all allegiance to the British Crown; and that all political connection between them and the State of Great Britain is, and ought to be dissolved."

Citizens, your fathers made good that resolution. They succeeded; and to-day you reap the fruits of their success. The freedom gained is yours; and you, therefore, may properly celebrate this anniversary. The 4th of July is the first great fact in your nation's history—the very ringbolt in the chain of your yet undeveloped destiny.

Pride and patriotism, not less than gratitude, prompt you to celebrate and to hold it in perpetual remembrance. I have said that the Declaration of Independence is the ringbolt to the chain of your nation's destiny; so, indeed, I regard it. The principles contained in that instrument are saving principles. Stand by those principles, be true to them on all occasions, in all places, against all foes, and at whatever cost. . . .

Fellow-citizens, pardon me, allow me to ask, why am I called upon to speak here today? What have I, or those I represent, to do with your national independence? Are the great principles of political freedom and of natural justice, embodied in the Declaration of Independence, extended to us? and am I, therefore, called upon to bring our humble offering to the national altar, and to confess the benefits and express devout gratitude for the blessings resulting from your independence to us?

Would to God, both for your sakes and ours, that an affirmative answer could be truthfully returned to these questions! Then would my task be light, and my burden easy and delightful. For who is there so cold, that a nation's sympathy could not warm him? Who so obdurate and dead to the claims of gratitude, that would not thankfully acknowledge such priceless benefits? Who so stolid and selfish, that would not give his voice to swell the hallelujahs of a nation's jubilee, when the chains of servitude had been torn from his limbs? I am not that man. In a case like that, the dumb might eloquently speak, and the "lame man leap as an hart."

But such is not the state of the case. I say it with a sad sense of the disparity between us. I am not included within the pale of this glorious anniversary! Your high independence only reveals the immeasurable distance between us. The blessings in which you, this day, rejoice, are not enjoyed in common.— The rich inheritance of justice, liberty, prosperity and independence bequeathed by your fathers, is shared by you, not by me. The sunlight that brought light and healing to you, has brought stripes and death to me. This Fourth of July is *yours,* not *mine. You* may *rejoice, I* must mourn. To drag a man in fetters into the grand illuminated temple of liberty, and call upon him to join you in joyous anthems, were inhuman mockery and sacrilegious irony. Do you mean, citizens, to mock me, by asking me to speak to-day? If so, there is a parallel to your conduct. And let me warn you that it is dangerous to copy the example of a nation whose crimes, towering up to heaven, were thrown down by the breath of the Almighty, burying that nation in irrevocable ruin! I can to day take up the plaintive lament of a peeled and woe-smitten people! . . .

My subject, then, fellow-citizens, is American slavery. I shall see this day and its popular characteristics from the slave's point of view. Standing there identified with the American bondsman, making his wrongs mine, I do not hesitate to declare, with all my soul, that the character and conduct of this nation never looked blacker to me than on this 4th of July! Whether we turn to the declarations of the past, or to the professions of the present, the conduct of the nation seems equally hideous and revolting. America is false to the past, false to the present, and solemnly binds herself to be false to the future. Standing with God and the crushed and bleeding slave on this occasion, I will, in the name of humanity which is outraged, in the name of liberty which is fettered, in the name of the constitution and the Bible which are disregarded and trampled upon, dare to call in question and to denounce, with all the emphasis I can command, everything that serves to perpetuate slavery—the great sin and shame of America! "I will not equivocate; I will not excuse"; I will use the severest language I can command; and yet not one word shall escape me that any man, whose judgment is not blinded by prejudice, or who is not at heart a slaveholder, shall not confess to be right and just.

But I fancy I hear some one of my audience say, "It is just in this circumstance that you and your brother abolitionists fail to make a favorable impression on the public mind. Would you argue more, and denounce less; would you persuade more, and rebuke less; your cause would be much more likely to succeed." But, I submit, where all is plain there is nothing to be argued. What point in the antislavery creed would you have me argue? On what branch of the subject do the people of this country need light? Must I undertake to prove that the slave is a man? That point is conceded already. Nobody doubts it. The slaveholders themselves acknowledge it in the enactment of laws for their government. They acknowledge it when they punish disobedience on the part of the slave. There are seventy-two crimes in the State of Virginia which, if committed by a black man (no matter how ignorant he be), subject him to the punishment of death; while only two of the same crimes will subject a white man to the like punishment. What is thus but the acknowledgment that the slave is a moral, intellectual, and responsible being? The manhood of the slave is conceded. It is admitted in the fact that Southern statue books are covered with enactments forbidding, under severe fines and penalties, the teaching of the slave to read or to write. When you can point to any such laws in reference to the beasts of the field, then I may consent to argue the manhood of the slave. When the dogs in your streets, when the fowls of the air, when the cattle on your hills, when the fish of the sea, and the reptiles that crawl, shall be unable to distinguish the slave from a brute, then will I argue with you that the slave is a man!

For the present, it is enough to affirm the equal manhood of the Negro race. It is not astonishing that, while we are ploughing, planting and reaping, using all kinds of mechanical tools, erecting houses, constructing bridges, building ships, working in metals of brass, iron, copper, silver and gold; that, while we are reading, writing and ciphering, acting as clerks, merchants and secretaries, having among us lawyers, doctors, ministers, poets, authors, editors, orators and teachers; that while we are engaged in all manner of enterprises common to other men, digging gold in California, capturing the whale in the Pacific, feeding sheep and cattle on the hillside, living, moving, acting, thinking, planning, living in families as husbands, wives and children, and, above all, confessing and worshipping the Christian's God, and looking hopefully for life and immortality beyond the grave, we are called upon to prove that we are men!

Would you have me argue that man is entitled to liberty? that he is rightful owner of his own body? You have already declared it. Must I argue the wrongfulness of slavery? Is that a question for Republicans? Is it to be settled by the rules of logic and argumentation, as a matter beset with great difficulty, involving a doubtful application of the principle of justice, hard to be understood? How should I look to-day, in the presence of Americans, dividing, and subdividing a discourse, to show that men have a natural right to freedom? speaking of it relatively and positively, negatively and affirmatively. To do so, would be to make myself ridiculous, and to offer an insult to your understanding.—There is not a man beneath the canopy of heaven that does not know that slavery is wrong *for him*. . . .

What, to the American slave, is your 4th of July? I answer; a day that reveals to him, more than all other days in the year, the gross injustice and cruelty to which he is the constant victim. To him, your celebration is a sham; your boasted liberty, an unholy license; your national greatness, swelling vanity; your sounds of rejoicing are empty and heartless; your denunciation of tyrants, brass fronted impudence; your shouts of liberty and equality, hollow mockery; your prayers and hymns, your sermons and thanskgivings, with all your religious parade and solemnity, are, to Him, mere bombast, fraud, deception, impiety, and hypocrisy—a thin veil to cover up crimes which would disgrace a nation of savages. There is not a nation on the earth guilty of practices more shocking and bloody than are the people of the United States, at this very hour. . . .

Behold the practical operation of this internal slave-trade, the American slave-trade, sustained by American politics and American religion. Here you will see men and women reared like swine for the market. You know what is a swine-drover? I will show you a man-drover. They inhabit all our Southern States. They perambulate the country, and crowd the highways of the nation, with droves of human stock. You will see one of these human flesh jobbers, armed with pistol, whip, and bowie-knife, driving a company of a hundred men, women, and children, from the Potomac to the slave market at New Orleans. These wretched people are to be sold singly, or in lots, to suit purchasers.

They are food for the cotton-field and the deadly sugar-mill. Mark the sad procession, as it moves wearily along, and the inhuman wretch who drives them. Hear his savage yells and his blood-curdling oaths, as he hurries on his affrighted captives! There, see the old man with locks thinned and gray. Cast one glance, if you please, upon that young mother, whose shoulders are bare to the scorching sun, her briny tears falling on the brow of the babe in her arms. See, too, that girl of thirteen, weeping, *yes!* weeping, as she thinks of the mother from whom she has been torn! The drove moves tardily. Heat and sorrow have nearly consumed their strength; suddenly you hear a quick snap, like the discharge of a rifle; the fetters clank, and the chain rattles simultaneously; your ears are saluted with a scream, that seems to have torn its way to the centre of your soul! The crack you heard was the sound of the slave-whip; the scream you heard was from the woman you saw with the babe. Her speed had faltered under the weight of her child and her chains! that gash on her shoulder tells her to move on. Follow this drove to New Orleans. Attend the auction; see men examined like horses; see the forms of women rudely and brutally exposed to the shocking gaze of American slave buyers. See this drove sold and separated forever; and never forget the deep, sad sobs that arose from that scattered multitude. Tell me, citizens, where, under the sun, you can witness a spectacle more fiendish and shocking. Yet this is but a glance at the American slave-trade, as it exists, at this moment, in the ruling part of the United States.

I was born amid such sights and scenes. To me the American slave-trade is a terrible reality. When a child, my soul was often pierced with a sense of its horrors. I lived on Philpot Street, Fell's Point, Baltimore, and have watched from the wharves the slave ships in the Basin, anchored from the shore, with their cargoes of human flesh, waiting for favorable winds to waft them down the Chesapeake. There was, at that time, a grand slave mart kept at the head of Pratt Street, by Austin Woldfolk. His agents were sent into every town and county in Maryland, announcing their arrival through the papers, and on flaming "*hand-bills,*" headed cash for Negroes. These men were generally well dressed men, and very captivating in their manners; ever ready to drink, to treat, and to gamble. The fate of many a slave has depended upon the turn of a single card; and many a child has been snatched from the arms of its mother by bargains arranged in a state of brutal drunkenness.

The flesh-mongers gather up their victims by dozens, and drive them, chained, to the general depot at Baltimore. When a sufficient number has been collected here, a ship is chartered for the purpose of conveying the forlorn crew to Mobile, or to New Orleans. From the slave prison to the ship, they are usually driven in the darkness of night; for since the anti-slavery agitation, a certain caution is observed.

In the deep, still darkness of midnight, I have been often aroused by the dead, heavy footsteps, and the piteous cries of the chained gangs that passed our door. The anguish of my boyish heart was intense; and I was often consoled, when speaking to my mistress in the morning, to hear her say that the custom was very wicked; that she hated to hear the rattle of the chains and the heart-rending cries. I was glad to find one who sympathized with me in my horror. . . .

* * *

For black men there is neither law nor justice, humanity nor religion. The Fugitive Slave *Law* makes mercy to them a crime; and bribes the judge who tries them. An American judge gets ten dollars for every victim he consigns to slavery, and five, when he fails to do so. The oath of any two villains is sufficient, under this hell-black enactment, to send the most pious and exemplary black man into the remorseless jaws of slavery! His own testimony is nothing. He can bring no witnesses for himself. The minister of American justice is bound by the law to hear but one side; that side is the side of the oppressor. Let this damning fact be perpetually told. Let it be thundered around the world that in tyrant-killing, king-hating, people-loving, democratic, Christian America the seats of justice are filled with judges who hold their offices under an open and palpable *bribe,* and are bound, in deciding the case of man's liberty, to hear only his *accusers!*

In glaring violation of justice, in shameless disregard of the forms of administering law, in cunning arrangement to entrap the defenceless, and in diabolical intent this Fugitive Slave Law stands alone in the annals of tyrannical legislation. I doubt if there be another nation on the globe having the brass and the baseness to put such a law on the statue-book. If any man in this assembly thinks differently from me in this matter, and feels able to disprove my statements, I will gladly confront him at any suitable time and place he may select.

I take this law to be one of the grossest infringements of Christian Liberty, and, if the churches and ministers of our country were not stupidly blind, or most wickedly indifferent, they, too, would so regard it.

At the very moment that they are thanking God for the enjoyment of civil and religious liberty, and for the right to worship God according to the dictates of their own consciences, they are utterly silent in respect to a law which robs religion of its chief significance and makes it utterly worthless to a world lying in wickedness. Did this law concern the "*mint, anise, and cummin*"—abridge the right to sing psalms, to partake of the sacrament, or to engage in any of the ceremonies of religion, it would be smitten by the thunder of a thousand

pulpits. . . . The fact that the church of our country (with fractional exceptions) does not esteem "the Fugitive Slave Law" as a declaration of war against
religious liberty, implies that that church regards religion simply as a form of
worship, an empty ceremony, and not a vital principle, requiring active benevolence, justice, love, and good will towards man. It esteems sacrifice above
mercy; psalm-singing above practical righteousness. A worship that can be
conducted by persons who refuse to give shelter to the houseless, to give bread
to the hungry, clothing to the naked, and who enjoin obedience to a law forbidding these acts of mercy is a curse, not a blessing to mankind. The Bible
addresses all such persons as "scribes, pharisees, hypocrites, who pay tithe of
mint, anise, and *cummin,* and have omitted the weightier matters of the law,
judgment, mercy, and faith."

But the church of this country is not only indifferent to the wrongs of the
slave, it actually takes sides with the oppressors. It has made itself the bulwark
of American slavery, and the shield of American slave-hunters. Many of its
most eloquent Divines, who stand at the very lights of the church, have shame-
lessly given the sanction of religion and the Bible to the whole slave system.
They have taught that man may, properly, be a slave; that the relation of master
and slave is ordained of God; that to send back an escaped bondman to his
master is clearly the duty of all the followers of the Lord Jesus Christ; and this
horrible blasphemy is palmed off upon the world for Christianity.

For my part, I would say, welcome infidelity! welcome atheism! welcome
anything! in preference to the gospel, *as preached by those Divines!* They con-
vert the very name of religion into an engine of tyranny and barbarous cruelty,
and serve to confirm more infidels, in this age, than all the infidel writings of
Thomas Paine, Voltaire, and Bolingbroke put together have done! These ministers make religion a cold and flinty-hearted thing, having neither principles
of right action nor bowels of compassion. They strip the love of God of its
beauty and leave the throne of religion a huge, horrible, repulsive form. It is a
religion for oppressors, tyrants, man-stealers, and *thugs.* It is not that "*pure and
undefiled religion*" which is from above, and which is "*first pure, then peaceable,
easy to be entreated,* full of mercy and good fruits, *without partiality,* and *without hypocrisy.*" But a religion which favors the rich against the poor; which exalts the proud above the humble; which divides mankind into two classes, tyrants and slaves; which says to the man in chains, stay there; and to the
oppressor, oppress on; it is a religion which may be professed and enjoyed by
all the robbers and enslavers of mankind; it makes God a respecter of persons,
denies his fatherhood of the race, and tramples in the dust the great truth of
the brotherhood of man. All this we affirm to be true of the popular church,
and the popular worship of our land and nation—a religion, a church, and a
worship which, on the authority of inspired wisdom, we pronounce to be an

abomination in the sight of God. In the language of Isaiah, the American church might be well addressed. "Bring no more vain oblations; incense is an abomination unto me; the new moons and Sabbaths, the calling of assemblies, I cannot away with; it is iniquity, even the solemn meeting. Your new moons, and your appointed feasts my soul hateth. They are a trouble to me; I am weary to bear them; and when ye spread forth your hands I will hide mine eyes from you. Yea! when ye make many prayers, I will not hear. Your hands are full of blood; cease to do evil, learn to do well; seek judgment; relieve the oppressed; judge for the fatherless; plead for the widow. . . ."

Americans! your republican politics, not less than your republican religion, are flagrantly inconsistent. You boast of your love of liberty, your superior civilization, and your pure Christianity, while the whole political power of the nation (as embodied in the two great political parties) is solemnly pledged to support and perpetuate the enslavement of three millions of your countrymen. You hurl your anathemas at the crowned headed tyrants of Russia and Austria and pride yourselves on your Democratic institutions, while you yourselves consent to be the mere tools and bodyguards of the tyrants of Virginia and Carolina. You invite to your shores fugitives of oppression from abroad, honor them with banquets, greet them with ovations, cheer them, toast them, salute them, protect them, and pour out your money to them like water; but the fugitives from your own land you advertise, hunt, arrest, shoot, and kill. You glory in your refinement and your universal education; yet you maintain a system as barbarous and dreadful as ever stained the character of a nation—a system begun in avarice, supported in pride, and perpetuated in cruelty. You shed tears over fallen Hungary, and make the sad story of her wrongs the theme of your poets, statesmen, and orators, till your gallant sons are ready to fly to arms to vindicate her cause against the oppressor; but, in regard to the ten thousand wrongs of the American slave, you would enforce the strictest silence, and would hail him as an enemy of the nation who dares to make those wrongs the subject of public discourse! You are all on fire at the mention of liberty for France or for Ireland; but are as cold as an iceberg at the thought of liberty for the enslaved of America. You discourse eloquently on the dignity of labor; yet, you sustain a system which, in its very essence, casts a stigma upon labor. You can bare your bosom to the storm of British artillery to throw off a three-penny tax on tea; and yet wring the last hard earned farthing from the grasp of the black laborers of your country. You profess to believe "that, of one blood, God made all nations of men to dwell on the face of all the earth," and hath commanded all men, everywhere, to love one another; yet you notoriously hate (and glory in your hatred) all men whose skins are not colored like your own. You declare before the world, and are understood by the world to declare that you "*hold these truths to be self-evident, that all men are created equal; and are endowed by their Creator with certain inalienable rights; and that among these are, life, liberty, and the pursuit of happiness;"* and yet, you hold securely, in a bondage which, according to your own Thomas Jefferson, *"is worse than ages of that which your fathers rose in rebellion to oppose,"* a seventh part of the inhabitants of your country.

Fellow-citizens, I will not enlarge further on your national inconsistencies. The existence of slavery in this country brands your republicanism as a sham, your humanity as a base pretense, and your Christianity as a lie. It destroys your moral power abroad: it corrupts your politicians at home. It saps the foundation of religion; it makes your name a hissing and a bye-word to a mocking earth. It is the antagonistic force in your government, the only thing that seriously disturbs and endangers your *Union.* It fetters your progress; it is the enemy of improvement; it breeds insolence; it promotes vice; it shelters it; and yet you cling to it as if it were the sheet anchor of all your hopes. Oh! be warned! be warned! a horrible reptile is coiled up in your nation's bosom; the venomous creature is nursing at the tender breast of your youthful republic; *for the love of God, tear away,* and fling from you the hideous monster, and *let the weight of twenty million crush and destroy it forever*!

But it is answered in reply to all this, that precisely what I have now denounced is, in fact, guaranteed and sanctioned by the Constitution of the United States; that, the right to hold, and to hunt slaves is a part of that Constitution framed by the illustrious Fathers of this Republic. . . .

Now, take the Constitution according to its plain reading, and I defy the presentation of a single pro-slavery clause in it. On the other hand, it will be found to contain principles and purposes, entirely hostile to the existence of slavery.

I have detained my audience entirely too long already. At some future period I will gladly avail myself of an opportunity to give this subject a full and fair discussion.

Allow me to say, in conclusion, notwithstanding the dark picture I have this day presented, of the state of the nation, I do not despair of this country. There are forces in operation which must inevitably work the downfall of slavery. "The arm of the Lord is not shortened," and the doom of slavery is certain. I, therefore, leave off where I began, with hope. While drawing encouragement from "the Declaration of Independence," the great principles it contains, and the genius of American Institutions, my spirit is also cheered by the obvious tendencies of the age. Nations do not now stand in the same relation to each other that they did ages ago. No nation can now shut itself up from the surrounding world and trot round in the same old path of its fathers without interference. The time was when such could be done. Long established customs of hurtful character could formerly fence themselves in, and do their evil work with social impunity. Knowledge was then confined and enjoyed by the privileged few, and the multitude walked on in mental darkness. But a change has now come over the affairs of mankind. Walled cities and empires have become unfashionable. The arm of commerce has borne away the gates of the strong city. Intelligence is penetrating the darkest corners of the globe. It makes its pathway over and under the sea, as well as on the earth. Wind, steam, and lightning are its chartered agents. Oceans no longer divide, but link nations together. From Boston to London is now a holiday excursion. Space is comparatively annihilated.—Thoughts expressed on one side of the Atlantic are distinctly heard on the other.

The far off and almost fabulous Pacific rolls in grandeur at our feet. The Celestial Empire, the mystery of ages, is being solved. The fiat of the Almighty, "Let there be Light," has not yet spent its force. No abuse, no outrage, whether in taste, sport or avarice, can now hide itself from the all-pervading light.

Abraham Lincoln

*As President of the United States, Abraham Lincoln (1809–1865) led his na-
tion through the worst crisis in its history, the Civil War. Born in Kentucky,
Lincoln moved to Indiana as a young child, a move his family undertook
partly because the Northwest Ordinance of 1787 forbade slavery there. In 1830
the family moved to Illinois, where Lincoln served briefly in the Black Hawk
War before running unsuccessfully for the Illinois legislature in 1832. In 1834
Lincoln ran again for legislative office in Illinois, winning the first of four
successive terms as a Whig. Lincoln aligned himself with many of the ideas
of the Whigs, including the party's opposition to slavery. Later, as a member
of the U.S. House of Representatives (1847–1849), Lincoln opposed any national expansion that would result in the spread of slavery into new areas.*

*Lincoln had married, withdrawn from political life, and settled into a
successful law practice when Congress passed the Kansas-Nebraska Act,
sponsored by Stephen A. Douglas, in 1854. The act effectively made all new
U.S. territories and states vulnerable to the spread of slavery. Lincoln ran
unsuccessfully for the U.S. Senate one year later, joined the newly-formed
Republican party in 1856, and in 1858 ran again for the Senate against
Douglas. Lincoln lost the campaign, but his performance in seven debates
against Douglas gained him national attention. In 1860 the Republican
party nominated him for president. Lincoln won the election and became
the sixteenth president of the United States. He was inaugurated in 1861; by
the eve of the inauguration seven states had seceded from the Union. Lincoln's two abiding goals became the preservation of the union and the reconciliation of the Constitution with the principle of equality proclaimed in
the Declaration of Independence, by the emancipation of slaves.*

"A House Divided," Speech before the 1858
Republican State Convention of Illinois
Springfield, June 17, 1858

Mr. President and Gentlemen of the Convention: If we could first know where
we are, and whither we are tending, we could better judge what to do, and how

to do it. We are now far into the fifth year since a policy was initiated with the avowed object and confident promise of putting an end to slavery agitation. Under the operation of that policy, that agitation has not only not ceased, but has constantly augmented. In my opinion, it will not cease until a crisis shall have been reached and passed. *"A house divided against itself cannot stand."* I believe this government cannot endure permanently half slave and half free. I do not expect the Union to be dissolved; I do not expect the house to fall; but I do expect it will cease to be divided. It will become all one thing, or all the other. Either the opponents of slavery will arrest the further spread of it, and place it where the public mind shall rest in the belief that it is in the course of ultimate extinction, or its advocates will push it forward till it shall become alike lawful in all the states, old as well as new, North as well as South.

Have we no tendency to the latter condition?

Let anyone who doubts, carefully contemplate that now almost complete legal combination—piece of machinery, so to speak—compounded of the Nebraska doctrine and the *Dred Scott* decision. Let him consider, not only what work the machinery is adapted to do, and how well adapted, but also let him study the history of its construction, and trace, if he can, or rather fail, if he can, to trace the evidences of design, and concert of action, among its chief architects, from the beginning.

The new year of 1854 found slavery excluded from more than half the states by state constitutions, and from most of the national territory by congressional prohibition. Four days later, commenced the struggle which ended in repealing that congressional prohibition. This opened all the national territory to slavery, and was the first point gained.

But, so far, Congress only had acted, and an endorsement by the people, real or apparent, was indispensable to save the point already gained, and give chance for more.

This necessity had not been overlooked, but had been provided for, as well as might be, in the notable argument of "squatter sovereignty," otherwise called "sacred right of self-government," which latter phrase, though expressive of the only rightful basis of any government, was so perverted in this attempted use of it as to amount to just this: That if any *one* man choose to enslave *another*, no *third* man shall be allowed to object. That argument was incorporated into the Nebraska bill itself, in the language which follows: "It being the true intent and meaning of this act not to legislate slavery into any territory or state, nor to exclude it therefrom, but to leave the people thereof perfectly free to form and regulate their domestic institutions in their own way, subject only to the Constitution of the United States." Then opened the roar of loose declamation in favor of "squatter sovereignty," and "sacred right of self-government." "But," said opposition members, "let us amend the bill so as to expressly declare that the people of the territory may exclude slavery." "Not we," said the friends of the measure, and down they voted the amendment.

While the Nebraska bill was passing through Congress, a *law case,* involving the question of a Negro's freedom, by reason of his owner having taken him first into a free state and then into a territory covered by the Congressional prohibition, and held him as a slave for a long time in each, was passing through the United States Circuit Court for the District of Missouri; and both Nebraska bill and lawsuit were brought to a decision in the same month of May 1854. The Negro's name was Dred Scott, which name now designates the decision finally made in the case. Before the then next presidential election, the law case came to, and was argued in, the Supreme Court of the United States; but the decision of it was deferred until after the election. Still, before the election, Senator Trumbull, on the floor of the Senate, requested the leading advocate of the Nebraska bill to state his opinion whether the people of a territory can constitutionally exclude slavery from their limits; and the latter answers: "That is a question for the Supreme Court."

The election came. Mr. Buchanan was elected, and the endorsement, such as it was, secured. That was the second point gained. The endorsement, however, fell short of a clear popular majority by nearly four hundred thousand votes, and so, perhaps, was not overwhelmingly reliable and satisfactory. The outgoing president, in his last annual message, as impressively as possible echoed back upon the people the weight and authority of the endorsement. The Supreme Court met again, did not announce their decision, but ordered a reargument. The presidential inauguration came, and still no decision of the court; but the incoming president, in his inaugural address, fervently exhorted the people to abide by the forthcoming decision, whatever it might be. Then, in a few days, came the decision.

The reputed author of the Nebraska bill finds an early occasion to make a speech at this capital endorsing the *Dred Scott* decision, and vehemently denouncing all opposition to it. The new president, too, seizes the early occasion of the Silliman letter to endorse and strongly construe that decision, and to express his astonishment that any different view had ever been entertained!

At length a squabble springs up between the president and the author of the Nebraska bill, on the mere question of fact, whether the Lecompton Constitution was or was not in any just sense made by the people of Kansas; and in that quarrel the latter declares that all he wants is a fair vote for the people, and that he cares not whether slavery be voted down or voted up. I do not understand his declaration, that he cares not whether slavery be voted down or voted up, to be intended by him other than as an apt definition of the policy he would impress upon the public mind—the principle for which he declares he has suffered so much, and is ready to suffer to the end. And well may he cling to it. That principle is the only shred left of his original Nebraska doctrine. Under the *Dred Scott* decision "squatter sovereignty" squatted out of existence, tumbled down like temporary scaffolding; like the mould at the foundry, served through one blast, and fell back into loose sand; held to carry an election, and then was kicked to the winds. His late joint struggle with the Republicans, against the Lecompton Constitution, involved nothing of the original Nebraska doctrine. That struggle was made on a point—the right of a people to make their own constitution—upon which he and the Republicans have never differed.

The several points of the *Dred Scott* decision, in connection with Senator Douglas's "care not" policy, constitute the piece of machinery, in its present state of advancement. This was the third point gained. The working points of that machinery are:

First, That no Negro slave, can ever be a citizen of any state, in the sense of that term as used in the Constitution of the United States. This point is made in order to deprive the Negro, in every possible event, of the benefit of that provision of the United States Constitution which declares that "the citizens of each state shall be entitled to all privileges and immunities of citizens in the several states."

Second, That, "subject to the Constitution of the United States," neither Congress nor a territorial legislature can exclude slavery from any United States territory. This point is made in order that individual men may fill up the territories with slaves, without danger of losing them as property, and thus to enhance the chances of permanency to the institution through all the future.

Third, That whether the holding a Negro in actual slavery in a free state makes him free, as against the holder, the United States courts will not decide, but will leave to be decided by the courts of any slave state the Negro may be forced into by the master. This point is made, not to be pressed immediately; but, if acquiesced in for a while, and apparently endorsed by the people at an election, then to sustain the logical conclusion that what Dred Scott's master might lawfully do with Dred Scott, in the free state of Illinois, every other master may lawfully do with any other one, or one thousand slaves, in Illinois, or in any other free state.

Auxiliary to all this, and working hand in hand with it, the Nebraska doctrine, or what is left of it, is to educate and mould public opinion, at least Northern public opinion, not to care whether slavery is voted down or voted up. This shows exactly where we now are; and partially, also whither we are tending.

It will throw additional light on the latter, to go back and run the mind over the string of historical facts already stated. Several things will now appear less dark and mysterious than they did when they were transpiring. The people were to be left "perfectly free," "subject only to the Constitution." What the Constitution had to do with it, outsiders could not then see. Plainly enough now—it was an exactly fitted niche, for the *Dred Scott* decision to afterwards come in, and declare the perfect freedom of the people to be just no freedom at all. Why was the amendment, expressly declaring the right of people, voted down? Plainly enough now—the adoption of it would have spoiled the niche for the *Dred Scott* decision. Why was the court decision held up? Why even a senator's individual opinion withheld, till after the presidential election? Plainly enough now—the speaking out then would have damaged the "perfectly free" argument upon which the election was to be carried. Why the outgoing president's felicitation on the endorsement? Why the delay of a reargument? Why the incoming president's advance exhortation in favor of the decision? These things look like the cautious patting and petting of a spirited horse preparatory to mounting him, when it is dreaded that he may give the rider a fall. And why the hasty afterendorsement of the decision by the president and others?

We cannot absolutely know that all these exact adaptations are the result of preconcert. But when we see a lot of framed timbers, different portions of which we know have been gotten out at different times and places and by different workmen—Stephen, Franklin, Roger, and James, for instance—and when we see these timbers joined together, and see they exactly make the frame of a house or a mill, all the tenons and mortises exactly fitting, and all the lengths and proportions of the different pieces too many or too few—not omitting even scaffolding—or, if a single piece be lacking, we see the place in the frame exactly fitted and prepared yet to bring such piece in—in such a case, we find it impossible not to believe that Stephen and Franklin and Roger and James all understood one another from the beginning, and all worked upon a common plan or draft drawn up before the first blow was struck.

It should not be overlooked that by the Nebraska bill the people of a state as well as territory were to be left "perfectly free," "subject only to the Constitution." Why mention a state? They were legislating for territories, and not for or about states. Certainly the people of a state are and ought to be subject to the Constitution of the United States; but why is mention of this lugged into this merely territorial law? Why are the people of a territory and the people of a state therein lumped together, and their relation to the Constitution therein treated as being precisely the same? While the opinion of the court, by Chief Justice Taney, in the *Dred Scott* case, and the separate opinions of all the concurring judges, expressly declare that the Constitution of the United States neither permits Congress nor a territorial legislature to exclude slavery from any United States territory, they all omit to declare whether or not the same Constitution permits a state, or the people of a state, to exclude it. Possibly, this is a mere omission; but who can be quite sure, if McLean or Curtis had sought to get into the opinion a declaration of unlimited power in the people of a state to exclude slavery from their limits, just as Chase and Mace sought to get such declaration, in behalf of the people of a territory, into the Nebraska bill—I ask, who can be quite sure that it would not have been voted down in the one case as it had been in the other? The nearest approach to the point of declaring the power of a state over slavery is made by Judge Nelson. He approaches it more than once, using the precise idea, and almost the language, too, of the Nebraska act. On one occasion, his exact language is "Except in cases where the power is restrained by the Constitution of the United States, the law of the state is supreme over the subject of slavery within its jurisdiction." In what cases the power of the states is so restrained by the United States Constitution, is left an open question, precisely as the same question, as to the restraint on the power of the territories, was left open in the Nebraska act. Put this and that together, and we have another nice little niche, which we may, ere long, see filled with another Supreme Court decision, declaring that the Constitution of the United States does not permit a state to exclude slavery from its limits. And this may especially be expected if the doctrine of "care not whether slavery be voted down or voted up" shall gain upon the public mind sufficiently to give promise that such a decision can be maintained when made.

Such a decision is all that slavery now lacks of being alike lawful in all the states. Welcome or unwelcome, such a decision is probably coming, and will soon be upon us, unless the power of the present political dynasty shall be met and overthrown. We shall lie down pleasantly dreaming that the people of Missouri are on the verge of making their state free, and we shall awake to the reality instead that the Supreme Court has made Illinois a slave state. To meet and overthrow the power of that dynasty is the work now before all those who would prevent that consummation. That is what we have to do. How can we best do this?

There are those who denounce us openly to their own friends, and yet whisper us softly that Senator Douglas is the aptest instrument there is with which to effect that object. They wish us to infer all, from the fact that he now has a little quarrel with the present head of the dynasty, and that he has regularly voted with us on a single point, upon which he and we have never differed. They remind us that he is a great man, and that the largest of us are very small ones. Let this be granted. But "a living dog is better than a dead lion." Judge Douglas, if not a dead lion, for this work is at least a caged and toothless one. How can he oppose the advances of slavery? He don't care anything about it. His avowed mission is impressing the "public heart" to *care nothing about it.*

A leading Douglas Democratic newspaper thinks Douglas's superior talent will be needed to resist the revival of the African slave trade. Does Douglas believe an effort to revive that trade is approaching us? He has not said so. Does he really think so? But if it is, how can he resist it? For years he has labored to prove it a sacred right of white men to take Negro slaves into the new territories. Can he possibly show that it is less a sacred right to buy them where they can be bought cheapest? And unquestionably they can be bought cheaper in Africa than in Virginia. He has done all in his power to reduce the whole question of slavery to one of a mere right of property; and, as such, how can he oppose the foreign slave trade—how can he refuse that trade in the "property" shall be "perfectly free"—unless he does it as a protection to the home production? And as the home producers will probably not ask the protection, he will be wholly without a ground of opposition.

Senator Douglas holds, we know, that a man may rightfully be wiser today than he was yesterday; that he may rightfully change when he finds himself wrong. But can we, for that reason, run ahead, and infer that he will make any particular change, of which he himself has given no intimation? Can we safely base our action upon any such vague inference?

The Emancipation Proclamation
January 1, 1863

Whereas, On the twenty-second day of September, A.D. 1862, a proclamation was issued by the president of the United States, containing, among other things, the following, to wit:

> That on the first day of January, A.D. 1863, all persons held as slaves within any state or designated part of a state the people whereof shall then be in rebellion against the United States shall be then, thenceforward, and forever free; and the executive government of the United States, including the military and naval authority thereof, will recognize and maintain the freedom of such persons and will do no act or acts to repress such persons, or any of them, in any efforts they may make for their actual freedom.
>
> That the executive will on the first day of January aforesaid, by proclamation, designate the states and parts of states, if any, in which the people thereof, respectively, shall then be in rebellion against the United States; and the fact that any state of the people thereof shall on the day be in good faith represented in the Congress of the United States by members chosen thereto at elections wherein a majority of the qualified votes of such state shall have participated shall, in the

absence of strong countervailing testimony, be deemed conclusive evidence that such state and the people thereof are not then in rebellion against the United States.

Now, therefore, I Abraham Lincoln, President of the United States, by virtue of the power in me vested as Commander in Chief of the Army and Navy of the United States in time of actual armed rebellion against the authority and government of the United States, and as a fit and necessary war measure for suppressing said rebellion, do, on this first day of January, A.D. 1863, and in accordance with my purpose so to do, publicly proclaimed for the full period of one hundred days from the first day above mentioned, order and designate as the states and parts of states wherein the people thereof, respectively, are this day in rebellion against the United States the following, to wit:

Arkansas, Texas, Louisiana (except the parishes of St. Bernard, Plaquemines, Jefferson, St. John, St. Charles, St. James, Ascension, Assumption, Terrebonne, Lafourche, St. Mary, St. Martin, and Orleans, including the city of New Orleans), Mississippi, Alabama, Florida, Georgia, South Carolina, North Carolina, and Virginia (except the forty-eight counties designated as West Virginia, and also the counties of Berkeley, Accomac, Northampton, Elizabeth City, York, Princess Anne, and Norfolk, including the cities of Norfolk and Portsmouth), and which excepted parts are for the present left precisely as if this proclamation were not issued.

And by virtue of the power and for the purpose aforesaid, I do order and declare that all persons held as slaves within said designated states and parts of states are, and henceforward shall be, free; and that the executive government of the United States, including the military and naval authorities thereof, will recognize and maintain the freedom of said persons.

And I hereby enjoin upon the people so declared to be free to abstain from all violence, unless in necessary self-defense; and I recommend to them that, in all cases when allowed, they labor faithfully for reasonable wages.

And I further declare and make known that such persons of suitable condition will be received into the armed service of the United States to garrison forts, positions, stations, and other places, and to man vessels of all sorts in said service.

And upon this act, sincerely believed to be an act of justice, warranted by the Constitution upon military necessity, I invoke the considerate judgment of mankind and the gracious favor of Almighty God.

In witness whereof I have hereunto set my hand and caused the seal of the United States to be affixed.

Done at the city of Washington, this first day of January, A.D. 1863, and of the independence of the United States of America the eighty-seventh.

The Gettysburg Address
November 19, 1863

Fourscore and seven years ago our fathers brought forth on this continent, a new nation, conceived in liberty, and dedicated to the proposition that all men are created equal.

Now we are engaged in a great civil war, testing whether that nation or any nation so conceived and so dedicated, can long endure. We are met on a great battlefield of that war. We have come to dedicate a portion of that field, as a final resting place for those who here gave their lives that that nation might live. It is altogether fitting and proper that we should do this.

But, in a larger sense, we cannot dedicate—we cannot consecrate—we cannot hallow—this ground. The brave men, living and dead, who struggled here, have consecrated it, far above our poor power to add or detract. The world will little note, nor long remember what we say here, but it can never forget what they did here. It is for us the living, rather, to be dedicated here to the unfinished work which they who fought here have thus far so nobly advanced. It is rather for us to be here dedicated to the great task remaining before us—that from these honored dead we take increased devotion to that cause for which they gave the last full measure of devotion—that we here highly resolve that these dead shall not have died in vain—that this nation, under God, shall have a new birth of freedom—and that government of the people, by the people, for the people, shall not perish from the earth.

Second Inaugural Address
March 4, 1865

Fellow Countrymen: At this second appearing to take the oath of the presidential office there is less occasion for an extended address than there was at the first. Then a statement somewhat in detail of a course to be pursued seemed fitting and proper. Now, at the expiration of four years, during which public declarations have been constantly called forth on every point and phase of the great contest which still absorbs the attention and engrosses the energies of the nation, little that is new could be presented. The progress of our arms, upon which all else chiefly depends, is as well known to the public as to myself, and it is, I trust, reasonably satisfactory and encouraging to all. With high hope for the future, no prediction in regard to it is ventured.

On the occasion corresponding to this four years ago all thoughts were anxiously directed to an impending civil war. All dreaded it, all sought to avert it. While the inaugural address was being delivered from this place, devoted altogether to saving the Union without war, insurgent agents were in the city seeking to destroy it without war—seeking to dissolve the Union and divide effects by negotiation. Both parties deprecated war, but one of them would make war rather than let the nation survive, and the other would accept war rather than let it perish, and the war came.

One eighth of the whole population was colored slaves, not distributed generally over the Union, but localized in the southern part of it. These slaves constituted a peculiar and powerful interest. All knew that this interest was somehow the cause of the war. To strengthen, perpetuate, and extend this interest was the object for which the insurgents would rend the Union even by war, while the government claimed no right to do more than to restrict the territorial enlargement of it. Neither party expected for the war the magnitude or the duration which it has already attained. Neither anticipated that the cause of the conflict might cease with or even before the conflict itself should cease. Each looked for an easier triumph, and a result less fundamental and astounding. Both read the same Bible and pray to the same God, and each invokes His aid against the other. It may seem strange that any men should dare to ask a just God's assistance in wringing their bread from the sweat of other men's faces, but let us judge not, that we be not judged. The prayers of both could not be answered. That of neither has been answered fully. The Almighty has His own purposes. "Woe unto the world because of offenses; for it must needs be that offenses come, but woe to that man by whom the offense cometh."

If we shall suppose that American slavery is one of those offenses which, in the providence of God, must needs come, but which, having continued through His appointed time, He now wills to remove, and that He gives to both North and South this terrible war as the woe due to those by whom the offense came, shall we discern therein any departure from those divine attributes which the believers in a living God always ascribe to Him? Fondly do we hope, fervently do we pray, that this mighty scourge of war may speedily pass away. Yet, if God wills that it continue until all the wealth piled by the bondsman's two hundred and fifty years of unrequited toil shall be sunk, and until every drop of blood drawn with the lash shall be paid by another drawn with the sword, as was said three thousand years ago, so still it must be said, "The judgments of the Lord are true and righteous altogether."

With malice toward none, with charity for all, with firmness in the right as God gives us to see the right, let us strive on to finish the work we are in, to bind up the nation's wounds, to care for him who shall have borne the battle and for his widow and his orphan, to do all which may achieve and cherish a just and lasting peace among ourselves and with all nations.

Martin Luther King, Jr.

Martin Luther King, Jr. (1929–1968) was one of the leading advocates for the black cause during the early phases of civil rights movement in the 1950s and early 1960s. Born in Atlanta, Georgia, King received his B.A. at Morehouse College, his B.Div. at Crozer Theological Seminary, and his Ph.D. in theology at Boston University.

In 1957 King and several other southern black clergy founded the Southern Christian Leadership Conference, which advocated nonviolent yet "direct" resistance to racial discrimination. King located the SCLC in Atlanta, where he became a co-pastor, with his father, of Ebenezer Baptist Church. King campaigned hard for integration and equal rights, lecturing in a brilliant and evangelical style across the country and encouraging blacks to participate in nonviolent tactics such as protest marches, "sit-ins," and freedom rides.

In the spring of 1963, King and the Reverend Fred Shuttlesworth encouraged and participated in a protest against segregation in Birmingham, Alabama. Hundreds of marchers were jailed, King himself on charges of parading without a permit. Knowing that many other clergy, including many black clergy, did not support his leadership of the Birmingham march, King wrote these peers the famous "Letter from Birmingham Jail," in which he spelled out his philosophy of nonviolent direct action.

Later that year King joined other civil rights leaders in organizing the historic March on Washington. There, on August 28, 1963, King delivered his masterful "I have a dream" speech to some 200,000 peacefully assembled civil-rights marchers.

The following year marked the passage of the Civil Rights Act of 1964, which authorized the federal government to enforce desegregation in employment and in any public accommodations. King was awarded the 1964 Nobel Peace Prize for his work in bringing that important legislation into fruition.

In April 1968 King took a hastily planned trip to Memphis, Tennessee, to support workers in a strike against the city sanitation agency. While standing on the balcony of a motel where he and other civil rights leaders were staying, King was assassinated by a sniper.

"I Have a Dream," Address at the March on Washington, August 1963

Five score years ago a great American, in whose symbolic shadow we stand, signed the Emancipation Proclamation. This momentous decree came as a great beacon light of hope to millions of Negro slaves who had been seared in the flames of withering injustice. It came as a joyous daybreak to end the long night of captivity.

But one hundred years later we must face the tragic fact that the Negro is still not free. One hundred years later the life of the Negro is still sadly crippled by the manacles of segregation and the chains of discrimination. One hundred years later the Negro lives on a lonely island of poverty in the midst of a vast ocean of material prosperity. One hundred years later the Negro still languishes in the corners of American society and finds himself an exile in his own land. So we have come here today to dramatize an appalling condition.

In a sense we have come to our nation's capital to cash a check. When the architects of our republic wrote the magnificent words of the Constitution and the Declaration of Independence, they were signing a promissory note to which every American was to fall heir. This note was a promise that all men would be guaranteed the unalienable rights of life, liberty, and the pursuit of happiness.

It is obvious today that America has defaulted on this promissory note insofar as her citizens of color are concerned. Instead of honoring this sacred obligation, America has given the Negro people a bad check; a check which has come back marked "insufficient funds." But we refuse to believe that the bank of justice is bankrupt. We refuse to believe that there are insufficient funds in the great vaults of opportunity of this nation. So we have come to cash this check—a check that will give us upon demand the riches of freedom and the security of justice. We have also come to this hallowed spot to remind America of the fierce urgency of *now*. This is no time to engage in the luxury of cooling off or to take the tranquilizing drugs of gradualism. *Now* is the time to make real promises of Democracy. *Now* is the time to rise from the dark and desolate valley of segregation to the sunlit path of racial justice. *Now* is the time to open the doors of opportunity to all of God's children. *Now* is the time to lift our nation from the quicksands of racial injustice to the solid rock of brotherhood.

It would be fatal for the nation to overlook the urgency of the moment and to underestimate the determination of the Negro. This sweltering summer of the Negro's legitimate discontent will not pass until there is an invigorating autumn of freedom and equality. 1963 is not an end, but a beginning. Those who hope that the Negro needed to blow off steam and will now be content will have a rude awakening if the nation returns to business as usual. There will be neither rest nor tranquillity in America until the Negro is granted his citizenship rights. The whirlwinds of revolt will continue to shake the foundations of our nation until the bright day of justice emerges.

But there is something that I must say to my people who stand on the warm threshold which leads into the palace of justice. In the process of gaining our rightful place we must not be guilty of wrongful deeds. Let us not seek to satisfy our thirst for freedom by drinking from the cup of bitterness and hatred. We must forever conduct our struggle on the high plane of dignity and discipline. We must not allow our creative protest to degenerate into physical violence. Again and again we must rise to the majestic heights of meeting physical force with soul force. The marvelous new militancy which has engulfed the Negro community must not lead us to a distrust of all white people, for many of our white brothers, as evidenced by their presence here today, have come to realize that their destiny is tied up with our destiny and their freedom is inextricably bound to our freedom. We cannot walk alone.

And as we walk, we must make the pledge that we shall march ahead. We cannot turn back. There are those who are asking the devotees of civil rights, "When will you be satisfied?" We can never be satisfied as long as the Negro is the victim of the unspeakable horrors of police brutality. We can never be satisfied as long as our bodies, heavy with the fatigue of travel, cannot gain lodging in the motels of the highways and the hotels of the cities. We cannot be satisfied as long as the Negro's basic mobility is from a smaller ghetto to a larger one. We can never be satisfied as long as a Negro in Mississippi cannot vote and a Negro in New York believes he has nothing for which to vote. No, no, we are not satisfied, and we will not be satisfied until justice rolls down like water and righteousness like a mighty stream.

I am not unmindful that some of you have come here out of great trials and tribulations. Some of you have come fresh from narrow jail cells. Some of you have come from areas where your quest for freedom left you battered by the storms of persecution and staggered by the winds of police brutality. You have been the veterans of creative suffering. Continue to work with the faith that unearned suffering is redemptive.

Go back to Mississippi, go back to Alabama, go back to South Carolina, go back to Georgia, go back to Louisiana, go back to the slums and ghettos of our modern cities, knowing that somehow this situation can and will be changed. Let us not wallow in the valley of despair.

I say to you today, my friends, that in spite of the difficulties and frustrations of the moment I still have a dream. It is a dream deeply rooted in the American dream.

I have a dream that one day this nation will rise up and live out the true meaning of its creed: "We hold these truths to be self-evident; that all men are created equal."

I have a dream that one day on the red hills of Georgia the sons of former slaves and the sons of former slaveowners will be able to sit down together at the table of brotherhood.

I have a dream that one day even the state of Mississippi, a desert state sweltering with the heat of injustice and oppression, will be transformed into an oasis of freedom and justice.

I have a dream that my four little children will one day live in a nation where they will not be judged by the color of their skin but by the content of their character.

I have a dream today.

I have a dream that one day the state of Alabama, whose governor's lips are presently dripping with the words of interposition and nullification, will be transformed into a situation where little black boys and black girls will be able to join hands with little white boys and white girls and walk together as sisters and brothers.

I have a dream today.

I have a dream that one day every valley shall be exalted, every hill and mountain shall be made low, the rough places will be made plains, and the crooked places will be made straight, and the glory of the Lord shall be revealed, and all flesh shall see it together.

This is our hope. This is the faith with which I return to the South. With this faith we will be able to hew out of the mountain of despair a stone of hope. With this faith we will be able to transform the jangling discords of our nation into a beautiful symphony of brotherhood. With this faith we will be able to work together, to pray together, to struggle together, to go to jail together, to stand up for freedom together, knowing that we will be free one day.

This will be the day when all of God's children will be able to sing with new meaning "My country 'tis of thee, sweet land of liberty, of thee I sing. Land where my fathers died, land of the pilgrim's pride, from every mountainside, let freedom ring."

And if America is to be a great nation this must become true. So let freedom ring from the prodigious hilltops of New Hampshire. Let freedom ring from the mighty mountains of New York. Let freedom ring from the heightening Alleghenies of Pennsylvania!

Let freedom ring from the snow-capped Rockies of Colorado!

Let Freedom ring from the curvaceous peaks of California!

But not only that; let freedom ring from Stone Mountain of Georgia!

Let freedom ring from Lookout Mountain of Tennessee!

Let freedom ring from every hill and molehill of Mississippi. From every mountainside, let freedom ring.

When we let freedom ring, when we let it ring from every village and every hamlet, from every state and every city, we will be able to speed up that day when all of God's children, black men and white men, Jews and Gentiles, Protestants and Catholics, will be able to join hands and sing in the words of the old Negro spiritual, "Free at last! free at last, thank God almighty, we are free at last!"

Letter from Birmingham Jail, 1963

My Dear Fellow Clergymen:

While confined here in the Birmingham city jail, I came across your recent statement calling my present activities "unwise and untimely." Seldom do I pause to answer criticism of my work and ideas. . . . But since I feel that you are men of genuine good will and that your criticisms are sincerely set forth, I want to try to answer your statement in what I hope will be patient and reasonable terms. . . .

I am here because I have organizational ties here . . . But more basically, I am in Birmingham because injustice is here. . . .

I am cognizant of the interrelatedness of all communities and states. I cannot sit idly by in Atlanta and not be concerned about what happens in Birmingham. Injustice anywhere is a threat to justice everywhere. We are caught in an inescapable network of mutuality, tied in a single garment of destiny. Whatever affects one directly, affects all indirectly. Never again can we afford to live with the narrow, provincial "outside agitator" idea. Anyone who lives inside the United States can never be considered an outsider anywhere within its bounds. It is unfortunate that demonstrations are taking place in Birmingham, but it is even more unfortunate that the city's white power structure left the Negro community with no alternative.

In any nonviolent campaign there are four basic steps: collection of the facts to determine whether injustices exist; negotiation; self-purification; and direct action. We have gone through all these steps in Birmingham.

There can be no gainsaying the fact that racial injustice engulfs this community. Birmingham is probably the most thoroughly segregated city in the

United States. Its ugly record of brutality is widely known. Negroes have experienced grossly unjust treatment in the courts. There have been more un-solved bombings of Negro homes and churches in Birmingham than in any other city in the nation. These are the hard, brutal facts of the case . . .

On the basis of these conditions, Negro leaders sought to negotiate with the city fathers. But the latter consistently refused to engage in good-faith ne-gotiation. Then, last September, came the opportunity to talk with leaders of Birmingham's economic community. In the course of the negotiations, certain promises were made by the merchants—for example, to remove the stores' hu-miliating racial signs.

On the basis of these promises, the Reverend Fred Shuttlesworth and the leaders of the Alabama Christian Movement for Human Rights agreed to a moratorium on all demonstrations. As the weeks and months went by, we re-alized that we were the victims of a broken promise. A few signs, briefly re-moved, returned; the others remained.

As in so many past experiences, our hopes had been blasted, and the shadow of deep disappointment settled upon us. We had no alternative except to prepare for direct action, whereby we would present our very bodies as a means of laying our case before the conscience of the local and the national community.

Mindful of the difficulties involved, we decided to undertake the process of self-purification. We began a series of workshops on nonviolence, and we repeatedly asked ourselves: "Are you able to accept blows without retaliation?" "Are you able to endure the ordeal of jail?"

You may well ask, "Why direct action? Why sit-ins, marches, and so forth? Isn't negotiation a better path?" You are quite right in calling for negotiation. Indeed, this is the very purpose of direct action. Nonviolent direct action seeks to create such a crisis and foster such a tension that a community which has constantly refused to negotiate is forced to confront the issue. It seeks so to dramatize the issue that it can no longer be ignored.

My citing the creation of tension as part of the work of the nonviolent resister may sound rather shocking. But I must confess that I am not afraid of the word "tension." I have earnestly opposed violent tension, but there is a type of constructive, nonviolent tension which is necessary for growth.

Just as Socrates felt that it was necessary to create a tension in the mind so that individuals could rise from the bondage of myths and half-truths to the unfettered realm of creative analysis and objective appraisal, so must we see the need for nonviolent gadflies to create the kind of tension in society that will help men rise from the dark depths of prejudice and racism to the majestic heights of understanding and brotherhood.

The purpose of our direct-action program is to create a situation so crisis-packed that it will inevitably open the door to negotiation. I therefore concur with you in your call for negotiation. Too long has our beloved Southland been bogged down in a tragic effort to live in monologue rather than dialogue.

One of the basic points in your statement is that the action that I and my associates have taken in Birmingham is untimely. Some have asked: "Why didn't you give the new city administration time to act?" The only answer that I can give to this query is that the new Birmingham administration must be prodded about as much as the outgoing one, before it will act. . . .

Lamentably, it is an historical fact that privileged groups seldom give up their privileges voluntarily. Individuals may see the moral light and voluntarily give up their unjust posture; but, as Reinhold Niebuhr has reminded us, groups tend to be more immoral than individuals.

We know through painful experience that freedom is never voluntarily given by the oppressor. It must be demanded by the oppressed. Frankly, I have yet to engage in a direct-action campaign that was "well timed" in view of those who have not suffered unduly from the disease of segregation.

For years now I have heard the word "Wait!" It rings in the ear of every Negro with piercing familiarity. This "Wait!" has almost always meant "Never." We must come to see, with one of our distinguished jurists, that "justice too long delayed is justice denied."

We have waited for more than 340 years for our constitutional and God-given rights. The nations of Asia and Africa are moving with jetlike speed toward gaining political independence, but we still creep at horse-and-buggy pace toward gaining a cup of coffee at a lunch counter. Perhaps it is easy for those who have never felt the stinging darts of segregation to say, "Wait."

But when you have seen vicious mobs lynch your mothers and fathers at will and drown your sisters and brothers at whim;

when you have seen hate-filled policemen curse, kick and even kill your black brothers and sisters;

when you see the vast majority of your twenty million Negro brothers smothering in an airtight cage of poverty in the midst of an affluent society;

when you suddenly find your tongue twisted and your speech stammering as you seek to explain to your six-year-old daughter why she can't go to the public amusement park that has just been advertised on television, and see tears welling up in her eyes when she is told the Funtown is closed to colored children, and see ominous clouds of inferiority beginning to form in her little mental sky, and see her beginning to distort her personality by developing an unconscious bitterness toward white people;

when you have to concoct an answer for a five-year-old son who is asking, "Daddy, why do white people treat colored people so mean?"

when you take a cross-country drive and find it necessary to sleep night after night in the uncomfortable corners of your automobile because no motel will accept you;

when you are humiliated day in and day out by nagging signs reading "white" and "colored";

when your first name becomes "nigger," your middle name becomes "boy" (however old you are) and your last name become "John," and your wife and mother are never given the respected title "Mrs.";

when you are harried by day and haunted by night by the fact that you are a Negro, living constantly at tiptoe stance, never quite knowing what to expect next, and are plagued with inner fears and outer resentments;

when you are forever fighting a degenerating sense of "nobodiness"—then you will understand why we find it difficult to wait.

There comes a time when the cup of endurance runs over, and men are no longer willing to be plunged into the abyss of despair. I hope, sirs, you can understand our legitimate and unavoidable impatience. . . .

One may well ask: "How can you advocate breaking some laws and obeying others?" The answer lies in the fact that there are two types of laws: just and unjust. I would be the first to advocate obeying just laws. One has not only a legal but a moral responsibility to obey just laws. Conversely, one has a moral responsibility to disobey unjust laws. I would agree with St. Augustine that "an unjust law is no law at all."

Now, what is the difference between the two? How does one determine whether a law is just or unjust? A just law is a man-made code that squares with the moral law or the law of God. An unjust law is a code that is out of harmony with the moral law.

To put it in the terms of St. Thomas Aquinas: An unjust law is a human law that is not rooted in eternal law and natural law. Any law that uplifts human personality is just. Any law that degrades human personality is unjust.

All segregation statutes are unjust because segregation distorts the soul and damages the personality. It gives the segregator a false sense of superiority and the segregated a false sense of inferiority . . .

Let us consider a more concrete example of just and unjust laws. An unjust law is a code that a numerical or power majority group compels a minority group to obey but does not make binding on itself. This is *difference* made legal. By the same token, a just law is a code that a majority compels a minority to follow and that it is willing to follow itself. This is *sameness* made legal.

Let me give another explanation. A law is unjust if it is inflicted on a minority that, as a result of being denied the right to vote, had no part in enacting or devising the law. Who can say that the legislature of Alabama which set up that state's segregation laws was democratically elected?

Throughout Alabama all sorts of devious methods are used to prevent Negroes from becoming registered voters, and there are some counties in which, even though Negroes constitute a majority of the population, not a single Negro is registered. Can any law enacted under such circumstances be considered democratically structured?

Sometimes a law is just on its face and unjust in its application. For instance, I have been arrested on a charge of parading without a permit. Now, there is nothing wrong in having an ordinance which requires a permit for a parade. But such an ordinance becomes unjust when it is used to maintain segregation and to deny citizens the First-Amendment privilege of peaceful assembly and protest.

I hope you are able to see the distinction I am trying to point out. In no sense do I advocate evading or defying the law, as would the rabid segregationist. That would lead to anarchy.

One who breaks an unjust law must do so openly, lovingly and with a willingness to accept the penalty. I submit that an individual who breaks a law that conscience tells him is unjust, and who willingly accepts the penalty of imprisonment in order to arouse the conscience of the community over its injustice, is in reality expressing the highest respect for law.

Of course, there is nothing new about this kind of civil disobedience. It was evidenced sublimely in the refusal of Shadrach, Meshach, and Abednego to obey the laws of Nebuchadnezzar, on the ground that a higher moral law was at stake. It was practiced superbly by the early Christians, who were willing to face hungry lions and the excruciating pain of chopping blocks rather than submit to certain unjust laws of the Roman Empire.

To a degree, academic freedom is a reality today because Socrates practiced civil disobedience. In our own nation, the Boston Tea Party represented a massive act of civil disobedience.

We should never forget that everything Adolf Hitler did in Germany was "legal" and everything the Hungarian freedom fighters did in Hungary was "illegal." It was "illegal" to aid and comfort a Jew in Hitler's Germany. Even so, I am sure that, had I lived in Germany at the time, I would have aided and comforted my Jewish brothers. If today I lived in a Communist country where certain principles dear to the Christian faith are suppressed, I would openly advocate disobeying that country's anti-religious laws.

I must make two honest confessions to you, my Christian and Jewish brothers. First, I must confess that over the past few years I have been gravely disappointed with the white moderate. I have almost reached the regrettable conclusion that the Negro's great stumbling block in his stride toward freedom is not the White Citizen's Counciler or the Ku Klux Klanner, but the white moderate, who is more devoted to "order" than to justice; who prefers a negative peace which is the absence of tension to a positive peace which is the presence of justice; who constantly says, "I agree with you in the goal you seek, but I cannot agree with your methods of direct action"; who paternalistically believes he can set the timetable for another man's freedom; who lives by a mythical concept of time and who constantly advises the Negro to wait for a "more convenient season."

Shallow understanding from people of good will is more frustrating than absolute misunderstanding from people of ill will. Lukewarm acceptance is much more bewildering than outright rejection.

I had hoped that the white moderate would understand that law and order exist for the purpose of establishing justice and that when they fail in this purpose they become the dangerously structured dams that block the flow of social progress.

I had hoped that the white moderate would understand that the present tension in the South is a necessary phase of the transition from an obnoxious negative peace, in which the Negro passively accepted his unjust plight, to a substantive and positive peace, in which all men will respect the dignity and worth of human personality.

Actually, we who engage in nonviolent direct action are not the creators of tension. We merely bring to the surface the hidden tension that is already alive. We bring it out in the open, where it can be seen and dealt with. Like a boil that can never be cured so long as it is covered up but must be opened with all its ugliness to the natural medicines of air and light, injustice must be exposed, with all the tension its exposure creates, to the light of human conscience and the air of national opinion, before it can be cured. . . .

Human progress never rolls in on wheels of inevitability; it comes through the tireless efforts of men willing to be co-workers with God, and without this hard work, time itself becomes an ally of the forces of stagnation. We must use time creatively, in the knowledge that the time is always ripe to do right.

Now is the time to make real the promise of democracy and transform our pending national elegy into a creative psalm of brotherhood. Now is the time to lift our national policy from the quicksand of racial injustice to the solid rock of human dignity.

You speak of our activity in Birmingham as extreme. At first I was rather disappointed that fellow clergymen would see my nonviolent efforts as those of an extremist. I began thinking about the fact that I stand in the middle of two opposing forces in the Negro community.

One is a force of complacency, made up in part of Negroes who, as a result of long years of oppression, are so drained of self-respect and a sense of "somebodiness" that they have adjusted to segregation; and in part of a few middle-class Negroes who, because of a degree of academic and economic security and because in some ways they profit by segregation, have become insensitive to the problems of the masses.

The other force is one of bitterness and hatred, and it comes perilously close to advocating violence. It is expressed in the various black nationalist groups that are springing up across the nation, the largest and best-known being Elijah Muhammad's Muslim movement. Nourished by the Negro's frustration over the continued existence of racial discrimination, this movement is made up of people who have lost faith in America, who have absolutely repudiated Christianity, and who have concluded that the white man is an incorrigible "devil."

I have tried to stand between these two forces, saying that we need emulate neither the "do-nothingism" of the complacent nor the hatred and despair of the black nationalist. For there is the more excellent way of love and nonviolent protest. I am grateful to God that, through the influence of the Negro church, the way of nonviolence became an integral part of our struggle . . .

Oppressed people cannot remain oppressed forever. The yearning for freedom eventually manifests itself, and that is what has happened to the American Negro. Something within has reminded him of his birthright of freedom, and something without has reminded him that it can be gained. Consciously or unconsciously, he has been caught up by the Zeitgeist, and with his black brothers of Africa and his brown and yellow brothers of Asia, South America and the Caribbean, the United States Negro is moving with a sense of great urgency toward the promised land of racial justice.

If one recognizes this vital urge that has engulfed the Negro community, one should readily understand why public demonstrations are taking place. The Negro has many pent-up resentments and latent frustrations, and he must release them. So let him march; let him make prayer pilgrimages to the city hall; let him go on freedom rides—and try to understand why he must do so.

If his repressed emotions are not released in nonviolent ways, they will seek expression through violence; this is not a threat but a fact of history. So I have not said to my people, "Get rid of your discontent." Rather, I have tried to say that this normal and healthy discontent can be channeled into the creative outlet of nonviolent direct action. And now this approach is being termed extremist . . .

Was not Jesus an extremist for love: "Love your enemies, bless them that curse you, do good to them that hate you, and pray for them which despitefully use you, and persecute you."

Was not Amos an extremist for justice: "Let justice roll down like waters and righteousness like an ever-flowing stream."

And John Bunyan: "I will stay in jail to the end of my days before I make a butchery of my conscience."

And Abraham Lincoln: "This nation cannot survive half slave and half free." And Thomas Jefferson: "We hold these truths to be self-evident, that all men are created equal . . . "

So the question is not whether we will be extremists, but what kind of extremists we will be. Will we be extremists for hate or for love? Will we be extremists for the preservation of injustice or for the extension of justice? . . . . Perhaps the South, the nation, and the world are in dire need of creative extremists.

I had hoped that the white moderate would see this need. Perhaps I was too optimistic; perhaps I expected too much. I suppose I should have realized that few members of the oppressor race can understand the deep groans and passionate yearnings of the oppressed race, and still fewer have the vision to see that injustice must be rooted out by strong, persistent, and determined action.

I am thankful, however, that some of our white brothers in the South have grasped the meaning of this social revolution and committed themselves to it. They are still all too few in quantity, but they are big in quality. Some—such as Ralph Mcgill, Lillian Smith, Harry Golden, James McBride Dabbs, Ann Braden, and Sarah Patton Boyle—have written about our struggle in eloquent and prophetic terms.

Others have marched with us down nameless streets of the South. They have languished in filthy, roach-infested jails, suffering the abuse and brutality of policemen who view them as "dirty nigger-lovers." Unlike so many of their moderate brothers and sisters, they have recognized the urgency of the moment and sensed the need for powerful "action" antidotes to combat the disease of segregation.

Let me take note of my other major disappointment. I have been so greatly disappointed with the white church and its leadership.

Of course, there are some notable exceptions. I am not unmindful of the fact that each of you has taken some significant stands on this issue. I commend you, Reverend Stallings, for your Christian stand on this past Sunday, in welcoming Negroes to your worship service on a nonsegregated basis. I commend the Catholic leaders of this state for integrating Spring Hill College several years ago . . .

In spite of my shattered dreams, I came to Birmingham with the hope that the white religious leadership of this community would see the justice of our cause and, with deep moral concern, would serve as the channel through which our just grievances could reach the power structure. I had hoped that each of you would understand. But again I have been disappointed.

I hope the church as a whole will meet the challenge of this decisive hour. But even if the church does not come to the aid of justice, I have no despair about the future. I have no fear about the outcome of our struggle in Birmingham, even if our motives are at present misunderstood. We will reach the goal of freedom in Birmingham and all over the nation, because the goal of America is freedom.

Abused and scorned though we may be, our destiny is tied up with America's destiny. Before the pilgrims landed at Plymouth, we were here. For more than two centuries our forebears labored in this country, without wages; they made cotton king; they built the homes of their masters while suffering gross injustice and shameful humiliation—and yet out of a bottomless vitality they continued to thrive and develop.

If the inexpressible cruelties of slavery could not stop us, the opposition we now face will surely fail. We will win our freedom because the sacred heritage of our nation and the eternal will of God are embodied in our echoing demands.

Before closing I feel impelled to mention one other point in your statement that has troubled me profoundly. You warmly commended the Birmingham police force for keeping "order" and "preventing violence."

I doubt that you would have so warmly commended the police force if you had seen its dogs sinking their teeth into unarmed, non-violent Negroes. I doubt that you would so quickly commend the policemen if you were to observe their ugly and inhumane treatment of Negroes here in the city jail; if you were to watch them push and curse old Negro women and young Negro girls; if you were to see them slap and kick old Negro men and young boys; if you were to observe them, as they did on two occasions, refuse to give us food because we wanted to sing our grace together. I cannot join you in your praise of the Birmingham police department.

It is true that the police have exercised a degree of discipline in handling the demonstrators. In this sense they have conducted themselves rather "non-violently" in public. But for what purpose? To preserve the evil system of segregation.

I wish you had commended the Negro sit-inners and demonstrators of Birmingham for their sublime courage, their willingness to suffer, and their amazing discipline in the midst of great provocation. One day the South will recognize its real heroes. They will be the James Merediths, with the noble sense of purpose that enables them to face jeering and hostile mobs, and with the agonizing loneliness that characterizes the life of the pioneer. They will be old, oppressed, battered Negro women, symbolized in a seventy-two-year-old woman in Montgomery, Alabama, who rose up with a sense of dignity and with her people decided not to ride segregated buses, and who responded with ungrammatical profundity to one who inquired about her weariness: "My feets is tired, but my soul is at rest."

They will be the young high school and college students, the young ministers of the gospel and a host of their elders, courageously and nonviolently sitting in at lunch counters and willingly going to jail for conscience' sake. One day the South will know that when these disinherited children of God sat down at lunch counters, they were in reality standing up for what is best in the American dream and for the most sacred values in our Judaeo-Christian heritage, thereby bringing our nation back to those great wells of democracy which were dug deep by the founding fathers in their formulation of the Constitution and the Declaration of Independence.

Never before have I written so long a letter. I'm afraid it is much too long to take your precious time. I can assure you that it would have been much shorter if I had been writing from a comfortable desk, but what else can one do when he is alone in a narrow jail cell, other than write long letters, think long thoughts and pray long prayers? . . .

Yours for the cause of peace and brotherhood,

Martin Luther King, Jr.

Woodrow Wilson

Thomas Woodrow Wilson, a Virginian, was born in 1856 and died in 1924. He studied at Davidson College, the College of New Jersey (Princeton), and the Virginia Law School, and earned a Ph.D. in political science at The Johns Hopkins University in 1886. He enjoyed a highly successful academic career, teaching at several colleges before becoming a professor and then president of Princeton in 1902. His prominence led him into politics and the governorship of New Jersey in 1910. In 1912 he was elected to his first of two terms as President of the United States. Wilson sponsored "progressive reform," reforms similar to those Theodore Roosevelt had espoused and intended to improve the day-to-day lives of ordinary people. Legislation passed during his tenure included establishment of the income tax, the Federal Reserve system, and the Federal Trade Commission; anti-trust legislation; and child labor laws. Such legislation consolidated a movement toward a stronger national state with a much enhanced role for the federal government. Wilson conceived of the presidency as an office of leadership to mobilize public opinion in support of national goals. He is remembered by most today primarily for his role in international politics, especially taking America into World War I, his role in the Paris Peace Conference Versailles Treaty, his work in establishing the League of Nations, and his failed attempt to bring the United States into the League. In 1919 Wilson campaigned tirelessly across America in support of the Versailles Treaty, but his health failed him and he suffered a massive stroke. Both in 1919 and in 1920 the Senate refused to ratify the Versailles Treaty. Wilson nevertheless was awarded the Nobel Peace Prize.

"Abraham Lincoln: A Man of the People," An Address on the Occasion of the Hundredth Anniversary of the Birth of Abraham Lincoln

. . . That year 1809 produced, as you know, a whole group of men who were to give distinction to its annals in many fields of thought and of endeavor. To mention only some of the great men who were born in 1809: the poet Tennyson was born in that year, our own poet Edgar Allan Poe, the great Sherman, the great Mendelssohn, Chopin, Charles Darwin, William E. Gladstone, and Abraham Lincoln. Merely read that list and you are aware of the singular variety of gifts and purposes represented . . .

When you read [Lincoln's] name you are at once aware of something that distinguished it from all the rest. There was in each of those other men some special gift, but not in Lincoln. You cannot pick Lincoln out for any special characteristic. He did not have any one of those peculiar gifts that the other men on this list possessed. He does not seem to belong in a list at all; he seems to stand unique and singular and complete in himself. The name makes the same impression upon the ear that the name of Shakespeare makes, because it is as if he contained a world within himself. And that is the thing which marks the singular stature and nature of this great—and, we would fain believe, typical—American. Because when you try to describe the character of Lincoln you seem to be trying to describe a great process of nature. Lincoln seems to have been of general human use and not of particular and limited human use. There was no point at which life touched him that he did not speak back to it instantly its meaning. There was no affair that touched him to which he did not give back life, as if he had communicated a spark of fire to kindle it. The man seemed to have, slumbering in him, powers which he did not exert of his own choice, but which woke the moment they were challenged, and for which no challenge was too great or comprehensive.

You know how slow, how almost sluggish the development of the man was. You know how those who consorted with him in his youth noted the very thing of which I speak. They would have told you that Abraham Lincoln was good for nothing in particular; and the singular fact is he *was* good for nothing in particular—he was good for everything in general. He did not narrow and concentrate his power, because it was meant to be diffused as the sun itself. And so he went through his youth like a man who has nothing to do, like a man whose mind is never halted at any point where it becomes serious, to seize upon the particular endeavor or occupation for which it is intended. He went from one sort of partial success to another sort of partial success, or, as his contemporaries would have said, from failure to failure, until—not until he found himself, but until, so to say, affairs found him, and the crisis of a country seemed suddenly to match the universal gift of his nature; until a great nature was summed up, not in any particular business or activity, but in the affairs of a whole country. It was characteristic of the man. . . .

Then we also say of Lincoln that he saw things with his own eyes. And it is very interesting that we can pick out individual men to say that of them. The opposite of the proposition is, that most men see things with other men's eyes. And that is the pity of the whole business of the world. Most men do not see things with their own eyes. If they did they would not be so inconspicuous as they consent to be. What most persons do is to live up to formulas and opinions and believe them, and never give themselves the trouble to ask whether they are true or not; so that there is a great deal of truth in saying what the trouble is, that men believe so many things that are not so, because they have taken them at second hand; they have accepted them in the form they were given to them. They have reexamined them. They have not seen the world with their own eyes. But Lincoln saw it with his own eyes. And he not only saw the surface of it, but saw beneath the surface of it; for the characteristic of the seeing eye is that it is a discerning eye, seeing also that which is not caught by the surface; it penetrates to the heart of the subjects it looks upon. . . .

 . . . Lincoln was a singularly studious man—not studious in the ordinary conventional sense. To be studious in the ordinary, conventional sense, if I may judge by my observation at a university, is to do the things you have to do and not understand them particularly. But to be studious, in the sense in which Mr. Lincoln was studious, is to follow eagerly and fearlessly the curiosity of a mind which will not be satisfied unless it understands. That is a deep studiousness; that is the thing which lays bare the map of life and enables men to understand the circumstances in which they live, as nothing else can do.

And what commends Mr. Lincoln's studiousness to me is that the result of it was he did not have any theories at all. Life is a very complex thing. No theory that I ever heard propounded will match its varied pattern and the men who are dangerous are the men who are not content with understanding, but go on to propound theories, things which will make a new pattern for society and a new model for the universe. Those are the men who are not to be trusted. Because, although you steer by the North Star, when you have lost the bearings of your compass, you nevertheless must steer in a pathway on the sea,—you are not bound for the North Star. The man who insists upon his theory insists that there is a way to the North Star, and I know, and every one knows, that there is not—at least none yet discovered. Lincoln was one of those delightful students who do not seek to tie you up in the meshes of any theory. . . .

Mr. Lincoln belonged to a type which is fast disappearing, the type of the frontiersman. And he belonged to a process which has almost disappeared from this country. Mr. Lincoln seemed slow in his development, but when you think of the really short span of his life and the distance he traversed in the process of maturing, you will see that it cannot be said to have been a slow process. Mr. Lincoln was bred in that part of the country—*this* part, though we can hardly conceive it now—where States were made as fast as men. Lincoln was made along with the States that were growing as fast as men were. States were born and came to their maturity, in that day, within the legal limit of twenty-one years, and the very pressure of that rapid change, the very imperious necessity of that quick process of maturing, was what made and moulded men with a speed and in a sort which have never since been matched. Here were the processes of civilization and of the building up of polities crowded into a single generation; and where such processes are crowded, men grow. Men could be picked out in the crude, and, if put in that crucible, could be refined out in a single generation into pure metal. That was the process which made Mr. Lincoln. We could not do it that way again, because that period has passed forever with us. . . .

Mr. Lincoln, in other words, was produced by processes which no longer exist anywhere in America, and therefore we are solemnized by this question: Can we have other Lincolns? We cannot do without them. This country is going to have crisis after crisis. God send they may not be bloody crises, but they will be intense and acute. No body politic so abounding in life and so puzzled by problems as ours is can avoid moving from crisis to crisis. We must have the leadership of sane, genial men of universal use like Lincoln, to save us from mistakes and give us the necessary leadership in such days of struggle and of difficulty. And yet, such men will hereafter have to be produced among us by processes which are not characteristically American, but which belong to the whole world. . . .

It seems to me serviceable, therefore, to ask ourselves what it is that we must reproduce in order not to lose the breed, the splendid breed, of men of this calibre. Mr. Lincoln we describe as "a man of the people," and he was a man of the people, essentially. But what do we mean by a "man of the people?" We mean a man, of course, who has his rootage deep in the experiences and the consciousness of the ordinary mass of his fellow-men; but we do not mean a man whose rootage is holding him at their level. We mean a man who, drawing his sap from such sources, has, nevertheless, risen above the level of the rest of mankind and has got an outlook over their heads, seeing horizons which they are too submerged to see; a man who finds and draws his inspiration from the common plane, but nevertheless has lifted himself to a new place of outlook and of insight; who has come out from the people and is their leader, not because he speaks from their ranks, but because he speaks for them and for their interests.

Browning has said:

> "A Nation is but the attempt of many
> To rise to the completer life of one;
> And they who live as models for the mass
> Are singly of more value than they all."

Lincoln was of the mass, but he was so lifted and big that all men could look upon him, until he became the "model for the mass" and was "singly of more value than they all."

It was in that sense that Lincoln was "a man of the people." His sources were where all the pure springs are, but his streams flowed down into other country and fertilized other plains, where men had become sophisticated with the life of an older age.

A great nation is not led by a man who simply repeats the talk of the street-corners or the opinions of the newspapers. A nation is led by a man who hears more than those things; or who, rather, hearing those things, understands them better, unites them, puts them into a common meaning; speaks, not the rumors of the street, but a new principle for a new age; a man in whose ears the voices of the nation do not sound like the accidental and discordant notes that come from the voice of the mob, but concurrent and concordant, like the united voices of a chorus, whose many meanings, spoken by melodious tongues, unite in his understanding in a single meaning and reveal to him a single vision, so that he can speak what no man else knows, the common meaning of the common voice. Such is the man who leads a great, free, democratic nation.

We must always be led by "men of the people," and therefore it behooves us to know them when we see them. How shall we distinguish them? Judged by this man, interpreted by this life, what is a "man of the people?" How shall we know him when he emerges to our view?

Well, in the first place, it seems to me that a man of the people is a man who sees affairs as the people see them, not as a man of particular classes or the professions sees them. You cannot afford to take the advice of a man who has been too long submerged in a particular profession,—not because you cannot trust him to be honest and candid, but because he has been too long immersed and submerged, and through the inevitable pressure and circumstances of his life has come to look upon the nation from a particular point of view. The man of the people is a man who looks far and wide upon the nation, and is not limited by a professional point of view. That may be a hard doctrine; it may exclude some gentlemen ambitious to lead; but I am not trying to exclude them by any arbitrary dictum of my own; I am trying to interpret so much as I understand of human history, and if human history has excluded them, you cannot blame me. Human history has excluded them, as far as I understand it, and that is the end of the matter. I am not excluding them. In communities like ours, governed by general opinion and not led by classes, not dictated to by special interests, they are of necessity excluded. You will see that it follows that a man of the people is not subdued by any stuff of life that he has happened to work in; that he is free to move in any direction his spirit prompts.

Are you not glad that Mr. Lincoln did not succeed too deeply in any particular calling; that he was sufficiently detached to be lifted to a place of leadership and to be used by the whole country? Are you not glad that he had not narrowed his view and understanding to any particular interest,—did not think in the terms of interest but in the terms of life? Are you not glad that he had a myriad of contacts with the growing and vehement life of this country, and that, because of that multiple contact, he was, more than any one else of his generation, the spokesman of the general opinion of his country? . . .

The tasks of the future call for men like Lincoln more audibly, more imperatively, than did the tasks of the time when civil war was brewing and the very existence of the Nation was in the scale of destiny. For the things that perplex us at this moment are the things which mark, I will not say a warfare, but a division among classes; and when a nation begins to be divided into rival and contestant interests by the score, the time is much more dangerous than when it is divided into only two perfectly distinguishable interests, which you can discriminate and deal with. If there are only two sides I can easily make up my mind which side to take, but if there are a score of sides then I must say to some man who is not immersed, not submerged, not caught in this struggle, "Where shall I go? What do you see? What is the movement of the mass? Where are we going? Where do you propose you should go?" It is then I need a man of the people, detached from this struggle yet cognizant of it all, sympathetic with it all, saturated with it all, to whom I can say, "How do you sum it up, what are the signs of the day, what does the morning say, what are the tasks that we must set our hands to?" We should pray, not only that we should be led by such men, but also that they should be men of the particular sweetness that Lincoln possessed.

The most dangerous thing you can have in an age like this is a man who is intense and hot. We have heat enough; what we want is light. Anybody can stir up emotions, but who is master of men enough to take the saddle and guide those awakened emotions? Anybody can cry a nation awake to the necessities of reform, but who shall frame the reform but a man who is cool, who takes his time, who will draw you aside for a jest, who will say: "Yes, but not to-day, to-morrow; let us see the other man and see what he has to say; let us hear everybody, let us know what we are to do. In the meantime I have a capital story for your private ear. Let me take the strain off, let me unbend the steel. Don't let us settle this thing by fire but let us settle it by those cool, incandescent lights which show its real nature and color."

The most valuable thing about Mr. Lincoln was that in the midst of the strain of war, in the midst of the crash of arms, he could sit quietly in his room and enjoy a book that led his thoughts off from everything American, could wander in fields of dreams, while every other man was hot with the immediate contest. Always set your faith in a man who can withdraw himself, because only the man who can withdraw himself can see the stage; only the man who can withdraw himself can see affairs as they are.

And so the lesson of this day is faith in the common product of the nation; the lesson of this day is the future as well as the past leadership of men, wise men, who have come from the people. We should not be Americans deserving to call ourselves the fellow-countrymen of Lincoln if we did not feel the compulsion that his example lays upon us—the compulsion, not to heed him merely but to look to our own duty, to live every day as if that were the day upon which America was to be reborn and remade; to attack every task as if we had something here that was new and virginal and original, out of which we could make the very stuff of life, by integrity, faith in our fellow-men, wherever it is deserved, absolute ignorance of any obstacle that is insuperable, patience, indomitable courage, insight, universal sympathy,—with that programme opening our hearts to every candid suggestion, listening to all the voices of the nation, trying to bring in a new day of vision and of achievement.

"Leaders of Men"

[June 17, 1890]

Only those are 'leaders of men,' in the general eye, who lead in action. The title belongs, if the whole field of the world be justly viewed, no more rightfully to the men who lead in action than to those who lead in silent thought. A book is often quite as quickening a trumpet as any made of brass and sounded in the field. But it is the estimate of the world that bestows their meaning upon words: and that estimate is not often very far from the fact. The men who act stand nearer to the mass of men than do the men who write; and it is at their hands that new thought gets its translation into the crude language of deeds. The very crudity of that language of deeds exasperates the sensibilities of the author; and his exasperation proves the world's point. He may be *back* of the leaders, but he is not the leader. In his thought there is due and studied proportion; all limiting considerations are set in their right places, as guards to ward off misapprehension. Every cadence of right utterance is made to sound in the careful phrases, in the perfect adjustments of sense. Translate the thought into action and all its shadings disappear. It stands out a naked, lusty thing, sure to rasp the sensibilities of every man of fastidious taste. Stripped for action, a thought must always shock those who cultivate the nice fashions of literary dress, as authors do. But it is only when thought does thus stand forth in unabashed force that it can perform deeds of strength in the arena round about which the great public sit as spectators, awarding the prizes by the suffrage of their applause.

Here, unquestionably, we come upon the heart of the perennial misunderstanding between the men who write and the men who act. The men who write love proportion; the men who act must strike out practicable lines of action, and neglect proportion. This would seem to explain the well-nigh universal repugnance felt by literary men towards Democracy. The arguments which induce popular action must always be broad and obvious arguments. Only a very gross substance of concrete conception can make any impression on the minds of the masses; they must get their ideas very absolutely put, and are much readier to receive a half truth which they can promptly understand than a whole truth which has too many sides to be seen all at once. How can any man whose method is the method of artistic completeness of thought and expression, whose mood is the mood of contemplation, for a moment understand or tolerate 'the majority,' whose purpose and practice it is to strike out broad, rough-hewn *policies,* whose mood is the mood of action? The great stream of freedom which

> "broadens down
> from precedent to precedent,"[9]

is not a clear mountain current such as the fastidious man of chastened taste likes to drink from: it is polluted with not a few of the coarse elements of the gross world on its banks; it is heavy with the drainage of a very material universe.

One of the nicest *tests* of the repugnance felt by the literary nature for the sort of leadership and action which commends itself to the world of common men you may yourself apply. Ask some author of careful, discriminative thought to utter his ideas to a *mass-meeting,* from a platform occupied by 'representative citizens.' He will shrink from it as he would shrink from being publicly dissected! Even to hear *some one else,* who is given to apt public speech, re-render his thoughts in oratorical phrase and make them acceptable to a miscellaneous audience, is often a mild, sometimes an accute [sic], form of torture for him. If the world would really know his thoughts for what they are, let them go to his written words, con his phrases, join paragraph with paragraph, chapter with chapter: then, the whole form and fashion of his conceptions

---

9. From Tennyson's "You Ask Me Why."

impressed upon their minds, they will know him as no platform speaker can ever make him known. Of course such preferences greatly limit his audience. Not many out of the multitudes who crowd about him buy his books. But, if the few who can understand read and are convinced, will not his thoughts finally leaven the mass? . . .

The competent leader of men cares little for the interior niceties of other people's characters: he cares much—everything for the external uses to which they may be put. His will seeks the lines of least resistance; but the whole question with him is a question *of the application of force.* There are men to be moved: how shall he move them? He supplies the power; others supply only the materials upon which that power operates. The power will fail if it be misapplied; it will be misapplied if it be not suitable both in kind and method to the nature of the materials upon which it is spent; but that nature is, after all, only its means. It is the *power* which dictates, dominates: the materials yield. Men are clay in the hands of the consummate leader. . . .

Some of the gifts and qualities which most commend the literary man to success would inevitably doom the would-be leader to failure. One could wish for no better proof and example of this than is furnished by the career of that most notable of great Irishmen, Edmund Burke. Everyone knows that Burke's life was spent in Parliament, and everyone knows that the eloquence he poured forth there is as deathless as our literature; and yet everyone is left to wonder in presence of the indubitable fact that he was of so little consequence in the actual direction of affairs. How noble a figure in the history of English politics; how large a man; how commanding a mind; and yet how ineffectual in the work of bringing men to turn their faces as he would have them, towards the high purposes he had ever in view! We hear with astonishment that after the delivery of that consummate speech on the Nabob of Arcot's debts, which everybody has read, Pitt and Grenville easily agreed that they need not trouble themselves to make any reply! His speech on conciliation with America is not only wise beyond precedent in the annals of debate, but marches also with a force of phrase which, it would seem, must have been irresistable;—and yet we know that it emptied the House of all audience! . . .

It is better to read Burke than to have heard him. The thoughts which miscarried in the parliaments of George III have had their triumphs in parliaments of a later day,—have established themselves at the heart of such policies as are to-day liberalizing the world. His power is literary, not forensic. He was no leader of men. He was an organizer of thought, but not of party victories. "Burke is a wise man," says Fox, "but he is wise too soon." He was wise also too much. He went on from wisdom of to-day to the wisdom of to-morrow,— to the wisdom which is for all time. It was impossible he should be followed so far. Men want the wisdom which they are expected to apply to be obvious, and to be conveniently limited in amount. They want a thoroughly trustworthy article, with very simple adjustments and manifest present uses. Elaborate it, increase the expenditure of thought necessary to obtain it, and they will decline to listen. You must keep it in stock for the use of the next generation.

Men are not led by being told what they do not know. *Persuasion* is a force, *but not information;* and persuasion is accomplished by creeping into the confidence of those you would lead. Their confidence is not gained by preaching new thoughts to them. It is gained by qualities which they can assimilate at once: by the things which find easy and immediate entrance into their minds, and which are easily transmitted to the palms of their hands or to the ends of their walking-sticks in the shape of applause. Burke's thoughts penetrate the mind and possess the heart of the quiet student. His style of saying things fills the attention as if it were finest music. But his are not thoughts to be shouted over; his is not a style to ravish the ear of the voter at the hustings. If you would be a leader of men, you must lead your own generation, not the next. . . .

The whole question of leadership receives sharp practical test in a popular legislative assembly. The revolutions which have changed the whole principle and method of government within the last hundred years have created a new kind of leadership in legislation: a leadership which is not yet, perhaps, fully understood. It used to be thought that legislation was an affair proper to be conducted only by the few who were instructed, for the benefit of the many who were uninstructed: that statesmanship was a function of origination for which only trained and instructed men were fit. Those who actually conducted legislation and undertook affairs were rather whimsically chosen by Fortune to illustrate this theory, but such was the ruling thought in politics. The Sovereignty of the People, however, that great modern dogma of politics, has erected a different conception—or, if so be that, in the slowness of our thought, we adhere to the old *conception,* has at least created a very different *practice.* . . . The evolution of [society's] institutions must take place by slow modification and nice all-around adjustment. And all this is but a careful and abstract way of saying that no reform may succeed for which the major thought of the nation is not prepared: that the instructed few may not be safe leaders except in so far as they have communicated their instruction to the many—except in so far as they have transmuted their thought into a common, a popular thought.

Let us fairly distinguish, therefore, the peculiar and delicate duties of the popular leader from the not very peculiar or delicate misdemeanors of the demagogue. Leadership, for the statesman, is *interpretation.* He must read the common thought: he must test and calculate very circumspectly the *preparation* of the nation for the next move in the progress of politics. If he fairly hit the popular thought, when we have missed it, are we to say that he is a demagogue? The nice point is to distinguish the firm and progressive popular *thought* from the momentary and whimsical popular *mood,* the transitory or mistaken popular passion. But it is fatally easy to blame or misunderstand the statesman.

Our temperament is one of logic, let us say. We hold that one and one make two and we see no salvation for the people except they receive the truth. The statesman is of another opinion, 'One and one doubtless make two,' he is ready to admit, 'but the people think that one and one make more than two and until they see otherwise we shall have to legislate on that supposition.' This is not to talk nonsense. The Roman augurs very soon discovered that sacred fowls drank water and pecked grain with no sage intent of prophecy, but from motives quite mundane and simple. But it would have been a revolution to say so in the face of a people who believed otherwise, and executive policy had to proceed on the theory of a divine method of fowl appetite and digestion. The divinity that once did hedge a king, grows not now very high about the latest Hohenzollern[10], but who that prefers growth to revolution would propose that legislation in Germany proceed independently of this accident of hereditary succession?

In no case may we safely hurry the organism away from its habit: for it is held together by that habit, and by it is enabled to perform its functions completely. The constituent habit of a people inheres in its thought, and to that thought legislation,—even the legislation that advances and modifies habit,— must keep very near. The ear of the leader must ring with the voices of the people. He cannot be the school of the prophets; he must be of the number of those who studiously serve the slow-paced daily demand . . .

. . . This function of interpretation, this careful exclusion of individual origination it is that makes it difficult for the impatient original mind to distinguish the popular statesman from the demagogue. The *demagogue* sees and seeks *self-interest* in an acquiescent reading of that part of the public thought upon which he depends for votes; the *statesman,* also reading the common inclination, also, when he reads aright, obtains the votes that keep him in power. But if you will justly observe the two, you will find the one trimming to the inclinations of the moment, the other obedient only to the permanent purposes of the public mind. The one adjusts his sails to the breeze of the day; the other makes his plans to ripen with the slow progress of the years. While the one solicitously watches the capricious changes of the weather, the other

10. Wilhelm II, who had acceded to the throne on June 15, 1888 and had dismissed Bismarck in 1890.

diligently sows the grains in their seasons. The one ministers to himself, the other to the race.

To the literary temperament leadership in both kinds is impossible. The literary mind conceives images, images rounded, perfect, ideal; unlimited and unvaried by accident. It craves outlooks. It handles such stuff as dreams are made of. It is not guided by principles, as statesmen conceive principles, but by conceptions. Principles, as statesmen conceive them, are threads to the labryinth of circumstances; principles, as the literary mind holds them, are unities, instrumental to nothing, sufficient unto themselves. Throw the conceiving mind, habituated to contemplating wholes, into the arena of politics, and it seems to itself to be standing upon shifting sands; where no sure foothold and no upright posture are possible. Its ideals are to it more real and more solid than any actuality of the world in which men are managed. . . .

You may say that if all this be truth: if practical political thought may not run in straight lines, but may twist and turn through all the sinuous paths of various circumstance, then compromise is the true gospel of politics. I cannot wholly gainsay the proposition. But it depends almost altogether upon how you conceive and define compromise whether it seem hateful or not,—whether it *be* hateful or not. I understand the biologists to say that all *growth* is a process of compromise: a compromise of the vital forces within the organism with the physical forces without, which constitute the environment. Yet growth is not dishonest. Neither need compromise in politics be dishonest,—if only it be progressive. Is not compromise the law of society in all things? Do we not in all dealings adjust views, compound differences, placate antagonisms? Uncompromising thought is the luxury of the closeted recluse. Untrammelled reasoning is the indulgence of the philosopher, of the dreamer of sweet dreams. We make always a sharp distinction between the literature of conduct and the literature of the imagination. 'Poetic justice' we recognize as being quite out of the common run of experience. . . .

There is and must be in politics a sort of pervasive sense of compromise, an abiding consciousness of the fact that there is in the general growth and progress of affairs no absolute initiative for any one man, but that each must both give and take. If I am so strenuous in every point of belief and conduct that I cannot meet those of opposite opinions in good fellowship wherever and whenever conduct does not tell immediately upon the action of the state, you may be sure that when you examine my schemes you will find them impracticable,—impracticable, that is, to be *voted* upon. You may be sure that I am a man who must have his own way wholly or not at all. Of course there is much in mere everyday association. Men of opposite parties, seeing each other every day, are enabled to discover that there are no more tails and cloven hoofs on one side in politics than on the other. But it is not all the effect of use and companionship. More than that, it is the effect of openness of mind to impressions of the general opinion, to the influences of the whole situation as to character and strategy. Now and again there arises the figure of a leader silent, reserved, intense, uncompanionable, shut in upon his own thoughts and plans; and such a man will oftentimes prove a great force; but you will find him generally useful for the advancement of but a single cause. He holds a narrow commission, and his work is soon finished. He may count himself happy if he escape the misfortune of being esteemed a fanatic.

What a lesson it is in the organic wholeness of Society, this study of leadership! How subtle and delicate is the growth of the organism, and how difficult initiative in it! Where is rashness? It is excluded. And raw invention? It is discredited. How, as we look about us into the great maze of Society, see its solidarity, its complexity, its restless forces surging amidst its delicate tissues, its hazards and its exalted hopes,—how can we but be filled with awe! Many are the functions that enter into its quick, unresting life. There is the lonely seer, seeking the truths that shall stand permanent and endure; the poet, tracing all perfected lines of beauty, sounding full-voiced all notes of love or hope, of duty or gladness; the toilers in the world's massy stuffs, moulders of meals, forgers of steel, refiners of gold; there are the winds of commerce; the errors and despairs of war; the old things and the new; the vast things that dominate and the small things that constitute the world; passions of men, loves of women; the things that are visible and which pass away and the things that are invisible and eternal. And in the midst of all stands the leader, gathering, as best he can, the thoughts that are completed, that are perceived, that have told upon the common mind; judging also of the work that is now at length ready to be completed; reckoning the gathered gain; perceiving the fruits of toil and of war,—and combining all these into words of progress, into acts of recognition and completion. Who shall say that this is not an exalted function? Who shall doubt or dispraise the title of leadership?

Shall we wonder, either, if the leader be a man open at all points to all men, ready to break into coarse laughter with the Rabelaisian vulgar; ready also to prose with the moralist and the reformer; with an eye of tolerance and shrewd appreciation for life of every mode and degree; a sort of sensitive dial registering all the forces that move upon the face of Society? I do not conceive the leader a trimmer, weak to yield what clamour claims, but the deeply human man, quick to know and to do the things that the hour and his people need.

Part IV

RECENT REFLECTIONS

The readings in this section address the question of leading and leadership in a noticeably self-conscious fashion. In earlier selections in this anthology, the question of leadership is often embedded in a larger context of political and moral philosophy, of military heroism or religious fulfillment, or of sweeping philosophies of focused history such as Hegel's. In the twentieth century, the idea of leadership increasingly became a separate topic of discussion of its own, even an academic field of study. Underlying much thought of the nineteenth and twentieth centuries is the conviction that ours is an era that is fundamentally different from every preceding one. In a world committed to individual rights and to democratic equality, leading seems to be a possibility in some degree attributed to all.

Leadership is also now looked at in historical perspective. Leading is understood in terms of what it has been and how it may have changed or is changing currently. Some writings in this section reflect this concern for how the concept of leadership has evolved, and how we think of leadership today compared to how it may have been understood in past periods. This tendency we have already seen in Woodrow Wilson's reflections, which have an affinity with those of Max Weber (the two contemporaries were both dedicated scholars of modern society and politics). Wilson asserted that a major transformation in the idea of a good leader had occurred in the past hundred years, and that Abraham Lincoln was indicative of that change.

Wilson feared that the kind of leadership needed in his era would be hard to find. This belief, that the need of leadership has never been greater, but the prospect of having it is uncertain, is a theme that runs through the most thoughtful of the writings on leadership in our time.

Max Weber

In the reading on "charismatic authority," one of the most famous analyses of German sociologist Max Weber, we see the historical perspective and the self-conscious concern for the conditions of our time, mentioned above. Weber worked out a theory of the types of authority by which leaders achieve recognition. Recognition or acknowledgement is the prerequisite to gaining directive influence over followers. In other words, Weber wanted to know what the bases of relationships of authority are, or what legitimates the exercise of authority in the eyes of followers.

To have "charisma" is to gain recognition based on a response in followers of trust and belief in the powers (perhaps divine) of the leader. This induces in followers a sense of duty and mission as articulated by the charismatic leader, and it involves "complete, personal devotion" and an "emotional form of communal relationship." "Charismatic authority is thus specifically outside the realm of everyday routine and the profane sphere." In that relationship, there is a quest for "spiritual" fulfillment, which often entails a disregard of material concerns. This is an ancient "primitive" relationship, found in many forms in many cultures, but we know that it can and does arise in our own time, although it is often feared as sectarian, aberrant, or "irrational."

Weber contrasts charismatic authority to "traditional" authority and to "bureaucratic" authority. Traditional and bureaucratic forms of authority are characterized by routine, habit, and dailiness; they emphasize procedure and do not foster the kind of inspired, enthusiastic transcendence of rules and procedures that goes with relationships of charismatic authority. This is echoed in the reading by Zaleznik, which analyzes the distinction between "leaders" and "managers."

Weber thought that with the displacement of charisma by tradition, and even more by modern bureaucracies, the process of disenchantment, taking the magic out of life, would impose despair and uncertainty upon many. At the same time, there is obvious danger in the charismatic relationship. The desire for transcendence is at odds with the rationalization of life under the auspices of scientific enlightenment. The impact of scientific enlightenment has been to chasten religious expression and the quest for divine meaning in life. The contemporary preoccupation with leadership is connected to the sense of loss of meaning, and how meaning is to be reestablished or recertified.

Ronald M. Glassman

In Ronald Glassman's commentary on Weber's concept of charisma, Glassman distinguishes "task" leadership from "charismatic" leadership (compare the distinction between "managers" and "leaders"). Bureaucracy tends to institutionalize and universalize the task orientation. In the task orientation, the emphasis is on addressing specific problems for which there are specific solutions that do not question the overall organizational assumptions and operations. Bureaucracy is indispensable to the operation of large complex organizations, but it also may have a deadening effect. Even when people benefit significantly from the operation of bureaucracy, they are not inspired by it; they take it for granted, even disdain it, while remaining dependent upon it.

The rise of the media further complicates the situation. In order to evade bureaucratization, it is increasingly necessary for a leader to achieve notice or celebrity through the effective use of media. But those who control the media, while offering a gateway to communication, may also filter messages independently, slanting the messages that are conveyed. In these circumstances, leadership can easily both be built up and torn down. We now face the paradox of "manufactured charisma," which is a curious amalgam of the miraculous and the manipulated. The scope and diversity of modern societies, moreover, ensure that no leader can be universally effective. Belief and cynicism, acceptance and rejection, are coexistent in the reactions of many to the attempted exercise of leadership. "Thus while bureaucratic political organization actively devalues and destroys charismatic leadership, it produces the concomitant longing for charisma in those individuals alienated by the structure of bureaucracy itself. . . ."

Given demythologizing tendencies in tension with the longings for charismatic leadership described by Glassman, it is worth suggesting that another conception of leadership might be that of mediator between these opposing tendencies. As mediator, a leader would lessen the tensions inherent to our situation. But this also implies the possibility of combining management and leadership or task and charisma. One can state this idea in the abstract, but achieving it in practice is another matter. Manuals of leadership technique cannot ensure this combination, because there is an art or an inspiration which cannot be taught. The best resources for coming to understand what the art might be are found in the study of history and philosophy.

Abraham Zaleznik

Abraham Zaleznik argues that managers and leaders are very different kinds of people. Leadership involves forceful efforts to change the way people think and act; management requires mutually sympathetic, collective action. Successful societies tend to downplay the importance of forceful leadership, emphasizing instead "rational methods" and "problem solving." Technique is increasingly emphasized over personality. The managerial style is to work incrementally within an evolving, accepted framework of action; the leadership style is to question received patterns and to look for striking, often unsettling, alternatives. The former is risk averse, the latter risk-taking.

Given Zaleznik's categories, it is easy to see why we would think we need both management and leadership, and why we might hope for "leaders" who combine the two styles. The question of how we recognize what we need and when we need it, and the question of how to discern who has what kinds of qualities, remain to be addressed. Is opening the way for both styles to emerge itself a question of management or of leadership?

Bertrand de Jouvenel

Bertrand de Jouvenel, a distinguished political economist and political philosopher, analyzes the operational paradoxes of a society in which the right to speak is universal, but is constrained both by the time available and by the varying capacities and intensities of the participants for significant debate. He is concerned with the "feasibility" issue. His essay is unusual and important for calling attention, not to bureaucratic constraints, but to constraints inherent to human communities which must use reasoning and speaking and where charismatic leadership, which would curtail the right to speak, is ruled out. Anyone attempting to orchestrate complex relationships in today's conditions can find enlightenment in this acute analysis of the "chairman's problem." It would seem to follow that there is a residual element of frustration that leadership cannot eliminate.

James MacGregor Burns

James MacGregor Burns emphasizes the reciprocity between leaders and followers. Leadership involves attention to the needs of followers, not only to the effort to mobilize them in some direction. Indeed, the former is a condition of success for the latter. Leadership involves both competition and conflict. This is a clear indication of the democratic environment in which leadership must operate.

Conflict is necessary to transformation, but harmonious adjustment is necessary to sustaining successful operations. Leadership must mediate between these (one example is the commonplace but important problem of conducting meetings such as those de Jouvenel analyzes). To lead thus means to accept, even to welcome conflict, and to find ways to shape and constrain conflict to useful ends. Those who seek to lead must learn to accept the tensions that are inherent to their role, and to find satisfaction in the achievements that emerge within a dynamic, interminable process.

John Gardner

John Gardner also emphasizes that leaders are always embedded in a context. The fascination people have for those in positions of leadership diverts attention from the conditions in which leaders must operate. As their achievements can be exaggerated, so they can be underrated. And, as Gardner points out, the verdicts of history can and do vary widely from one generation to the next.

Gardner also emphasizes the reciprocal nature of the relationship between leaders and followers. This is true in all historical contexts, but it is most prominent in democratic societies where the demand for consultation is in tension with the need for leaders to be clear and decisive. To be clear and decisive is often to appear to be indifferent to numerous wishes and demands of constituents. On the other hand, to be attentive and inclusive often leads to the accusation of "mixed signals" and confusing messages. Gardner's conclusion is that there are no simple answers to these difficulties. The best leaders are those who can move from attentiveness to decisiveness as may be required in different situations, and who embody or symbolize the meaning and purpose of the organizations or communities they lead. They must be both "problem-solving" and "intuitive." Here again we meet a way of thinking that is expressed in a variety of ways in most of the recent reflections on leadership.

Gardner is disturbed by what he sees as a powerful tendency to emphasize tasks or management at the expense of personal skill and genius. This fear is coeval with the rise of democracy and has been expressed in one form or another since the time of Tocqueville. It is worth noting that more effort has been made in our century to analyze leadership than ever before. So far the result is to rediscover the mysterious character of leadership in the peculiar circumstances of democratic society where leadership is no less needed than ever, but where it is met with ambivalent expectations. In his conclusion on the "anti-leadership vaccine," Gardner expresses the same fear that Woodrow Wilson did about the need for more Lincolns in an era unlikely to produce them. Like Wilson, he points out the difference between the "literary" or the "intellectuals" and those who act in practical life. The intellectuals may want to advise leaders with their putatively scientific knowledge. But who will educate leaders to assess and shape what they are given by the experts?

There are no obvious answers to these questions. However, the deepening of our reflections in historical and philosophical terms, and a patience to seek wisdom without rushing to easy answers, is essential if we are to do the best we can in the dispensation of our time and place.

Max Weber, "Charismatic Authority"

Max Weber (1864–1921) was a German sociologist, political economist, and historian. He is often described as the father of twentieth-century social science. He developed a powerful philosophical account of the methods of the social sciences which continues to influence those disciplines nearly a hundred years later. Among the topics of greatest importance to Weber were those of religion and the secularization or "disenchantment" of the modern age.

10: The Principal Characteristics of Charismatic Authority and Its Relation to Forms of Communal Organization

The term 'charisma' will be applied to a certain quality of an individual personality by virtue of which he is set apart from ordinary men and treated as endowed with supernatural, superhuman, or at least specifically exceptional powers or qualities. These are such as are not accessible to the ordinary person, but are regarded as of divine origin or as exemplary, and on the basis of them the individual concerned is treated as a leader. In primitive circumstances this peculiar kind of deference is paid to prophets, to people with a reputation for therapeutic or legal wisdom, to leaders in the hunt, and heroes in war. It is very often thought of as resting on magical powers. How the quality in question would be ultimately judged from any ethical, aesthetic, or other such point of view is naturally entirely indifferent for purposes of definition. What is alone important is how the individual is actually regarded by those subject to charismatic authority, by his 'followers' or 'disciples.'

For present purposes it will be necessary to treat a variety of different types as being endowed with charisma in this sense. It includes the state of a 'berserker' whose spells of maniac passion have, apparently wrongly, sometimes been attributed to the use of drugs. In Medieval Byzantium a group of people endowed with this type of charismatic war-like passion were maintained as a kind of weapon. It includes the 'shaman,' the kind of magician who in the pure type is subject to epileptoid seizures as a means of failing into trances. Another type is that of Joseph Smith, the founder of Mormonism, who, however, cannot be classified in this way with absolute certainty since there is a possibility that he was a very sophisticated type of deliberate swindler. Finally it includes the type of intellectual, such as Kurt Eisner, who is carried away with his own demagogic success. Sociological analysis, which must abstain from value judgments, will treat all these on the same level as the men who, according to conventional judgments, are the 'greatest' heroes, prophets, and saviours.

I. It is recognition on the part of those subject to authority which is decisive for the validity of charisma. This is freely given and guaranteed by what is held to be a 'sign' or proof, originally always a miracle, and consists in devotion to the corresponding revelation, hero worship, or absolute trust in the leader. But where charisma is genuine, it is not this which is the basis of the claim to legitimacy. This basis lies rather in the conception that it is the duty of those who have been called to a charismatic mission to recognize its quality and to act accordingly. Psychologically this 'recognition' is a matter of complete personal devotion to the possessor of the quality, arising out of enthusiasm, or of despair and hope. No prophet has ever regarded his quality as dependent on the attitudes of the masses toward him. No elective king or military leader has ever treated those who have resisted him or tried to ignore him otherwise than as delinquent in duty. Failure to take part in a military expedition under such a leader, even though recruitment is formally voluntary, has universally been met with disdain.

2. If proof of his charismatic qualification fails him for long, the leader endowed with charisma tends to think his god or his magical or heroic powers have deserted him. If he is for long unsuccessful, above all if his leadership fails to benefit his followers, it is likely that his charismatic authority will disappear. This is the genuine charismatic meaning of the 'gift of grace.' Even the old Germanic kings were sometimes rejected with scorn. Similar phenomena are very common among so-called 'primitive' peoples. In China the charismatic quality of the monarch, which was transmitted unchanged by heredity, was upheld so rigidly that any misfortune whatever, not only defeats in war, but drought, floods, or astronomical phenomena which were considered unlucky, forced him to do public penance and might even force his abdication. If such things occurred it was a sign that he did not possess the requisite charismatic virtue, he was thus not a legitimate 'Son of Heaven.'

3. The corporate group which is subject to charismatic authority is based on an emotional form of communal relationship. The administrative staff of a charismatic leader does not consist of 'officials'; at least its members are not technically trained. It is not chosen on the basis of social privilege nor from the point of view of domestic or personal dependency. It is rather chosen in terms of the charismatic qualities of its members. The prophet has his disciples; the war lord his selected henchmen; the leader, generally, his followers. There is no such thing as 'appointment' or 'dismissal,' no career, no promotion. There is only a 'call' at the instance of the leader on the basis of the charismatic qualification of those he summons. There is no hierarchy; the leader merely intervenes in general or in individual cases when he considers the members of his staff inadequate to a task with which they have been entrusted. There is no such thing as a definite sphere of authority and of competence, and no

appropriation of official powers on the basis of social privileges. There may, however, be territorial or functional limits to charismatic powers and to the individual's 'mission.' There is no such thing as a salary or a benefice. Disciples or followers tend to live primarily in a communistic relationship with their leader on means which have been provided by voluntary gift. There are no established administrative organs. In their place are agents who have been provided with charismatic authority by their chief or who possess charisma of their own. There is no system of formal rules, of abstract legal principles, and hence no process of judicial decision oriented to them. But equally there is no legal wisdom oriented to judicial precedent. Formally concrete judgments are newly created from case to case and are originally regarded as divine judgments and revelations. From a substantive point of view, every charismatic authority would have to subscribe to the proposition, 'It is written . . . but I say unto you. . . .' The genuine prophet, like the genuine military leader and every true leader in this sense, preaches, creates, or demands new obligations. In the pure type of charisma, these are imposed on the authority of revolution by oracles, or of the leader's own will, and are recognized by the members of the religious, military, or party group, because they come from such a source. Recognition is a duty. When such an authority comes into conflict with the competing authority of another who also claims charismatic sanction, the only recourse is to some kind of a contest, by magical means or even an actual physical battle of the leaders. In principle, only one side can be in the right in such a conflict; the other must be guilty of a wrong which has to be expiated.

Charismatic authority is thus specifically outside the realm of everyday routine and the profane sphere. In this respect, it is sharply opposed both to rational, and particularly bureaucratic, authority, and to traditional authority, whether in its patriarchal, patrimonial, or any other form. Both rational and traditional authority are specifically forms of everyday routine control of action; while the charismatic type is the direct antithesis of this. Bureaucratic authority is specifically rational in the sense of being bound to intellectually analysable rules; while charismatic authority is specifically irrational in the sense of being foreign to all rules. Traditional authority is bound to the precedents handed down from the past and to this extent is also oriented to rules. Within the sphere of its claims, charismatic authority repudiates the past, and is in this sense a specifically revolutionary force. It recognizes no appropriation of positions of power by virtue of the possession of property, either on the part of a chief or of socially privileged groups. The only basis of legitimacy for it is personal charisma, so long as it is proved; that is, as long as it receives recognition and is able to satisfy the followers or disciples. But this lasts only so long as the belief in its charismatic inspiration remains.

The above is scarcely in need of further discussion. What has been said applies to the position of authority of such elected monarchs as Napoleon, with his use of the plebiscite. It applies to the 'rule of genius,' which has elevated people of humble origin to thrones and high military commands, just as much as it applies to religious prophets or war heroes.

4. Pure charisma is specifically foreign to economic considerations. Whenever it appears, it constitutes a 'call' in the most emphatic sense of the word, a 'mission' or a 'spiritual duty.' In the pure type, it disdains and repudiates economic exploitation of the gifts of grace as a source of income, though, to be sure, this often remains more an ideal than a fact. It is not that charisma always means the renunciation of property or even of acquisition, as under certain circumstances prophets and their disciples do. The heroic warrior and his followers actively seek 'booty'; the elective ruler or the charismatic party leader requires the material means of power. The former in addition requires a brilliant display of his authority to bolster his prestige. What is despised, so long as the genuinely charismatic type is adhered to, is traditional or rational everyday economizing, the attainment of a regular income by continuous economic activity devoted to this end. Support by gifts, sometimes on a grand scale involving foundations, even by bribery and grand-scale honoraria, or by begging, constitute the strictly voluntary type of support. On the other hand, 'booty,' or coercion, whether by force or by other means, is the other typical form of charismatic provision for needs. From the point of view of rational economic activity, charisma is a typical anti-economic force. It repudiates any sort of involvement in the everyday routine world. It can only tolerate, with an attitude of complete emotional indifference, irregular, unsystematic, acquisitive acts. In that it relieves the recipient of economic concerns, dependence on property income can be the economic basis of a charismatic mode of life for some groups; but that is not usually acceptable for the normal charismatic 'revolutionary.'

The fact that incumbency of church office has been forbidden to the Jesuits is a rationalized application of this principle of discipleship. The fact that all the 'virtuosi' of asceticism, the mendicant orders, and fighters for a faith belong in this category, is quite clear. Almost all prophets have been supported by voluntary gifts. The well-known saying of St. Paul, 'If a man does not work, neither shall he eat,' was directed against the swarm of charismatic missionaries. It obviously has nothing to do with a positive valuation of economic activity for its own sake, but only lays it down as a duty of each individual somehow to provide for his own support. This because he realized that the purely charismatic parable of the lilies of the field was not capable of literal application, but at best 'taking no thought for the morrow' could be hoped for. On the other hand, in such a case as primarily an artistic type of charismatic discipleship, it is conceivable that insulation from economic struggle should mean limitation of those who were really eligible to the 'economically independent'; that is, to persons living on income from property. This has been true of the circle of Stefan George, at least in its primary intentions.

5. In traditionally stereotyped periods, charisma is the greatest revolutionary force. The equally revolutionary force of 'reason' works from without by altering the situations of action, and hence its problems finally in this way changing men's attitudes toward them; or it intellectualizes the individual. Charisma, on the other hand, may involve a subjective or internal reorientation born out of suffering, conflicts, or enthusiasm. It may then result in a radical alteration of the central system of attitudes and directions of action with a completely new orientation of all attitudes toward the different problems and structures of the 'world.' In prerationalistic periods, tradition and charisma between them have almost exhausted the whole of the orientation of action.

Ronald M. Glassman,
"Manufactured Charisma and Legitimacy"

Ronald M. Glassman is professor of sociology and anthropology at William Paterson College in New Jersey.

For Max Weber, as Reinhard Bendix has suggested, charisma was more than a sociological category. In his despair over the trends he saw emerging in the modern world, Weber turned to charisma as a potential savior. However, he was always a realist; thus he described two anticharismatic trends in the contemporary world—the "depersonalization" of charisma that occurs after the routinization of charisma, and the "disenchantment" with charisma that emerges from a rational worldview.

The production of "depersonalized" charisma and the inhibition of "pure" charisma in today's rationalized world will be the focus of this analysis. I shall argue that depersonalized charisma, a manufactured form of charisma, becomes critical in the legitimation processes of contemporary political systems of all kinds. The influence of the mass media on mass populations becomes a central factor—one that Weber could not have fully foreseen but which fits in neatly as an extension of his theoretical formulations.

Administrative Leadership

In terms of human political leadership, we may at the outset differentiate between "task" leadership and "charismatic" leadership. Task leadership is based purely on the skill of an individual at a given task which the group needs to accomplish. There will be many leaders in a group depending on the number of tasks necessitated and the specific differential skills of the individuals in the group. This kind of leadership is never absent from human politics.

Bureaucracy, in its essence, represents the total institutionalization of task leadership. It is an effective, if not always efficient, way to organize and accomplish specific tasks in large-scale, complex societies. Weber has described its structure, Mumford its origins. But since task-accomplishment is never one of the central issues of the political process, humans are always singularly unimpressed by task-officialdom. This attitude is a mixture of blasé acceptance of the necessity of task-officialdom and annoyance when this officialdom impinges upon them and in turn prods them to accomplish some specific task. Bureaucracy gains legitimacy simply because people accept the fact that complex tasks need to be done in large-scale societies.

In fact, bureaucracy is always attached to some other legitimation system. Historically, it has been attached to both traditional kingly authority and to legal-democratic authority. It has also been attached to communist party power in contemporary communist states. Whether bureaucratic leadership can stand alone as a fully legitimated "power elite" in a future technocratic-industrial society, we cannot yet know, though this may be one of the critical questions of our age.

Charismatic Leadership

. . . A test of a political leader's charisma in the modern world is whether his or her charisma can be projected through the media. The kind of charismatic techniques that worked well in the era of public speaking, microphones, and radio do not usually translate well in a television appearance. That is, as McLuhan has pointed out brilliantly, television is a "cool" medium in which "hot" oratory looks out of place—it becomes annoying, grating. The gesticulations seem too flamboyant, facial expressions too twisted and forced, and the voice too small to justify such bodily histrionics. Therefore, the "great orator" does not do well on television. In fact, such oratory is rarely shown directly. Instead, with the speaker in the background and the speaker's voice tuned out, the television newsperson summarizes the main points of the speech with only a few sentences of the speaking allowed to go on the air. Not only is the oratorical charisma neutralized, but the newscaster's interpretation of the main points of the speech is all that is conveyed. Only the President, and less often, party chiefs, get uninterrupted speech time on the media in the United States, and even then commentators provided by the networks engage in "instant analysis" and critical summations of the address.

Furthermore, television is unkind to many leaders in that the close-up lens tends to highlight blemishes, pimples, and other physical imperfections. Leaders used the "the stump," but unskilled in the media, often look furrowed, pockmarked, or uncertain on television. Very often they look smaller than life, as contrasted with media stars, who appear larger than life. The lack of media skill, along with a clinging to older oratorical styles, can decharismatize a candidate who cannot adapt to its technical demands. Television in this sense is a decharismatizing medium.

Some candidates, of course, have just the right combination of good looks, oratorical restraint, wit, and style for the new medium. John Kennedy's looks and style were so well suited to television that he became charismatized through it, while Nixon was so ill-suited to this medium that whatever office charisma the vice-presidency might have carried was largely neutralized by his poor television "presence." The projection of genuine charisma through television is not impossible, then, but demands a different set of techniques than those which enhanced charisma prior to television. Few political leaders have been able to imitate Kennedy's success. There is good reason for this, having more to do with television coverage of political leaders than the leaders' failure to imitate Kennedy.

Certain further decharismatizing processes have become typical in the television medium. It is now evident that even when a political leader learns to master television technique, if television's opinion-forming agents wish to decharismatize such a candidate, they very often can. Television newspeople tend to be cynical and frequently attempt to debunk a candidate. They can be formidable opponents in this regard because they manipulate the media situation. They may set out on a careful campaign of slandering the leader's programs, impugning the leader's judgments and choice of aides and friends, or uncovering embarrassing incidents from his or her personal life. They can ask hostile questions during interviews, put the leader on the defensive and never ask the questions which would allow the leader to present a positive, personal point of view. Failure to submit to this ordeal is itself treated as a "news event," while even sponsored programming may subsequently be subjected to critical analysis.

It is because of these problems that modern political leaders have had to learn how to utilize the media to their advantage. They have had to learn how to present themselves on television in both spontaneous and arranged situations, and they have had to hire public relations "image makers" and Madison Avenue "marketing experts" to create television commercials in which their image, their message, and the situation can be manipulated on their behalf. Madison Avenue image making and political commercials are now commonplace phenomena. Media experts can make or break a candidate. "Packaged" versions of candidates are presented to the public regularly. All of these image-making processes represent attempts at media-manufactured charisma. The real candidate is hidden behind the facade as surely as the kings were hidden behind their crowns, robes, and scepters.

This is a "rationalized" world, of course, and therefore the candidates' actions and policies can be analyzed beyond their manufactured images. Thus, sometimes the image-making works, and sometimes it does not. But in either case, the presentation of the leader in today's media dominated world is often a packaged product. Television, then, inhibits the projection of pure charisma and sometimes debunks it when it does emerge, while at the same time structurally encouraging the manufacture of charisma through media techniques.

Finally, if television debunks the pure charisma of political leaders, it also produces charismatic figures of its own. Television, like the movies, produces stars, who are themselves, of course, packaged personalities. We do not know much about the "real" person. The star possesses some modicum to charm, beauty, or other characteristic of importance. Not everyone who is packaged catches on, but the greater part of the personality is manufactured image.

Stars have become potentially powerful as political leaders. C. Wright Mills, so far ahead of his time, wrote of celebrities and how easily they mingled with the politically powerful figures of the United States. He was clearly right when he suggested the "power elite" would include figures from the world of the celebrities. Figures like Ronald Reagan, Jane Fonda, and Ed Asner have emerged as political leaders. Even before Ronald Reagan became president, people were talking about Walter Cronkite as a possible candidate. During the Carter-Ford election of 1976, the general opinion in the nation was that Cronkite, in fact, would be more trustworthy and capable than either of them.

Media celebrities, be they movie stars, television stars, sports figures (like Jack Kemp) or astronauts (like John Glenn) are taken seriously as political leaders even though they have no political experience. They are taken seriously because they possess media-manufactured charisma. This manufactured charisma produces an irrational bond between such a figure and a mass audience in typical charismatic fashion. This irrational bond can be utilized to create mass acceptance in the political sphere. The example of Walter Cronkite shows how newscasters can become stars in their own right.

As media celebrities emerged as political leaders, television newscasters also began to stand out as stars—and therefore as potential political leaders. Television news ratings have skyrocketed and news shows have expanded considerably. The newscasters' faces are everywhere, and they command prime time as they "chaperone" and define every critical event. Not only do they debunk the charisma of political leaders, they also can become political leaders themselves, not for their political experience or expertise but as media "personalities." The age of television is truly in its infancy. Size, color, and cable, if newly combined, could produce a "hot" medium of the future in which the manufacture of charisma could reach heady heights indeed.

Instead of leading toward "1984" media-manufactured charismatic political leadership, however, television technology could alternatively lead toward a new kind of rational legitimacy process. Through local and national cable TV hook-ups, a new kind of participation could be generated in which media-monitored town meetings and debates could create a new form of democratic politics. I am not suggesting that the media are neutral entities through which we can do whatever we existentially will—this is not the case. Media definitely affect the process of human interaction. But the use of the media is often variable rather than rigidly singular, and human input and intent are as critical in media adaptation as the structure and effect of the media themselves. The media are only half the message; human participation and will potential are the other half.

Some Impediments to the Manufacture of Charisma in the Modern World

The impediments to the media-manufacture of charisma in the modern world all come under Weber's heading of "rationality." TV commentators in their cynical and probing style, along with newspaper reporters and columnists, tend to produce a kind of debunking rationality in our approach to political life.

Science and social science produce a rational, skeptical, empirical worldview in which humans become an object to themselves. Therefore, attempts at manufactured charisma are analyzed and unveiled by the constant probing and analytical processes of the rational scientific worldview. Of course, at the same time scientists and social scientists are also coopted by elites and utilized to help create manufactured charisma and the new media through which to manufacture charisma. Nonetheless, there will always be other scientists who are not coopted and who will continue to analyze such processes rationally. Thus attempts both to manufacture charisma and to unmask such manufacture will occur in the scientific community. As a worldview, science itself produces a general rationality through which the "average" individual becomes cynical and decharismatized easily, even though media and audience manipulation become ever more sophisticated.

Another factor which makes the media-manufacture of charisma difficult is that modern society is a multigroup, multiclass society. Because of this, any charismatic leader will fail to charismatize certain portions of the population. Such a leader can be, then, decharismatized through active propaganda used against him or her. This process did occur occasionally in traditional societies, but it is intensified today by the rationality of modern groups and by the possibilities of quick travel and media communications. Repression can be used against such activities, but repression does not charismatize the repressed; so the effect of manufactured charisma is never total in multigroup societies of any kind.

Finally, the rise and extension of bureaucratic political organization creates a situation in which charisma is purposefully eliminated from leadership roles and creates instead a structure in which leadership offices are divided and subdivided and organized in a maze of hierarchies. Charismatic leadership is not necessary for cohesion and is instead discouraged. But bureaucratic political leadership creates no legitimacy structure of its own except in terms of performance evaluation, and the alienation and lack of cohesion humans feel

when confronted with or absorbed into bureaucratic organizations often drive
them toward the desire for charismatic leadership. Thus while bureaucratic political organization actively devalues and destroys charismatic leadership, it
produces the concomitant longing for charisma in those individuals alienated
by the structure of bureaucracy itself. . . .

Conclusion

Two contradictory trends are emerging powerfully in the modern world:
the rational, decharismatizing trend, demanding active participation in the political process and producing alienation where this does not fully occur; and
the irrational, infantile trend toward desiring a charismatic leader, genuine or
manufactured, who will take care of the individual totally and reintegrate society into a single, loving, cohesive, cooperative group. The tension between
the rational and the irrational processes of political action will always exist,
and the outcome of this tension can produce very different political structures
even in technologically similar societies, depending on the historical, cultural,
and structural circumstances of those societies at a given time and upon the
existential desires of the individuals within those societies, if they choose to
act beyond the limitations which culture, structure, and history impose. Nonetheless, the cohesion problems of large-scale societies are so complex that pres-
sures toward some kind of irrational unification figure or symbol become almost a necessity, if anomie and social conflict are to be reduced to manageable
levels. It is still possible that rational processes of consent getting can be re-
vived and innovated so as to minimize the irrational processes, even if they
cannot be discarded, and reciprocal and cooperative rather than usurping and
coercive relationships can exist between people and their leaders.

Abraham Zaleznik, "Managers and Leaders: Are They Different?"

Abraham Zaleznik is Konosuke Matsushita Professor of Leadership, Emeritus, at the Harvard Business School. Zaleznik earned his M.B.A. from Harvard in 1947 and his Ph.D. in commercial science there four years later. A stint as a research assistant led Zaleznik to consider research as a career; he remained in academe for four decades, generating fourteen books and over forty articles on leadership and group psychology. In addition to his professorship at Harvard Business School, Zaleznik is certified as a clinical psychoanalyst by the American Psychoanalytic Association. In 1996, Zaleznik won the Harvard Business School's Distinguished Service Award for his contributions to research and teaching.

What is the ideal way to develop leadership? Every society provides its own answers, defines its deepest concerns about the purposes, distributions, and uses of power. Business has contributed its answer to the leadership question by evolving a new breed called the manager. Simultaneously, business has established a new power ethic that favors collective over individual leadership, the cult of the group over that of personality. While ensuring the competence, control, and the balance of power relations among groups with the potential for rivalry, managerial leadership unfortunately does not necessarily ensure imagination, creativity, or ethical behavior in guiding the destinies of corporate enterprises.

Leadership inevitably requires using power to influence the thoughts and actions of other people. Power in the hands of an individual entails human risks: first, the risk of equating power with the ability to get immediate results; second, the risk of ignoring the many different ways people can legitimately accumulate power: and third, the risk of losing self-control in the desire for power. The need to hedge these risks accounts in part for the development of collective leadership and the managerial ethic. . . .

Out of this conservatism and inertia organizations provide succession to power through the development of managers rather than individual leaders. And the irony of the managerial ethic is that it fosters a bureaucratic culture in business, supposedly the last bastion protecting us from the encroachments and controls of bureaucracy in government and education. Perhaps the risks associated with power in the hands of an individual may be necessary ones for business to take if organizations are to break free of their inertia and bureaucratic conservatism. . . .

What it takes to ensure the supply of people who will assume practical responsibility may inhibit the development of great leaders. Conversely, the presence of great leaders may undermine the development of managers who become very anxious in the relative disorder that leaders seem to generate. The antagonism in aim (to have many competent managers as well as great leaders) often remains obscure in stable and well-developed societies. But the antagonism surfaces during periods of stress and change, as it did in the Western countries during both the Great Depression and World War II. The tension also appears in the struggle for power between theorists and professional managers in revolutionary societies.

It is easy enough to dismiss the dilemma I pose (of training managers while we may need new leaders, or leaders at the expense of managers) by saying that the need is for people who can be *both* managers and leaders. The truth of the matter as I see it, however, is that just as a managerial culture is different from the entrepreneurial culture that develops when leaders appear in organizations, managers and leaders are very different kinds of people. They differ in motivation, personal history, and in how they think and act.

A technologically oriented and economically successful society tends to depreciate the need for great leaders. Such societies hold a deep and abiding faith in rational methods of solving problems, including problems of value, economics, and justice. Once rational methods of solving problems are broken down into elements, organized, and taught as skills, then society's faith in technique over personal qualities in leadership remains the guiding conception for a democratic society contemplating its leadership requirements. But there are times when tinkering and trial and error prove inadequate to the emerging problems of selecting goals, allocating resources, and distributing wealth and opportunity. During such times, the democratic society needs to find leaders who use themselves as the instruments of learning and acting, instead of managers who use their accumulation of collective experience to get where they are going.

Managers and leaders differ fundamentally in their world views. The dimensions for assessing these differences include managers' and leaders' orientations toward their goals, their work, their human relations, and their selves.

Attitudes Toward Goals

Managers tend to adopt impersonal, if not passive, attitudes toward goals. Managerial goals arise out of necessities rather than desires, and therefore, are deeply embedded in the history and culture of the organization. . . .

Leaders adopt a personal and active attitude toward goals. The influence a leader exerts in altering moods, evoking images and expectations, and in establishing specific desires and objectives determines the direction a business takes. The new result of this influence is to change the way people think about what is desirable, possible, and necessary.

Conceptions of Work

What do managers and leaders do? What is the nature of their respective work? Leaders and managers differ in their conception. Managers tend to view work as an enabling process involving some combination of people and ideas interacting to establish strategies and make decisions. Managers help the process along by a range of skills, including calculating the interests in opposition, staging and timing the surfacing of controversial issues, and reducing tensions. In this enabling process, managers appear flexible in the use of tactics: they negotiate and bargain, on the one hand, and use rewards and punishments, and other forms of coercion, on the other. Machiavelli wrote for managers and not necessarily for leaders. . . .

What about leaders, what do they do? Where managers act to limit choices, leaders work in the opposite direction, to develop fresh approaches to long-standing problems and to open issues for new options. Stanley and Inge Hoffmann, the political scientists, liken the leader's work to that of the artist. But unlike most artists, the leader himself is an integral part of the aesthetic product. One cannot look at a leader's art without looking at the artist. On Charles de Gaulle as a political artist, they wrote: "And each of his major political acts, however tortuous the means or the details, has been whole, indivisible and unmistakably his own, like an artistic act."[1]

Leaders work from high risk positions, indeed often are temperamentally disposed to seek out risk and danger, especially where opportunity and reward appear high. From my observations, why one individual seeks risks while another approaches problems conservatively depends more on his or her personality and less on conscious choice. For some, especially those who become managers, the instinct for survival dominates their need for risk, and their ability to tolerate mundane, practical work assists their survival. The same cannot be said for leaders who sometimes react to mundane work as to an affliction.

Relations with Others

Managers prefer to work with people; they avoid solitary activity because it makes them anxious. Several years ago, I directed studies on the psychological aspects of career. The need to seek out others with whom to work and col-

1. Stanley and Inge Hoffmann, "The Will for Grandeur: de Gaulle as Political Artist," *Daedalus* (Summer 1968): 849.

laborate seemed to stand out as important characteristics of managers. When asked, for example, to write imaginative stories in response to a picture showing a single figure (a boy contemplating a violin, or a man silhouetted in a state of reflection), managers populated their stories with people. The following is an example of a manager's imaginative story about the young boy contemplating a violin:

> Mom and Dad insisted that junior take music lessons so that someday he can become a concert musician. His instrument was ordered and had just arrived. Junior is weighing the alternatives of playing football with the other kids or playing with the squeak box. He can't understand how his parents could think a violin is better than a touchdown.
>
> After four months of practicing the violin, junior has had more than enough, Daddy is going out of his mind, and Mommy is willing to give in reluctantly to the men's wishes. Football season is now over, but a good third baseman will take the field next spring.[2]

This story illustrates two themes that clarify managerial attitudes toward human relations. The first, as I have suggested, is to seek out activity with other people (i.e. the football team), and the second is to maintain a low level of emotional involvement in these relationships. The low emotional involvement appears in the writer's use of conventional metaphors, even clichés, and in the depiction of the ready transformation of potential conflict into harmonious decisions. In this case, Junior, Mommy, and Daddy agree to give up the violin for manly sports.

These two themes may seem paradoxical, but their coexistence supports what a manager does, including reconciling differences, seeking compromises, and establishing a balance of power. A further idea demonstrated by how the manager wrote the story is that managers may lack empathy, or the capacity to sense intuitively the thoughts and feelings of others. To illustrate attempts to be emphatic, here is another story written to the same stimulus picture by someone considered by his peers to be a leader.

> This little boy has the appearance of being a sincere artist, one who is deeply affected by the violin, and has an intense desire to master the instrument.
>
> He seems to have just completed his normal practice session and appears to be somewhat crestfallen at his inability to produce the sounds which he is sure lie within the violin.

2. Abraham Zaleznik, Gene W. Dalton, and Louis B. Barnes, *Orientation and Conflict in Career* (Boston: Division of Research, Harvard Business School, 1970), p. 326.

He appears to be in the process of making a vow to himself to expend the necessary time and effort to play this instrument until he satisfies himself that he is able to bring forth the qualities of music which he feels within himself.

With this type of determination and carry through, this boy became one of the great violinists of his day.[3]

Empathy is not simply a matter of paying attention to other people. It is also the capacity to take in emotional signals and to make them mean something in a relationship with an individual. People who describe another person as "deeply affected" with "intense desire," as capable of feeling "crestfallen" and as one who can "vow to himself," would seem to have an inner perceptiveness that they can use in their relationships with others.

Managers relate to people according to the role they play in a sequence of events or in a decision-making *process,* while leaders, who are concerned with ideas, relate in more intuitive and empathetic ways. The manager's orientation to people, as actors in a sequence of events, deflects his or her attention away from the substance of people's concerns and toward their role in a process. The distinction is simply between a manager's attention to *how* things get done and a leader's to *what* the events and decisions mean to participants. . . .

One often hears subordinates characterize managers as inscrutable, detached, and manipulative. These adjectives arise from the subordinates' perception that they are linked together in a process whose purpose, beyond simply making decisions, is to maintain a controlled as well as rational and equitable structure. These adjectives suggest that managers need order in the face of the potential chaos that many fear in human relationships.

In contrast, one often hears leaders referred to in adjectives rich in emotional content. Leaders attract strong feelings of identity and difference, or of love and hate. Human relations in leader-dominated structures often appear turbulent, intense, and at times even disorganized. Such an atmosphere intensifies individual motivation and often produces unanticipated outcomes. Does this intense motivation lead to innovation and high performance, or does it represent wasted energy?

Senses of Self

In the *Varieties of Religious Experience,* William James describes two basic personality types, "once-born" and "twice-born."[4] People of the former personality type are those for whom adjustments to life have been straightforward

3. Ibid., p. 294.
4. William James, *Varieties of Religious Experience* (New York: Mentor Books, 1958).

and whose lives have been more or less a peaceful flow from the moment of their births. The twice-borns, on the other hand, have not had an easy time of it. Their lives are marked by a continual struggle to attain some sense of order. Unlike the once-borns they cannot take things for granted. According to James, these personalities have equally different world views. For a once-born personality, the sense of self, as a guide to conduct and attitude, derives from a feeling of being at home and in harmony with one's environment. For a twice-born, the sense of self derives from a feeling of profound separateness.

A sense of belonging or of being separate has a practical significance for the kinds of investments managers and leaders make in their careers. Managers see themselves as conservators and regulators of an existing order of affairs with which they personally identify and from which they gain rewards. Perpetuating and strengthening existing institutions enhances a manager's sense of self-worth: he or she is performing in a role that harmonizes with the ideals of duty and responsibility. William James had this harmony in mind—this sense of self as flowing easily to and from the outer world—in defining a once-born personality. If one feels oneself as a member of institutions, contributing to their well-being, then one fulfills a mission in life and feels rewarded for having measured up to ideals. This reward transcends material gains and answers the more fundamental desire for personal integrity which is achieved by identifying with existing institutions.

Leaders tend to be twice-born personalities, people who feel separate from their environment, including other people. They may work in organizations, but they never belong to them. Their sense of who they are does not depend upon memberships, work roles, or other social indicators of identity. What seems to follow from this idea about separateness is some theoretical basis for explaining why certain individuals search out opportunities for change. The methods to bring about change may be technological, political, or ideological, but the object is the same: to profoundly alter human, economic, and political relationships.

Sociologists refer to the preparation individuals undergo to perform in roles as the socialization process. Where individuals experience themselves as an integral part of the social structure (their self-esteem gains strength through participation and conformity), social standards exert powerful effects in maintaining the individual's personal sense of continuity, even beyond the early years in the family. The line of development from the family to schools, then to career is cumulative and reinforcing. When the line of development is not reinforcing because of significant disruptions in relationships or other problems experienced in the family or other social institutions, the individual turns inward and struggles to establish self-esteem, identity, and order. Here the psychological dynamics center on the experience with loss and the efforts at recovery.

In considering the development of leadership, we have to examine two different courses of life history: (1) development through socialization, which prepares the individual to guide institutions and to maintain the existing balance of social relations; and (2) development through personal mastery which impels an individual to struggle for psychological and social change. Society produces its managerial talent through the first line of development, while through the second leaders emerge.

Development of Leadership

The development of every person begins in the family. Each person experiences the traumas associated with separating from his or her parents, as well as the pain that follows such frustration. In the same vein, all individuals face the difficulties of achieving self-regulation and self-control. But for some, perhaps a majority, the fortunes of childhood provide adequate gratifications and sufficient opportunities to find substitutes for rewards no longer available. Such individuals, the "once-borns," make moderate identifications with parents and find a harmony between what they expect and what they are able to realize from life.

But suppose the pains of separation are amplified by a combination of parental demands and the individual's need to the degree that a sense of isolation, of being special, and of wariness disrupts the bonds that attach children to parents and other authority figures? Under such conditions, and given a special aptitude, the origins of which remain mysterious, the person becomes deeply involved in his or her inner world at the expense of interest in the outer world. For such a person, self-esteem no longer depends solely upon positive attachments and real rewards. A form of self-reliance takes hold along with expectations of performance and achievement, and perhaps even the desire to do great works.

Such self-perceptions can come to nothing if the individual's talents are negligible. Even with strong talents, there are no guarantees that achievement will follow, let alone that the end result will be for good rather than evil. Other factors enter into development. For one thing, leaders are like artists and other gifted people who often struggle with neuroses; their ability to function varies considerably even over the short run, and some potential leaders may lose the struggle altogether. Also, beyond early childhood, the patterns of development that affect managers and leaders involve the selective influence of particular people. Just as they appear flexible and evenly distributed in the types of talents available for development, managers form moderate and widely distributed attachments. Leaders, on the other hand, establish, and also break off, intensive one-to-one relationships.

It is a common observation that people with great talents are often only indifferent students. No one, for example, could have predicted Einstein's great achievements on the basis of his mediocre record in school. The reason for mediocrity is obviously not the absence of ability. It may result, instead, from self-absorption and the inability to pay attention to the ordinary tasks at hand. The only sure way an individual can interrupt reverie-like preoccupation and self-absorption is to form a deep attachment to a great teacher or other benevolent person who understands and has the ability to communicate with the gifted individual.

Whether gifted individuals find what they need in one-to-one relationships depends on the availability of sensitive and intuitive mentors who have a vocation in cultivating talent. Fortunately, when the generations do meet and the self-selections occur, we learn more about how to develop leaders and how talented people of different generations influence each other.

While apparently destined for a mediocre career, people who form important one-to-one relationships are able to accelerate and intensify their development through an apprenticeship. The background for such apprenticeships, or the psychological readiness of an individual to benefit from an intensive relationship, depends upon some experience in life that forces the individual to turn inward. A case example will make this point clearer. This example comes from the life of Dwight David Eisenhower, and illustrates the transformation of a career from competent to outstanding.[5]

Dwight Eisenhower's early career in the Army foreshadowed very little about his future development. During World War I, while some of his West Point classmates were already experiencing the war firsthand in France, Eisenhower felt "embedded in the monotony and unsought safety of the Zone of the Interior . . . that was intolerable punishment."[6]

Shortly after World War I, Eisenhower, then a young officer somewhat pessimistic about his career chances, asked for a transfer to Panama to work under General Fox Connor, a senior officer whom Eisenhower admired. The army turned down Eisenhower's request. This setback was very much on Eisenhower's mind when Ikey, his first-born son, succumbed to influenza. By some sense of responsibility for its own, the army transferred Eisenhower to Panama, where he took up his duties under General Connor with the shadow of his lost son very much upon him.

In a relationship with the kind of father he would have wanted to be, Eisenhower reverted to being the son he lost. In this highly charged situation,

---

5. This example is included in Abraham Zaleznik and Manfred F. R. Kets de Vries, *Power and the Corporate Mind* (Boston: Houghton Mifflin, 1975).

6. Dwight D. Eisenhower, *At Ease: Stories I Tell to Friends* (New York: Doubleday, 1967), p. 136.

Eisenhower began to learn from his mentor. General Connor offered, and Eisenhower gladly took, a magnificent tutorial on the military. The effects of this relationship on Eisenhower cannot be measured quantitatively, but, in Eisenhower's own reflections and the unfolding of his career, one cannot overestimate its significance in the reintegration of a person shattered by grief. As Eisenhower wrote later about Connor,

> Life with General Connor was a sort of graduate school in military affairs and the humanities, leavened by a man who was experienced in his knowledge of men and their conduct. I can never adequately express my gratitude to this one gentleman. . . . In a lifetime of association with great and good men, he is the one more or less invisible figure to whom I own an incalculable debt.[7]

Some time after his tour of duty with General Connor, Eisenhower's breakthrough occurred. He received orders to attend the Command and General Staff School at Fort Leavenworth, one of the most competitive schools in the army. It was a coveted appointment, and Eisenhower took advantage of the opportunity. Unlike his performance in high school and West Point, his work at the Command School was excellent; he was graduated first in his class.

Psychological biographies of gifted people repeatedly demonstrate the important part a mentor plays in developing an individual. Andrew Carnegie owed much to his senior, Thomas A. Scott. As head of the Western Division of the Pennsylvania Railroad, Scott recognized talent and the desire to learn in the young telegrapher assigned to him. By giving Carnegie increasing responsibility and by providing him with the opportunity to learn through close personal observation, Scott added to Carnegie's self-confidence and sense of achievement. Because of his own personal strength and achievement, Scott did not fear Carnegie's aggressiveness. Rather, he gave it full play in encouraging Carnegie's initiative.

Mentors take risks with people. They bet initially on talent they perceive in younger people. Mentors also risk emotional involvement in working closely with their juniors. The risks do not always pay off, but the willingness to take them appears crucial in developing leaders.

Can Organizations Develop Leaders?

The examples I have given of how leaders develop suggest the importance of personal influence and the one-to-one relationship. For organizations to encourage consciously the development of leaders as compared with managers

7. Ibid., p. 187.

would mean developing one-to-one relationships between junior and senior executives and, more important, fostering a culture of individualism and possibly elitism. The elitism arises out of the desire to identify talent and other qualitites suggestive of the ability to lead and not simply to manage.

The Jewel Companies, Inc., enjoy a reputation for developing talented people. The chairman and chief executive officer, Donald S. Perkins, is perhaps a good example of a person brought along through the mentor approach. Franklin J. Lunding, who was Perkins's mentor, expressed the philosophy of taking risks with young people this way: "Young people today want in on the action. They don't want to sit around for six months trimming lettuce."[8]

The statement runs counter to the culture that attaches primary importance to slow progression based on experience and proved competence. It is a high-risk philosophy, one that requires time for the attachment between senior and junior people to grow and be meaningful, and one that is bound to produce more failures than successes.

The elitism is an especially sensitive issue. At Jewel the MBA degree symbolized the elite. Lunding attracted Perkins to Jewel at a time when business school graduates had little interest in retailing in general, and food distribution in particular. Yet the elitism seemed to pay off: not only did Perkins become the president at age 37, but also, under the leadership of young executives recruited into Jewel with the promise of opportunity for growth and advancement, Jewel managed to diversify into discount and drug chains and still remain strong in food retailing. By assigning each recruit to a vice president who acted as sponsor, Jewel evidently tried to build a structure around the mentor approach to developing leaders. To counteract the elitism implied in such an approach, the company also introduced an "equalizer" in what Perkins described as "the first assistant philosophy." Perkins stated:

> Being a good first assistant means that each management person thinks of himself not as the order-giving, domineering boss, but as the first assistant to those who "report" to him in a more typical organizational sense. Thus we mentally turn our organizational charts upside-down and challenge ourselves to seek ways in which we can lead . . . by helping . . . by teaching . . . by listening . . . and by managing in the true democratic sense . . . that is, with the consent of the managed. Thus the satisfactions of leadership come from helping others to get things done and changed—and not from getting credit for doing and changing things ourselves.[9]

---

8. "Jewel Lets Young Men Make Mistakes," *Business Week,* January 17, 1970, p. 90.
9. "What Makes Jewel Shine So Bright," *Progressive Grocer,* September 1973, p. 76.

While this statement would seem to be more egalitarian than elitist, it does reinforce a youth-oriented culture since it defines the senior officer's job as primarily helping the junior person.

A myth about how people learn and develop that seems to have taken hold in the American culture also dominates thinking in business. The myth is that people learn best from their peers. Supposedly, the threat of evaluation and even humiliation recedes in peer relations because of the tendency for mutual identification and the social restraints on authoritarian behavior among equals. Peer training in organizations occurs in various forms. The use, for example, of task forces made up of peers from several interested occupational groups (sales, production, research, and finance) supposedly removes the restraints of authority on the individual's willingness to assert and exchange ideas. As a result, so the theory goes, people interact more freely, listen more objectively to criticism and other points of view and, finally, learn from this healthy interchange.

Another application of peer training exists in some large corporations, such as Philips, N.V. in Holland, where organization structure is built on the principle of joint responsibility of two peers, one representing the commercial end of the business and the other the technical. Formally, both hold equal responsibility for geographic operations or product groups, as the case may be. As a practical matter, it may turn out that one or the other of the peers dominates the management. Nevertheless, the main interaction is between two or more equals.

The principal question I would raise about such arrangements is whether they perpetuate the managerial orientation, and preclude the formation of one-to-one relationships between senior people and potential leaders. . . .

Bertrand de Jouvenel, "The Chairman's Problem"

Bertrand de Jouvenel (1903–1987) was born in France into a family of liter-
ary and political acclaim. He studied law and mathematics at the Sorbonne
but later became interested in economic and political studies. Working as a
journalist, de Jouvenel funneled his interests into a long list of publications.
In 1935 he scored a journalistic coup with an interview of Adolf Hitler.
He also conducted interviews with Benito Mussolini, Winston Churchill,
Neville Chamberlain, and Pierre Laval. Disturbed by effects of the Great
Depression in the United States, de Jouvenel discoursed on the problem of
poverty, the practice of economic planning, and the effects of international
conflict on domestic prosperity. During World War II, de Jouvenel volun-
teered for service first in the French Army's Intelligence Branch and later in
the infantry, joining a regiment from his native Corrèze. He was called into
service for army intelligence again, serving until 1943, when he learned that
the Germans had become aware of his activities. He fled to Switzerland,
where he remained until the end of the war. Even while working for the
army, de Jouvenel wrote profusely on economic and political issues. Among
his best known works are three volumes, separated in time, but linked in
thought: Du pouvoir: Historie naturelle de sa croissance *(1945);* De la sou-
*veraineté: A la recherche du bien politique *(1955); and* The Pure Theory
of Politics *(1963).*

One of the major obstacles to the progress of political theory lies in the fact
that people speak of rights without paying attention to the feasibility of their
exercise. I propose to raise here some elementary problems relating to the right
of speech. It is one of the basic tenets of our democratic political philosophy
that all people (over a given age) have an equal right of speech. Making this
right operational, however, gives rise to difficulties which have not been faced.

The Chairman's Problem

I shall start out with a very simple problem, which moreover has the advantage of evoking familiar pictures: this is the chairman's problem. I find myself chairman of an assembly, and regard all participants as formally equal,
which commits me to treating them equally. Feeling bound by this principle,
I decide as follows: the duration of the meeting is m, the number of participants n: I shall give the floor to each participant for a time m/n; thus the equal
right of speech will receive practical application. Assume that the meeting is

to be crowned by a vote (the time of actual voting not figuring in *m*): before the participants cast their equal votes, they will have had equal opportunities to influence the voting; that is, they shall have had, insofar as depends upon me, equal voices.

Now if *m* the duration of the meeting (in speaking time) is three hours, and if *n* the number of participants is 12, my procedure is susceptible of being applied: it grants the floor to each participant for a quarter of an hour. This is not a long time but still it may be enough.

But, keeping *m* at three hours, let us set the value of *n* at 5,400. Then, adhering to the same rule for the allocation of time, I shall give the floor to each participant for 2 seconds, which is absurd. Aware of this absurdity, I shall have to scrap my rule. On what principles shall I then exercise my chairmanship? Assuming that I cannot stretch the duration of the discussion (*m* is a datum), time is my scarce resource. How shall I divide it up? My ideal denominator, the number of participants, will not do. I shall then use as my denominator the minimum time (call it *k*) required to develop a meaningful argument. But the consequence thereof is immediately apparent: my number of speakers shall now be $s=m/k$; which means that it will be *indifferent to the number of participants* formally entitled to speak.

Let us leave *m* at three hours, and set *k* at a quarter of an hour: then I shall have a maximum of twelve speakers no matter how great the assembly. Which means that the greater the assembly, the greater the proportion of those who are denied in fact the right granted to them in principle. In an assembly of forty-eight, three out of four will be denied the effective exercise of their formal right. In an assembly of 5,400 no less than 449 out of 450 will be denied in practice their theoretical right.

I had a reason for using a figure in the five-thousand range. In that range, according to historians, stood the number of the Athenian citizens, who, on the most important occasions, responded to the calling of the popular assembly in the days when it was the sovereign decision-making body of the City. We are told that this body met from sunrise to sundown; call it twelve hours. But all the speeches which have come down to us suggest that the time taken by an individual orator was at least one hour. Thus, at the outside, there were twelve orators, probably less. We must conclude that in this direct democracy, the right to speak was in fact exercised only by a very small minority, and that there must have been some principle of selection of this small minority.

Looking to figures has yielded us three important results: (1) With an upper time limit for discussion *m* and a lower time limit for the formulation of a speech *k*, the feasible maximum number of people exercising the right of speech is determined. (2) Therefore with an increasing number *n*, the formal right to speak is a delusion for an increasing proportion of those entitled to this formal right. (3) In any system which grants formal rights to more than can effectively be given the opportunity of exercising them, there must be some device whereby those who are allowed the actual right are singled out from those to whom it formally belongs.

These remarks lead us to consider a number of problems.

The *m* Limit

Going back to my position as chairman, let us assume that I greatly take to heart the principle that each participant, entitled to the same right, should have an equal opportunity to expound his views. The one thing I cannot do is to share out the time into units so small that nobody can make sense. Therefore my first obligation is to set the value of k, of which more anon. Supposing I have set it at fifteen minutes, I now feel impelled to break the m limit. I shall thus tell the assembly that having made up my mind that fifteen minutes is, the minimum time for an opinion, I propose that each member should have his fifteen minutes. Supposing that I have 5,400 participants, this means that we must sit for 1,350 hours in all, or, assuming 9 hours a day, a session of 150 working days. . . .

But obviously the suggestion is absurd. First, in some cases, a decision must be reached before this great space of time. Second, in all cases, the participants will prove unwilling to sit through this long succession of speeches. If they are a body of citizens, as in Athens, they have private affairs to attend to. If they are a professional decision-making body, as in the case of our parliaments, they have other issues to decide. . . .

The *k* Constraint

Let us now turn to the k constraint. This letter designates the time which I, as chairman, deem to be the minimum necessary to develop adequately an opinion on the subject under discussion. I offer no justification for my setting of k because I would find it difficult to explain the complicated computations which intervene in my mind and of which I am hardly aware. First I make some assessment of the difficulty of the subject. The more complex it seems to me, the more prone I am to raise k. Though my assessment of the difficulty of the subject is inevitably subjective, I am apt to take it as objective, and there is no practical harm in so calling it. But now I must take into account the quali-fication of the audience. . . . I must then take into account the fact that the ex-penditure of words required to convey an argument increases as the qualifica-tion of the listener decreases. An expert can convey his argument to a fellow expert in the same field with an economy of words or symbols, which makes his message incomprehensible to a layman. When speaking to the latter, the shorthand of jargon or conventional signs must be made explicit, and redundance must be introduced to increase the probability of understanding.

Therefore, the lower the qualification of the audience, the more I must raise k. We have now reached a conclusion which is capable of two alternative formulations. One: the more complex the subject and the less qualified the audience, the higher I must set k. Two: the greater the difficulty of the subject for the given audience, the more I must raise k. The two formulations are of course equivalent and the choice between them depends upon one's desire to include or exclude the notion of "intrinsic" difficulty. . . .

I am constrained by an inelastic m: total discussion time is fixed. Therefore the higher I set k, the fewer the speakers I can allow. Already, if the subject be one of some complexity and the audience of low qualification, I have to set k pretty high. I now want to set k so as to allow a maximum number of speakers. It is clear that I can maximize my number of speakers only by restricting my choice of speakers to those who require least time to develop their argument. . . .

Criteria for the Selection of Speakers

Thus attention to k, with m held constant, gives me a recipe for choosing those who will be called upon to exercise the right of speech; that is, those who can formulate their argument, under given conditions, with maximum economy.

But while we considered m, it became apparent that, apart from cases where the duration of the assembly is exogenously determined, which are many, m can be considered as somewhat elastic, rising if the speakers be men who are capable of retaining attention. Here is another distinct criterion for the selection of speakers. It may occur that the two criteria coincide—a clear and concise speaker is apt to retain attention—but also the two criteria may not coincide because a "big name" is apt to attract attention even if its bearer be a diffuse speaker.

The two criteria which have been formulated arise logically from the problem examined. These criteria are in fact applied when for instance the BBC organizes a broadcast discussion: the name which appeals to the audience, and the ability to make points swiftly are both taken into consideration. But another consideration also arises, and is of major importance. If a discussion is wanted, different opinions must be advanced. How is the chairman to choose bearers of different opinions, without making a prior selection of opinions on his own account? The procedure generally accepted is to choose bearers of opinions, different from each other, but of which every one is accepted by a notable portion of the body politic. The men's individual opinions are then severally representative of a body of opinion.

This completes our cursory examination of "the chairman's problem": he recognizes men whose names are apt to retain attention, who are representative of different bodies of opinion, and who are apt to present their argument with maximum economy.

The Criteria Seen From the Angle of the *Bonum Commune*

The criteria we have found for dealing with the chairman's problem are in no way surprising. They are those which any reasonably competent chairman applies in fact. They can however be assailed from two angles, from the *bonum commune* viewpoint and also from the individual rights viewpoint.

Beginning with the first, it may be said: (1) that a glamorous name, capable of retaining attention is not a guarantee of wisdom; (2) that the several opinions which are widely held may all be wrong, and that the best opinion may not be representative of a body of opinion; (3) that an argument may be presented tersely, thanks to the neglect of important considerations, and that its economy of words may correspond to a poverty of substance.

To the first point, the answer must be brief. The chairman, should he feel entitled to pick out the wisest, may well doubt his ability to discern them, and if he does not doubt it, the congregation may well call it into question. The second point will be dealt with as we come to discuss the criteria from the angle of individual rights. The third point is well taken.

We like our problems to be simple and our decisions to require little thought. Therefore if speaker A presents a problem as complicated and B as simple, we are apt to prefer B's argument. Rightly so, if B has taken the complexities into account and reduced them to simplicity, but wrongly if B has made the problem simple by overlooking important aspects, which is most frequently the case. There is a sure recipe for presenting any problem as simple: it is to disregard factual information and to reason discursively from general principles. The principles and the reasoning are easily grasped by listeners who are thus readily convinced, while many are apt to resent the effort required from them by speaker A who pours out and marshals a great deal of factual information.

We are prone to buy our opinions in the cheapest market: and that is the market where particular opinions are mass produced from general principles. This is a major danger which afflicts assemblies: it can be guarded against only by the chairman's closest attention to providing participants with the factual information relevant to the issue; and if the assembly cannot be asked to digest the adequate amount of factual information, then it is not the proper body for deciding the specific issue.

The Viewpoint of the Individual Rights

We started out, concerned not with the problem of reaching the right decision (a *bonum commune* problem) but with the gap which may occur between the right of speech and its exercise. Our examination of the chairman's problem has made it clear to us that the gap cannot fail to be considerable.

Our main point throughout this discussion has been that time is a scarce commodity; that is, the time during which a congregation can be held together attentive to speakers from a floor or pulpit, or the time during which an audience can be expected to remain attentive to a broadcast, is a limited quantity. The problem is not different in kind if we think, not of speakers competing for the opportunity of addressing a gathering, but of people addressing letters for the correspondence column of a newspaper: here it is the space which is limited. The editor who returns to the letter writer a printed note expressing regret that his communication could not be printed due to lack of space refers to a real concrete problem. There is a bottleneck of space in the correspondence column (or columns) as there is a bottleneck of time in an assembly. However the editor's answer by no means satisfies the letter writer who sees other letters printed while his has not been. Nor does lack of time pleaded by the chairman satisfy the would-be speaker who has not been recognized while others have had their say.

There is no place (as far as I know) in the political theory of democracy for the simple and glaring fact of bottlenecks. Individuals are told at every moment that they have an equal right of speech, and they find out in any concrete instance that the opportunity of expression is denied to them. This breeds the feeling that democratic principles are a lie. And indeed if the principle of right of speech is so formulated as to convey the impression "you shall have the opportunity of being heard by the congregation, equal to anyone else's" then it is a lie, because it is impossible to give such an opportunity. This comes back to the old idea so often forgotten that any right is meaningless which does not have as its counterpart an obligation in someone else toward whom the claim must be directed. Now, giving to everyone the right of being heard by the congregation would mean settling upon the congregation the obligation of listening to each and everyone; and that is not feasible.

People who are taught and told that they have an equal right of speech find out in fact that the avenues of expression are guarded by people who turn down their application. They do not realize that this is a necessity since here we are dealing with a scarce commodity which cannot be divided into less than given quantities. They are merely aware of being turned down, and are apt to believe that the guardians of the avenues of speech have turned them down personally: from there it is just one jump to thinking that the right to speech which rightly belongs to all (is this not tirelessly stated?) is in fact confiscated by a few, who form an Establishment. Whether or not the guardians of the many different avenues of expression do in some loose manner form one company, and can be called an Establishment, or whether in fact such guardians are in the several cases ad hoc and are linked in one body by our innate tendency to mythologize, is a sociological problem which does not concern us here. I personally lean to the second view. Different avenues are guarded by different people, and the only sameness which obtains is the sameness of the denial of the exercise of the right of speech.

Clearly this denial applies to a greater proportion of applicants, the greater the concentration of the avenues of expression. Say that every day one out of ten thousand readers of a newspaper feels moved to write to the paper. And say that there is room for ten readers' letters. A newspaper with a circulation of three hundred thousand will deny two out of three letter writers. A newspaper with a circulation of three million will deny two hundred and ninety out of three hundred.

Thus if you have ten of the smaller circulation newspaper instead of the one with the large circulation, you have less frustration. The same of course holds for assemblies. Thus every phenomenon of concentration in the media of expression or in the centers of discussion and decision making tends to decrease the percentage of received candidates among those who postulate for the exercise of the right of speech.

If one does not want people to feel that they are cheated it is important to explain to them this phenomenon of "scarcity" and also to make reasonably clear the criteria of selection used to choose among the many who have a formal right the few who are called to exercise it. It is better to stress the positive scarcity features of the system and the criteria used to allocate this scarce resource than to stress the formal right which can in so few cases be exercised. In fact a system of expression is characterized by just these two things: its bottlenecks and the criteria for admission through the bottlenecks.

The Right to Buttonhole

There is however a sense in which the right of speech can be exercised by each and everyone; it is the right to buttonhole, to address a fellow citizen, one to one, and convince him to hear you out (that is the speaker's business in which he may succeed or fail) and having done so to convince him of your opinion (that again is the speaker's business in which he may succeed or fail). By such "artisan" procedure, you may command successively the attention of n people, and in consequence you may collect these n people in a hall, and so fire them with your opinion that they shall go abroad and collect n^2 and then n^3 people, and so on. You may thus constitute a congregation of your own. That this should be allowed is essential to a free society; that, and not that anyone should be given the right to address any congregation.

Now consider the problem which arises in the case of Primus who has collected through toil and trouble a congregation of his own doing. An outsider, Secundus, comes in and claims the right to address this congregation on grounds of the right of free speech. Is Primus bound to give him the floor? I doubt it. He can reply to Secundus: "I have made up this congregation. Go thou and do likewise."

Conclusion

It is essential to lay stress upon feasibility problems. Exclusive emphasis upon formal rights must inevitably breed in citizens the feeling that they are deceived, since the enunciation of such formal rights leads them to think that they should be enabled to exercise rights which in fact give rise to scarcity situations, frustrating the hopes aroused by the enunciation of formal rights.

With increasing centralization we move from the viewpoint of the right of speech to situations of increasing scarcity, which make the actual enjoyment of the formal right more and more subject to narrower bottlenecks. This is not generally understood and people feel mystified. This can be remedied only by speaking increasingly in terms of feasibility.

James MacGregor Burns,
"Conflict and Consciousness"

James MacGregor Burns (1918–) is Professor Emeritus of Williams College. An author, teacher and political activist, Burns has done extensive scholarship on political leadership. In addition to his biographies of political leaders, Burns has published numerous works on democracy, including The Workshop of Democracy *(1985) and a widely-used textbook on government,* Government by the People. *Born in Melrose, Massachusetts, Burns received his B.A. at Williams College and his M.A. and Ph.D. at Harvard. He spent the bulk of his teaching career in the government department at Williams College; he currently serves as Senior Scholar at the Center for Political Leadership and Participation at the University of Maryland at College Park.*

Leadership is a process of morality to the degree that leaders engage with followers on the basis of shared motives and values and goals—on the basis, that is, of the followers' "true" needs as well as those of leaders: psychological, economic, safety, spiritual, sexual, aesthetic, or physical. Friends, relatives, teachers, officials, politicians, ministers, and others will supply a variety of initiatives, but only the followers themselves can ultimately define their own true needs. And they can do so only when they have been exposed to the competing diagnoses, claims, and values of would-be leaders, only when the followers can make an informed choice among competing "prescriptions," only when—in the political arena at least—followers have had full opportunity to perceive, comprehend, evaluate, and finally experience alternatives offered by those professing to be their "true" representatives. Ultimately the moral legitimacy of transformational leadership, and to a lesser degree transactional leadership, is grounded in *conscious choice among real alternatives.* Hence leadership assumes competition and conflict, and brute power denies it.

Conflict has become the stepchild of political thought. Philosophical concern with conflict reaches back to Hobbes and even Heraclitus, and men who spurred revolutions in Western thought—Machiavelli and Hegel, Marx and Freud—recognized the vital role of conflict in the relations among persons or in the ambivalences within them. The seventeenth-century foes of absolute monarchy, the eighteenth-century Scottish moralists, the nineteenth-century Social Darwinists—these and other schools of thought dealt directly with questions of power and conflict, and indirectly at least with the nature of leadership. The theories of Pareto, Durkheim, Weber, and others, while not centrally concerned with problems of social conflict "contain many concepts, assumptions, and hypotheses which greatly influenced later writers who did attempt to deal with conflict in general." Georg Simmel and others carried theories of conflict into the twentieth century.

It was, curiously, in this same century—an epoch of the bloodiest world wars, mightiest revolutions, and most savage civil wars—that social science, at least in the West, became most entranced with doctrines of harmony, adjustment, and stability. Perhaps this was the result of relative affluence, or of the need to unify people to conduct total war or consolidate revolutions, or of the co-option of scholars to advise on mitigating hostility among interest groups such as labor and management or racial groups such as blacks and whites. Whatever the cause, the "static bias" afflicted scholarly research with a tendency to look on conflict as an aberration, if not a perversion, of the agreeable and harmonious interactions that were seen as actually making up organized society. More recently Western scholarship has shown a quickened interest in the role of conflict in establishing boundaries, channeling hostility, counteracting social ossification, invigorating class and group interests, encouraging innovation, and defining and empowering leadership.

The static bias among scholars doubtless encouraged and reflected the pronouncements of political authority. Communist leaders apotheosized conflict as the engine of the process of overthrowing bourgeois regimes and then banned both the profession and the utilization of conflict in the new "classless" societies. Western leaders, especially in the United States, make a virtual fetish of "national unity," "party harmony," and foreign policy bipartisanship even while they indulge in—and virtually live off—contested elections and divisive policy issues. Jefferson proclaimed at his first Inaugural, "We are all Federalists, we are all Republicans." Few American presidents have aroused and inflamed popular attitudes as divisively as Franklin D. Roosevelt with his assaults on conservatives in both parties, his New Deal innovations, and his efforts to pack the Supreme Court and purge the Democratic party, yet few American presidents have devoted so many addresses to sermonlike calls for transcending differences and behaving as one nation and one people.

The potential for conflict permeates the relations of humankind, and that potential is a force for health and growth as well as for destruction and barbarism. No group can be wholly harmonious, as Simmel said, for such a group would be empty of process and structure. The smooth interaction of people is continually threatened by disparate rates of change, technological innovation, mass deprivation, competition for scarce resources, and other ineluctable social forces and by ambivalences, tensions, and conflicts within individuals' personalities. One can imagine a society—in ancient Egypt, perhaps, or in an isolated rural area today—in which the division of labor, the barriers against external influence, the structure of the family, the organization of the value system, the acceptance of authority, and the decision-making by leaders all interact smoothly and amiably with one another. But the vision of such a society would be useful only as an imaginary construct at one end of a continuum from cohesion to conflict. Indeed, the closer, the more intimate the relations within a group, the more hostility as well as harmony may be generated. The smaller the cooperative group—even if united by language and thrown closely together by living arrangements—"the easier it is for them to be mutually irritated and to flare up in anger," Bronislaw Malinowski said. Some conflict over valued goals and objects is almost inevitable. Even small, isolated societies cannot indefinitely dike off the impact of internal changes such as alteration of the birth rate or the disruption caused by various forms of innovation.

The question, then, is not the inevitability of conflict but the function of leadership in expressing, shaping, and curbing it. Leadership as conceptualized here is grounded in the seedbed of conflict. Conflict is intrinsically compelling; it galvanizes, prods, motivates people. Every person, group, and society has latent tension and hostility, forming a variety of psychological and political patterns across social situations. Leadership acts as an inciting and triggering force in the conversion of conflicting demands, values, and goals into significant behavior. Since leaders have an interest of their own, whether opportunistic or ideological or both, in expressing and exploiting followers' wants, needs, and aspirations, they act as catalytic agents in arousing followers' consciousness. They discern signs of dissatisfaction, deprivation, and strain; they take the initiative in making connections with their followers; they plumb the character and intensity of their potential for mobilization; they articulate grievances and wants; and they act for followers in their dealings with other clusters of followers.

Conflicts vary in origin—in and between nations, races, regions, religions, economic enterprises, labor unions, communities, kinship groups, families, and individuals themselves. Conflicts show various degrees and qualities of persistence, direction, intensity, volatility, latency, scope. The last alone may be pivotal; the outcome of every conflict, E. E. Schattschneider wrote, "is determined by the scope of its contagion. The number of people involved in any conflict determines what happens; every change in the number of participants . . . affects the results. . . . The moral of this is: If a fight starts, watch the crowd, because the crowd plays the decisive role." But it is leadership that draws the crowd into the incident, that changes the number of participants, that closely affects the manner of the spread of the conflict, that constitutes the main "processes" of relating the wider public to the conflict.

The root causes of conflict are as varied as their origins. No one has described these causes as cogently as James Madison.

> The latent causes of faction are thus sown in the nature of man; and we see them every where brought into different degrees of activity, according to the different circumstances of civil society. A zeal for different opinions concerning religion, concerning government and many other points, as well of speculation as of practice; an attachment to different leaders ambitiously contending for preeminence and power; or to persons of other descriptions whose fortunes have been interesting to the human passions, have in turn divided mankind into parties, inflamed them with mutual animosity, and rendered them much more disposed to vex and oppress each other, than to cooperate for their common good. So strong is this propensity of mankind to fall into mutual animosities, that where no substantial occasion presents itself, the most frivolous and fanciful distinctions have been sufficient to kindle their unfriendly passions, and excite their most violent conflicts. But the most common and durable source of factions, has been the various and unequal distribution of property.

Not only "attachment to different leaders" but all these forces for conflict are expressed and channeled through many different types of leaders "ambitiously contending for preeminence and power."

Leaders, whatever their professions of harmony, do not shun conflict; they confront it, exploit it, ultimately embody it. Standing at the points of contact among latent conflict groups, they can take various roles, sometimes acting directly for their followers, sometimes bargaining with others, sometimes overriding certain motives of followers and summoning others into play. The smaller and more homogeneous the group for which they act, the more probable that they will have to deal with the leaders of other groups with opposing needs and values. The larger, more heterogeneous their collection of followers, the more probable that they will have to embrace competing interests and goals within their constituency. At the same time, their marginality supplies them with a double leverage, since in their status as leaders they are expected by their followers and by other leaders to deviate, to innovate, and to mediate between the claims of their groups and those of others.

But leaders shape as well as express and mediate conflict. They do this largely by influencing the intensity and scope of conflict. Within limits they can soften or sharpen the claims and demands of their followers, as they calculate their own political resources in dealing with competing leaders within their own constituencies and outside. They can amplify the voice and pressure of their followers, to the benefit of their bargaining power perhaps, but at the possible price of freedom to maneuver—less freedom to protect themselves against their followers—as they play in games of broader stakes. Similarly, they can narrow or broaden the scope of conflict as they seek to limit or multiply the number of entrants into a specific political arena.

John Gardner, Various Selections

John Gardner (1912–) spent a number of years teaching psychology at both private and public colleges before assuming an administrative position at the Carnegie Corporation in 1946. He became president of that organization in 1955. In 1965, Gardner joined President Johnson's cabinet as Secretary of Health, Education, and Welfare, a post he held until 1968, when he took over the administration of the National Urban Coalition. In 1970, Gardner founded Common Cause, a citizen's lobby, which he headed for seven years.

On Leadership, "Judgments of Leaders"

In curious ways, people tend to aggrandize the role of leaders. They tend to exaggerate the capacity of leaders to influence events. Jeffrey Pfeffer says that people want to achieve a feeling of control over their environment, and that this inclines them to attribute the outcomes of group performance to leaders rather than to context. If we were to face the fact—so the argument goes—that outcomes are the result of a complex set of interactions among group members plus environmental and historical forces, we would feel helpless. By attributing outcomes to an identifiable leader we feel, rightly or not, more in control. There is at least a chance that one can fire the leader; one cannot "fire" historical forces.

Leaders act in the stream of history. As they labor to bring about a result, multiple forces beyond their control, even beyond their knowledge, are moving to hasten or hinder the result. So there is rarely a demonstrable causal link between a leader's specific decisions and consequent events. Consequences are not a reliable measure of leadership. Franklin Roosevelt's efforts to bolster the economy in the middle-to-late-1930s were powerfully aided by a force that did not originate with his economic brain trust—the winds of war. Leaders of a farm workers' union fighting for better wages may find their efforts set at naught by a crop failure.

Frank Lloyd Wright said, "A doctor can bury his mistakes. An architect can only advise his client to plant vines." Unlike either doctor or architect, leaders suffer from the mistakes of predecessors and leave some of their own misjudgments as time bombs for successors. Many of the changes sought by leaders take time: lots of years, long public debate, slow shifts in attitude. In their lifetimes, leaders may see little result from heroic efforts yet may be setting the stage for victories that will come after them. Reflect on the long, slow unfolding of the battles for racial equality or for women's rights. Leaders who did vitally important early work died without knowing what they had wrought.

Leaders may appear to have succeeded (or failed) only to have historians a generation later reverse the verdict. The "verdict of history" has a wonderfully magisterial sound, but in reality it is subject to endless appeals to later generations of historians—with no court of last resort to render a final judgment.

On Leadership, "The Heart of the Matter: Leader-Constituent Interaction"

The Role of Followers

Leaders are almost never as much in charge as they are pictured to be, followers almost never as submissive as one might imagine. That influence and pressure flow both ways is not a recent discovery. The earliest sociologists who wrote on the subject made the point. Max Weber (1864–1920), in discussing charismatic leaders, asserted that such leaders generally appear in times of trouble and that their followers exhibit "a devotion born of distress." In other words, the state of mind of followers is a powerful ingredient in explaining the emergence of the charismatic leader.

Weber's great contemporary, Georg Simmel (1858–1918), was even more explicit, suggesting that followers have about as much influence on their leaders as their leaders have on them. Leaders cannot maintain authority, he wrote, unless followers are prepared to believe in that authority. In a sense, leadership is conferred by followers. To say that followers have substantial influence on leaders sounds like the view of someone steeped in the democratic tradition. But Weber and Simmel were writing in pre-World War I Germany; their views were hardly the product of a populist environment.

. . . Even monarchs and dictators have discovered that it is costly to take measures that offend the deeply held beliefs of their subjects, and that it is substantially less costly to attain their ends in ways that do not offend. Corporate executives learn comparable lessons today. They learn to operate within the framework of the culture, which is to say within the limits people in the system can accept in terms of their norms, beliefs and expectations. Leaders can go against the grain of the culture, but not without cost.

Contemporary research confirms the two-way character of the relationship. It is this reciprocal aspect that underlies one of the soundest of political maxims: *good constituents tend to produce good leaders.*

There is a striking difference between the situation of political leaders and that of line executives in business or government. In the political process, constituents have a measure of choice—and leaders must compete for approval. In corporate and governmental bureaucracies employees are supposed to accept their superiors in the hierarchy as their leaders. But, of course, quite often they do not. The assumption by line executives that, given their rank and authority, they can lead without being leaders is one reason bureaucracies stagnate. As I pointed out earlier, *executives are given subordinates; they have to earn followers.* . . .

Structure and Control

. . . Given our cultural framework, what patterns of leader-constituent interaction are most effective in accomplishing the purposes of the group? Does the group function most effectively when leaders make the decisions without consultation and impose their wills, or when they invite varying degrees of participation in the decision? The tension between the two approaches is nicely illustrated in a story (probably apocryphal) told of Woodrow Wilson when he was president of Princeton University. "How can I democratize this university," he demanded, "if the faculty won't do what I ask?"

Should there be a high degree of structure in the relationship—a sharp differentiation between the roles of leaders and followers, a clear hierarchy of authority with emphasis on detailed assignments and task specifications? Or should the relationship be more informal, less structured, with leaders making the goals clear and then letting constituents help determine the way of proceeding?

Should there be an atmosphere of discipline, constraints, controls—in Navy parlance, a tight ship—or should there be autonomy, individual responsibility and freedom for growth, with the leader in the role of nurturer, supporter, listener and helper?

Should the leader focus on the job to be done—task-oriented as the researchers put it—or should the leader be concerned primarily with the people performing the task, with their needs, their morale, their growth?

More than four decades of objective research have not produced dramatically clear answers to these questions, but they have yielded improved understanding of a set of very complicated relationships. . . .

One reason simple answers have not emerged from the research is that there are no simple answers, only complicated answers hedged by conditions and exceptions. Followers do like being treated with consideration, do like to have their say, do like a chance to exercise their own initiative—and participation does increase acceptance of decisions. But there are times when followers welcome rather than reject authority, want prompt and clear decisions from the leader, and want to close ranks around the leader. The ablest and most effective leaders do not hold to a single style; they may be highly supportive in personal relations when that is needed, yet capable of a quick, authoritative decision when the situation requires it. . . .

Two-Way Communication

One generalization that is supported both by research and experience is that effective two-way communication is essential to proper functioning of the leader-follower relationship. It is a point that corporations have emphasized increasingly in recent years. There must be not only easy communication from leaders to constituents but also ample return communication, including dissent. Leaders, to be effective, must pick up the signals coming to them from constituents. And the rule is: If the messages from below says you are doing a flawless job, send back for a more candid assessment. . . .

The Multilevel Dialogue

. . . Effective leaders deal not only with the explicit decisions of the day—to approve a budget, announce a policy, discipline a subordinate—but also with that partly conscious, partly buried world of needs and hopes, ideals and symbols. They serve as models; they symbolize the group's unity and identity; they retell the stories that carry shared meanings. Their exemplary impact is great. There are messages for followers in what leaders pay attention to, in how they deal with critical incidents, in the correspondence between their words and acts, in the ethical tone of their behavior.

Edmund Wilson wrote:

The poetry of Lincoln has not all been put into his writings. It was acted out in his life. . . . He created himself as a poetic figure, and he thus imposed himself on the nation. For the molding by Lincoln of American opinion was a matter of style and imagination as well as of moral authority, of cogent argument and obstinate will. . . . When we put ourselves back into the period, we realize that it was not at all inevitable to think of it as Lincoln thought.

... To analyze complex problems, leaders must have a capacity for rational problem solving; but they must also have a penetrating intuitive grasp of the needs and moods of followers. The ablest leaders understand, rationally and intuitively, the expectations of people with respect to their leadership. And they are adept at meeting those expectations not only with rational verbal pronouncements but also with symbolic acts, ritual observances, and the like. . . .

That leaders and followers share a culture (i.e., share norms and values) enhances communication between the two, but is not an unmixed blessing. When the system is in grave need of renewal, leaders who wear the same blinders as their followers may be of little help in renewing.

Perception and Reality

Leaders develop their styles as they interact with their constituencies. They move toward the style that seems most effective in dealing with the mixture of elements that make up their constituencies.

Conventional wisdom says that there is, on the one hand, the public image of the leader as perceived by followers; and on the other hand, the reality of what the leader truly is. But many researchers agree that how the followers perceive the leader is also reality—and in matters of leadership a more important reality than what the leader is really like. . . .

Shaper and Shaped

. . . People who have not thought much about it are likely to believe that all influence originates with the leader, that the leader is the shaper, never the object of shaping by followers.

Having brought leaders down from that pedestal, one can all too readily fall into the opposite error of supposing that leaders are clay in the hands of followers. Not really. Leaders, because of their significant positions, because of their inevitable symbolic roles, because of their natural persuasive gifts, wield undeniable influence. . . .

Trust

There is much to be gained for any leader in winning the trust of constituents. A leader capable of inspiring trust is especially valuable in bringing about collaboration among mutually suspicious elements in the constituency. The trust the contending groups have for such a leader can hold them together until they begin to trust one another.

It is not easy to sort out the ingredients of trust in leadership. I recall the senior partner of a law firm stressing to younger men and women in his firm the importance of client trust. One ambitious young lawyer asked how one went about winning trust, and the senior partner said dryly, "Try being trustworthy."

One of the most important prerequisites for trust in a leader is steadiness. The need for reliability is not only ethically desirable, it is generally a practical necessity. A leader who is unpredictable poses a nerve-wracking problem for followers. They cannot rally around a leader if they do not know where he or she stands. A businessman friend of mine, commenting on his congressman, said, "It isn't that he's crooked, it's just that I can't keep track of him. He's too swift for me—I wish he'd stay in one place." . . .

Strengthening Followers

If both leaders and constituents are significant actors in the relationship, we must talk not only about failures of leadership but also about failures of followership. There is a vast literature on the failures of leadership—on the abuse of power, injustice, indecisiveness, shortsightedness, and so on. Who will write the essay on individual and collective failures among followers? When it is written the essay will have to cover two matters at some length.

First, there are qualities such as apathy, passivity, cynicism, and habits of spectatorlike noninvolvement that invite the abuse of power by leaders. Bertrand de Jouvenel said, "A society of sheep must in time beget a government of wolves."

Second, there is the inclination of followers in some circumstances to collaborate in their own deception. Given the familiar fact that what people want and need often determines what they see and hear, the collaboration comes easily. But a citizenry that wants to be lied to will have liars as leaders. Have we not tested that generalization at every level of government?

Rather than dwell on the failings, we would do well to focus on how to ensure better performance. Perhaps the most promising trend in our thinking about leadership is the growing conviction that the purposes of the group are best served when the leader helps followers to develop their own initiative, strengthens them in the use of their own judgment, enables them to grow, and to become better contributors. Industrial concerns are experimenting with such an approach because of their hard-won awareness that some matters (for example, quality control, productivity, morale) simply cannot be dealt with unless lower levels of leadership are actively involved. This is a subject to which I shall return.

To the extent that leaders enable followers to develop their own initiative, they are creating something that can survive their own departure. Some individuals who have dazzling powers of personal leadership create dependency in those below them and leave behind a weakened organization staffed by weakened people. Leaders who strengthen their people may create a legacy that will last for a very long time. . . .

On Leadership, "Sharing Leadership Tasks"

. . . The leadership tasks involved in keeping a community going are richly varied and extend far beyond the deciding function. We must find a way of thinking which reflects that variety, and the concept of sharing leadership tasks does just that.

The Leadership Team

One manifestation of sharing is the leadership team, the few individuals who work closely with the leader. Most of the conversation and writing about leadership deals with The Leader, splendidly alone. But even a cursory glance at the real world reveals that most leadership involves a number of individuals acting in a team relationship. Teams have leaders, of course, and most ventures fare better if one person is in charge, but not as a solo performer, not as a giant surrounded by pygmies.

Team leadership enhances the possibility that different styles of leadership—and different skills—can be brought to bear simultaneously. If the leader is a visionary with little talent for practical steps, a team member who is a naturally gifted agenda setter can provide priceless support. The important thing is not that the leader cover all bases but that the team collectively do so. . . .

Advantages of Sharing Leadership Tasks

. . . The only hope for vitality in large-scale organization is the willingness of a great many people scattered throughout the organization to take the initiative in identifying problems and solving them. Without that, the organization becomes another of those sodden, inert, nonadaptive bureaucracies that are the bane of modern corporate and government life-rigid, unimaginative, and fatally unequipped to deal with a swiftly changing environment.

The taking of responsibility is at the heart of leadership. To the extent that leadership tasks are shared, responsibility is shared. The wider sharing of leadership tasks could sharply lower the barriers to leadership. For every person now leading, there are many more who could share leadership tasks, testing their skills, enjoying the lift of spirit that comes with assuming responsibility, and putting their feet on the lower rungs of a ladder that rises to higher leadership responsibilities. Many who lack the self-assurance to think of themselves as leaders would find within themselves the confidence to test the lower rungs of the ladder. Others who now feel excluded, or shut out from the possibility of leadership, would find that the entry points were numerous and welcoming.

"The Antileadership Vaccine"

. . . Of all our deficiencies with respect to leadership, one of the gravest is that we are not doing what we should to encourage potential leaders. In the late eighteenth century we produced out of a small population a truly extraordinary group of leaders—Washington, Adams, Jefferson, Franklin, Madison, Monroe, and others. Why is it so difficult today, out of a vastly greater population, to produce men of that caliber? It is a question that most reflective people ask themselves sooner or later. There is no reason to doubt that the human material is still there, but there is excellent reason to believe that we are failing to develop it—or that we are diverting it into nonleadership activities.

The Antileadership Vaccine

Indeed, it is my belief that we are immunizing a high proportion of our most gifted young people against any tendencies to leadership. It will be worth our time to examine how the antileadership vaccine is administered.

The process is initiated by the society itself. The conditions of life in a modern, complex society are not conducive to the emergence of leaders. The young person today is acutely aware of the fact that he is an anonymous member of a mass society, an individual lost among millions of others. The processes by which leadership is exercised are not visible to him, and he is bound to believe that they are exceedingly intricate. Very little in his experience encourages him to think that he might some day exercise a role of leadership.

This unfocused discouragement is of little consequence compared with the expert dissuasion the young person will encounter if he is sufficiently bright to attend a college or university. In those institutions today, the best students are carefully schooled to avoid leadership responsibilities.

Most of our intellectually gifted young people go from college directly into graduate school or into one of the older and more prestigious professional schools. There they are introduced to—or, more correctly, powerfully indoctrinated in—a set of attitudes appropriate to scholars, scientists, and professional men. This is all to the good. The students learn to identify themselves strongly with their calling and its ideals. They acquire a conception of what a good scholar, scientist, or professional man is like.

As things stand now, however, that conception leaves little room for leadership in the normal sense; the only kind of leadership encouraged is that which follows from the performing of purely professional tasks in a superior manner. Entry into what most of us would regard as the leadership roles in the society at large is discouraged.

In the early stages of a career, there is a good reason for this: becoming a first-class scholar, scientist, or professional requires single-minded dedication. Unfortunately, by the time the individual is sufficiently far along in his career to afford a broadening of interests, he often finds himself irrevocably set in a narrow mold.

The antileadership vaccine has other more subtle and powerful ingredients. The image of the corporation president, politician, or college president that is current among most intellectuals and professionals today has some decidedly unattractive features. It is said that such men compromise their convictions almost daily, if not hourly. It is said that they have tasted the corrupting experience of power. They must be status seekers, the argument goes, or they would not be where they are.

Needless to say, the student picks up such attitudes. It is not that professors propound these views and students learn them. Rather, they are in the air and students absorb them. The resulting unfavorable image contrasts dramatically with the image these young people are given of the professional who is almost by definition dedicated to his field, pure in his motives, and unencumbered by worldly ambition.

My own extensive acquaintance with scholars and professionals on the one hand and administrators and managers on the other does not confirm this contrast in character. In my experience, each category has its share of opportunists. Nevertheless, the negative attitudes persist. As a result the academic world appears to be approaching a point at which everyone will want to educate the technical expert who advises the leader, or the intellectual who stands off and criticizes the leader, but no one will want to educate the leader himself. . . .

SOURCES AND CREDITS

The editor and publisher thank the owners of copyright for their permission to include selections within this anthology.

Bacon, Francis. "Of Great Place," from *Francis Bacon: A Selection of His Works,* edited by Sidney Warhaft. New York: Macmillan Publishing Company; London: Collier Macmillan Publishers, 1965, pp. 70–73.

Burckhardt, Jacob. *Force and Freedom: An Interpretation of History,* edited by James Hastings Nichols. New York: Meridian Books, 1955, pp. 288, 289, 291–92, 293–94, 301–2, 305–6.

Burns, James MacGregor. "Conflict and Consciousness," in *Leadership.* New York and London: Harper & Row, 1978, pp. 36–39. © 1978 by James MacGregor Burns. Reprinted by permission of HarperCollins Publishers, Inc.

Cicero. *De Officiis,* translated by Walter Miller, vol. 21 of *Cicero in Twenty-Eight Volumes.* Cambridge, Mass.: Harvard University Press; London: William Heinemann, 1968, pp. 69, 71, 73, 75, 81, 83, 87, 89, 91. Reprinted by permission of Harvard University Press and the Loeb Classical Library.

Confucius. Excerpts from *The Essential Confucius: A Compendium of Ethical Wisdom,* translated and edited by Thomas Cleary. San Francisco: Harper-SanFrancisco, 1992. © 1992 by Thomas Cleary. Reprinted by permission of HarperCollins Publishers, Inc.

Constant, Benjamin. "The Liberty of the Ancients Compared with That of the Moderns." Originally delivered as a speech at the Athènèe Royal in Paris in 1819. From *Political Writings of Benjamin Constant,* translated and edited by Biancamaria Fontana. Cambridge: Cambridge University Press, 1988, pp. 309–23, 325–26. Reprinted with permission of Cambridge University Press.

de Tocqueville, Alexis. "Why There Are So Many Men of Ambition in the United States But So Few Lofty Ambitions," from *Democracy in America,* Part II: *The Influence of Democracy on the Sentiments of the Americans.* Originally published in 1840. Translated by George Lawrence and edited by J. P. Mayer and Max Lerner. New York: Harper & Row, 1966, pp. 627–32. English translation © 1965 by Harper & Row Publishers, Inc., copyright renewed. Reprinted by permission of HarperCollins Publishers, Inc.

Douglass, Frederick. "Fourth of July Oration, 1852," in *The Life and Writings of Frederick Douglass,* edited by Philip S. Foner. New York: International Publishers, 1950.

Gardner, John. "The Antileadership Vaccine." President's essay from the 1965 Carnegie Corporation of New York Annual Report. Reprinted by permission of the Carnegie Corporation of New York.

———. *On Leadership.* New York: Free Press, 1990, pp. 7–9, 23–36, 149–52. © 1990 by John W. Gardner. Reprinted with the permission of The Free Press, a division of Simon & Schuster, Inc.

Glassman, Ronald M. "Manufactured Charisma and Legitimacy," in *Charisma, History, and Social Structure,* edited by Ronald M. Glassman and William H. Swatos, Jr. Contributions in Sociology, no. 58. New York and Westport, Conn.: Greenwood Press, 1987, pp. 114–16, 121–27, 128. © 1987 by Ronald Glassman and William H. Swatos, Jr. Reprinted with permission of Greenwood Publishing Group, Inc.

Gracián, Baltasar. *The Wisdom of Baltasar Gracián: A Practical Manual for Good and Perilous Times,* adapted and edited by J. Leonard Kaye. New York: Pocket Books, 1992, pp. 70, 72–75, 81, 92–93, 101–2, 117–18, 125, 129, 134–36, 145–46, 149, 152, 155, 157–59, 162, 181. © 1992 by J. Leonard Kaye. Reprinted with permission of Pocket Books, a division of Simon & Schuster, Inc.

Hegel, Georg Wilhelm Friedrich. "Reason in History," in *Lectures on the Philosophy of World History,* translated from the German edition of Johannes Hofmeister by H. B. Nisbet. Cambridge: Cambridge University Press, 1975, pp. 82–88. Reprinted with permission of Cambridge University Press.

Homer. *The Iliad,* translated with an introduction by Richard Lattimore. Chicago and London: University of Chicago Press, 1961, pp. 202–3, 204, 205, 206–9. © 1951 by University of Chicago Press. Reprinted by permission of the University of Chicago Press.

Jouvenel, Bertrand de. "The Chairman's Problem," in *American Political Science Review,* vol. 55, no. 2 (June 1961). Reprinted with permission of the American Political Science Association.

Keats, John. "On Fame," from *John Keats: Complete Poems,* edited by Jack Stillinger. Cambridge, Mass., and London: The Belknap Press of Harvard University Press, 1982, p. 277.

Kierkegaard, Søren. "The Individual and 'the Public,'" in *The Present Age.* Originally published in 1846. Reprinted in *A Kierkegaard Anthology,* edited by Robert Bretall. Princeton: Princeton University Press, 1946, pp. 260–69. © 1946 by Princeton University Press. Reprinted by permission of Princeton University Press.

King, Martin Luther, Jr. "I Have a Dream," from *Southern Christian Leadership Conference Newsletter,* September 1963. © 1963 by Martin Luther King, Jr., copyright renewed 1991 by Coretta Scott King. Reprinted by arrangement with The Heirs to the Estate of Martin Luther King, Jr., c/o Writers House, Inc., as agent for the proprietor.

———. "Letter from Birmingham Jail," from *Why We Can't Wait*. New York: Harper & Row, 1963. © 1963 by Martin Luther King, Jr., copyright renewed 1991 by Coretta Scott King. Reprinted by arrangement with The Heirs to the Estate of Martin Luther King, Jr., c/o Writers House, Inc., as agent for the proprietor.

Lao-Tzu. Excerpts from *Tao-te-Ching*, in John Heider, "The Leader Who Knows How Things Happen." *Journal of Humanistic Psychology*, vol. 27, no. 3 (Summer 1982): 33–39. Reprinted with permission of Sage Publications, Inc.

Lincoln, Abraham. "A House Divided," The Emancipation Proclamation, The Gettysburg Address, Second Inaugural Address, in *The Essential Abraham Lincoln*, edited by John Gabriel Hunter. New York: Gramercy Books, 1993.

Machiavelli, Niccolò. *The Prince*, translated with an introduction by Harvey C. Mansfield, Jr. Chicago and London: University of Chicago Press, 1985, pp. 61–63, 65–67, 68–71. Reprinted with permission of the University of Chicago Press.

Montaigne, Michel de. "Of Glory," from *The Complete Essays of Montaigne*, translated by Donald M. Frame. Stanford: Stanford University Press, 1958, pp. 468–78. © 1958 by the Board of Trustees of the Leland Stanford Junior University. Reprinted with permission of Stanford University Press.

Morgenthau, Hans J. "Love and Power," in *Politics in the Twentieth Century*, vol. 3: *The Restoration of American Politics*. Chicago: University of Chicago Press, 1962. Reprinted with permission of the University of Chicago Press.

Plato. *Epistles: A Translation with Critical Essays and Notes*. Edited by Glenn R. Morrow. New York: Bobbs-Merrill, 1962, pp. 217, 223–24.

Plutarch. Excerpts from *Moralia in Sixteen Volumes*, translated by Frank Cole Babbitt. Cambridge, Mass.: Harvard University Press; London: William Heinemann, 1971. Reprinted by permission of Harvard University Press and the Loeb Classical Library.

Shelley, Percy Bysshe. "Mutability" and "Ozymandias," from *Shelley Poems*, selected by Isabel Quigly. Penguin Poetry Library, Penguin Books, 1956.

Thomas Aquinas. "On Princely Government," from *Aquinas: Selected Political Writings*, edited by A. P. D'Entrèves, translated by J. G. Dawson. Oxford: Basil Blackwell, 1948, pp. 79, 81, 83.

Washington, George. "Farewell Address to Americans, 1796," in *Major Problems in the Era of the American Revolution 1760–1791: Documents and Essays*, edited by Richard D. Brown. Lexington, Mass., and Toronto: D. C. Heath and Company, 1992.

Weber, Max. "Charismatic Authority," from *The Theory of Social and Economic Organization*, translated by A. M. Henderson and Talcott Parsons, edited with an introduction by Talcott Parsons. New York: Free Press; London: Collier-Macmillan, 1947, pp. 358–63. © 1947, copyright renewed in 1975 by

Talcott Parsons. Reprinted with the permission of The Free Press, a division of Simon & Schuster, Inc.

Wilson, Woodrow. "Abraham Lincoln: A Man of the People," in *College and State Educational, Literary, and Political Papers (1875–1913)*, edited by Ray Stannard Baker and William E. Dodd. New York and London: Harper & Brothers Publishers, 1925, vol. 2, pp. 83–101.

———. "Leaders of Men," in *The Papers of Woodrow Wilson*, vol. 6: *1888–1890*, edited by Arthur S. Link. Princeton: Princeton University Press, 1969, pp. 644–671.

Zaleznik, Abraham. "Managers and Leaders: Are They Different?" *Harvard Business Review*, vol. 55 (June 1977). © 1977 by the President and Fellows of Harvard College; all rights reserved. Reprinted by permission of *Harvard Business Review*.